ESSAY ANNUAL
1933

1933

Essay Annual

*A Yearly Collection of Signif-
icant Essays, Personal, Critical,
Controversial, and Humorous*

ERICH A. WALTER

Department of English, University of Michigan

SCOTT, FORESMAN AND COMPANY

CHICAGO — ATLANTA — DALLAS — NEW YORK

Editor's Note

The editor of this volume has for some time felt the need of an annual publication which should give a cross section of the outstanding essays of each year. The editor has not been alone in this feeling. The desire for such an annual collection for university classes and for the general reader has also been expressed by students, teachers, and librarians. This book, the first of a series to be issued each year, accordingly has as its purpose the presentation of significant essays—personal, critical, controversial and humorous—published between the dates January 1, 1932 and June 1, 1933. Because it is obviously impossible to include every desirable selection in a book of this size, a bibliography of further remarkable American essays published in American periodicals in 1932 and 1933 has been added.

The reader should note that the present collection includes two essays published in 1931, Christopher Morley's "Alice and the Aquitania" and the essay by Lincoln Steffens. The former is Mr. Morley's own selection for this anthology; while "I Get a Colt to Break In" appears in Lincoln Steffens's *Autobiography,* announced as a Pulitzer Prize winner in 1932. In the future, a strict adherence to chronology will be the rule for the *Essay Annual.*

Although the essays are not grouped under various headings, the following scheme was operative in the arrangement of the table of contents. Burton Rascoe's "Montaigne and the Average man" was placed first because it fittingly marks the four-hundredth anniversary of Montaigne's birth. The seven essays beginning with "On Learning to Read" and ending with "Universities and Religious Indifference" cover various aspects of the question, *What Is Education?* Henry Hazlitt, Dorothy Canfield, Walter Hard, and Helen Keller look toward an *Objective View of Ourselves.* Then follow eleven answers to the question, *What Is Happening in the World of Art and Letters?*

Herbert Reed and Paul Gallico write about America's national games. Mrs. Anderson and Messrs. Halper and Morley present the familiar essay. The last eight pieces, with one exception (a commentary on the German situation), may be considered a symposium upon *Our "New Nation."*

To the authors, editors, and publishers who have helped in the completion of this anthology, the editor expresses his sincere gratitude.

E. A. W.

Table of Contents

TABLE OF CONTENTS

ESSAY ANNUAL
1933

Montaigne
And the Average Man

By BURTON RASCOE

Burton Rascoe was born in Fulton, Kentucky, in 1892. After studying for two years at the University of Chicago, he joined the staff of THE CHICAGO TRIBUNE, *of which paper he successively became literary and dramatic editor. He has been editor or associate editor at various times of* McCALL'S MAGAZINE, *Johnson Features Inc.,* THE BOOKMAN, *and* PLAIN TALK. *For four years, 1924-1928, Burton Rascoe wrote a syndicated column,* "The Day-book of a New Yorker." *This column appeared in more than four hundred daily papers.*

Note—This essay is particularly apropos this year, since the world celebrated Montaigne's four-hundredth birthday anniversary last February. Michel Eyquem de Montaigne was born February 28, 1533.

RABELAIS had the Gallic spirit, a tonic quality of earthiness and levity which identifies French literature and sets it slightly apart from all other literatures of the world. Villon, Rabelais, and Montaigne may be said to have formed the French mind and there is nothing in the subsequent literature of France which is alien to these three writers. In Proust, who aspired to write an Arabian Nights entertainment in terms of the *Memoires* of Saint-Simon, we see the same inner necessity which set Montaigne meticulously to examine, expose, and record himself. Verlaine is almost like a reincarnation of Villon, and the rasping, plaintive, sardonic voice of

Tristan Corbière is that of the wayward starveling of medieval Paris re-echoing in the rainswept streets of a more modern Montmartre. Ronsard is a lyrical Rabelais; Voltaire is the creator of Gargantua speaking always in the person of Friar John of Entommeures; Renan and Anatole France are heirs to the irony, frankness, and freedom of Montaigne and to the surprising turn of thought invented by Rabelais; Molière is the homeliness of Montaigne and the satire of Rabelais done into good theater; Rousseau is a soul tortured by a Calvinistic conscience and eager, like Montaigne, to learn the meaning of existence by examination of self. La Fontaine, Racine, what are they but, in the one case, the concision and condensation, and in the other of the rarification, of the wit of Rabelais? What was the origin of that seeking after truth that is found in the first great psychological novels of Balzac, Flaubert, Stendhal, and Zola, but the urge which made Montaigne day after day, over a long period of years, set down even the most trivial matters about himself?

No man is a hero to his valet and Montaigne was valet to himself. Therein lies his greatness: he deigned and dared to proclaim that in no single thing was he a hero. Persons who suffer from a feeling of inferiority should read Montaigne. Whatever they think is holding them back, Montaigne had in double measure. He had, so he tells us, everything wrong with him except his health, and even that went bad on him in his middle life, for he suffered from stone in the kidneys which modern surgery would have relieved. He was undersized; and this seems to have bothered him considerably: "My height is rather below the average. This defect hath not only the drawback of ugliness, but, in addition, that of inconvenience. A beautiful figure, in truth, is the only beauty allowed to men. . . . I am of something lower than middle stature, a defect that not only borders upon deformity, but carries withal a great deal of inconvenience along with it, especially to those who are in command; for the authority which a graceful presence, and a majestic mien beget, is wanting. . . . I am, as to the rest, strong and well knit, my face is not puffed, but full, and my complexion betwixt jovial and melancholic, moderately sanguine and hot." *

One cannot be sure that Le Duc de La Rochefoucauld ever read Montaigne, but we can be sure that Montaigne put something in the air when we find Rochefoucauld writing this sketch of himself as a preface to his *Maximes:*

> I am of medium stature: I am well proportioned and my gestures are easy. My coloring is dark but harmonious. My forehead is high and rather broad; my eyes black, small and deep set; my eyebrows are dark and bushy, but well shaped. I am at a loss what to say of my nose, for it is neither hooked nor aquiline, heavy, nor yet, to my knowledge, sharp; all that I can say of it is that it is large rather than small, and that it is a trifle too long. My mouth is large and my lips are usually fairly red and neither well or ill shaped. My teeth are white and moderately regular. People have told me that my chin is too pronounced. I have just examined myself in the mirror to ascertain the truth of the matter, and I do not quite know what judgment to pronounce. My face is certainly square or oval—I hardly know which. My hair is black, curls naturally and is sufficiently abundant to sustain my pretensions to a fine head.
>
> My expression is both haughty and sad, which leads most persons to deem me supercilious, although in reality quite the reverse. My gestures are easy, perhaps too easy, for I gesticulate freely when speaking. Such, quite frankly do I consider my exterior, and I fancy one will find that my opinion is not far from the truth. . . .
>
> —Tr. John Heard.

Le Duc de La Rochefoucauld, whose particular responsibility seems to have been the distillation of his experience in terms of epigrams, not for pay, not for advancement, not for anything except a satisfaction to himself, followed Montaigne in subjecting himself to relentless self-scrutiny.

---

* Tr. Trechmann, Oxford Univ. Press.

Montaigne, long before Rochefoucauld, realized that it is "easier to understand mankind than to understand a man." Therefore, he set out to understand himself, or rather to reveal himself and let others make what they could out of it.

Michel Eyquem de Montaigne had one of the most glorious fathers in the history of literature, and, in a way, the famous Essays of Montaigne are a long comparison of the son with the father to the great disadvantage of the son. Montaigne's father was, in many respects, everything Montaigne would like to have been, and failing to be like his father, he celebrated the virtues his father possessed. This, I may remark, is extremely rare. Sons of well-endowed fathers frequently bear toward them a special grudge. The Freudians call it an Œdipus complex and say that it is the result of a sense of rivalry on the part of a son for the love a father enjoys from the son's mother which the son cannot share. But this, I think, is far-fetched. There are only about fifteen years in a man's life or a woman's in which a passional interest is paramount. After that, extreme passion is an aberration. In one's middle years and after, one is happy enough for any eventuality which recalls to one that the only conceivable aim of life is the perpetuation of life—or going through the motions of perpetuating it. After forty the war may not be won or the enthusiasm for it quite diminished; but at least, in general, the motives are clear, the aim is in mind, the outcome (win or lose) is discounted. After forty one may see qualities in one's father that one wishes one had, and to wish it one may have only an esthetic interest.

Montaigne's father was a virgin when he married a Jewess in his thirty-third year on his return from Italy after campaigning as a soldier under Francis I. (The wars of Charles VIII, Louis XII, and Francis I upon Italy were idiotic from a practical standpoint, for they brought no money into the French treasury and ran up a considerable debt, but they did acquaint the victorious French with a civilization from which they were able to learn something.) That a man may remain a virgin until his thirty-third year and that he might remain thereafter a singularly monogamous husband may seem incredible to the youngsters of our generation; but such, it appears, was a fact which Montaigne, who had been deflowered in puberty, had to face. There was no reason for his father's chastity, for the age was especially licentious, beyond a certain fastidiousness in his nature and an inclination toward physical exercise. Montaigne's father was an athlete: he could vault, leap, run, swim, box, fence, dance, play tennis, lift weights, and curb a horse in a fashion so expert as to excite the wonder and admiration of his son, Michel, who could do none of these things with any credit to himself.

Montaigne's father, in the report of his adoring son, was grave, humble, and modest in his behavior; swart, well-proportioned, and well-knit, though of small stature, of pleasing countenance, and capable of miracles of vaulting, running, and leaping. He was, it seems, a bundle of wiry nerves all in perfect co-ordination with his muscles. Such a constitution Montaigne admired because he himself was fumbling, phlegmatic, self-indulgent, weak, unambitious, forgetful, and without any physical prowess whatever. As a youth he was dandified, seeking to make up in clothes the deficiencies he felt about his appearance. The only physical exercise he ever enjoyed was that of horseback riding, and since he tells us that he was pretty good at this, we can take it that he was very good indeed, because there is no man in the history of literature so inclined as Montaigne is to belittle his abilities. He tells us that he has no memory and that he cannot remember things he has read two hours after he has read them, but when he quotes from memory he is much more nearly perfect than scholars who pride themselves on the accuracy of their scholastic attainments. (The late Stuart P. Sherman revealed in an essay that he did not know such a common thing as the authorship of the words, "She walks in beauty ——." Irving Babbitt attributes to Bacon the words of Lucian about there being no beauty without some strangeness in it. Ambrose Bierce said about Brander Matthews: "He is nothing if not accurate; and he is not accurate.") In the glosses on Montaigne there are but few corrections in his scholarship and such few as there are remain equivocal. He had a library of a thousand books and these thousand books he knew intimately. For the rest, he did nothing after forty, except to examine himself for our benefit and report his findings faithfully.

Besides Montaigne, there have been but two men in the history of literature who have had this pressing sense of the value of the true record of what a man sees, thinks, feels, and does—Samuel Pepys and James Boswell. Boswell, who was a great man, had the charming humility of believing he was a mere agent for recording the minutiæ of an intellectual dictator of his period, and he never for a moment realized that his *Life of Samuel Johnson* was vastly superior to anything Johnson had ever written. And Pepys seems to have had only a tenuous apprehension that a record of his most trivial doings was much more important to a fine mind, like Marcel Schwob's, than any of the vainglorious conquests of Alexander the Great.

Lytton Strachey, when he wrote *Landmarks of French Literature,* was still a young man, and it is only on the score of youth that we can excuse him for saying that Montaigne was "neither a great artist, nor a great philosopher; he was not great at all." Strachey, when he wrote that, was under the popular delusion that greatness consists in doing something flamboyantly discreditable, like leading an army against a defenseless people, achieving great wealth by tricks, usury, and extortion, or maintaining nonsense by a great show of syllogisms. In his later years, Strachey reversed his position so thoroughly that he discredited the motives which enable one to become a cardinal, a founder of English public school education, an angel to the wounded in war, and a conquerer of barbaric tribes. But, meanwhile, he neglected to revise his verdict that Montaigne was "not great."

Montaigne's greatness is visible in nearly every great work of French prose; he and Rabelais gave final form to the still plastic French language, before the standardizing of it set it under the direction of the French Academy. He invented the familiar essay; he was the father of the spirit of inquiry which

produced Voltaire and the French revolution. If the word
"philosophy" means anything, Montaigne's philosophy of
"loyal enjoyment of being" is as valid as any philosophical
system I know. Montaigne aspired to simplicity, clarity, and
easiness in writing; he strove to use only those words "which
are current in the Paris markets." He was one of the first to
espouse the doctrine of equality of the sexes; one of the first
to combat that idealization of woman which so hampered the
freedom of all women. As Buckle said, "Under the guise of
a mere man of the world expressing natural thoughts in a common language, Montaigne concealed a spirit of lofty and
audacious inquiry." He immeasurably increased the estimate
of the dignity and worth of human life, by showing us the
kinship between great spirits and the average man. Montaigne was the first, and almost the last, to search out his
soul, "to penetrate the dark profundities of its intricate wind-
ings; to choose and lay hold of so many little nimble motions,"
with complete honesty and fidelity to the record. He was a
great artist in the greatest of arts, the art of living.

Let me tell you how easy it is to take Montaigne to your
heart: You can scarcely open a page of, say, the translations by
E. J. Trechmann or by Thomas Cotton, or of Dr. Armaingaud's
text, without coming upon something which causes you to exclaim, "That is like me." I am not so foolish as to imagine
that I am very like Montaigne or so careless of the truth as to
try to create Montaigne in my image. But Montaigne tells us
in one place something that has struck some commentators as
trivial but rather curious; he says that at first he did like radishes
very much, then he could not eat them at all for a long time,
and now he likes radishes again. And, dear reader, that is
what happened to me. As a boy I was so fond of radishes that
my mother told everybody that I could "eat a barrel of them";
then my taste for radishes vanished for a long period of time;
and now I am very fond of them again.

Does that sound trivial? If it does, you are incapable of understanding Montaigne. For that is a paradigm of Montaigne's
great contribution to thought. Listen to the great French critic,

Jules Lemaître (translated by A. W. Evans in the collection of essays, *Literary Impressions*):

> One of Montaigne's favorite thoughts is that we can have no certain knowledge since nothing is immutable, neither things nor intelligences, and the mind and its object are both borne along in perpetual movement. Ourselves changing, we behold a changing world. And even when the object under observation is for ever fixed in its forms, the mind in which it is reflected is mutable and multifarious, and this is enough to make it impossible for us to be responsible for anything more than our momentary impression.
>
> How, therefore, could literary criticism constitute itself into a doctrine? Works pass in procession before the mirror of our minds; but, as the procession is long, the mirror becomes modified in the interval, and when by chance the same work returns, it no longer projects the same image.
>
> Any one can try the experiment on himself. I have adored Corneille, and I have been within an ace of despising Racine; at the present moment I adore Racine and Corneille is almost indifferent to me. The transports into which Musset's verses used to throw me, I can recapture now no longer. I have lived with my ears and eyes filled by Victor Hugo's resonance and enchantments, and today I feel Victor Hugo's soul almost alien from mine. I dare not read again the books that delighted me and captured my tears at the age of fifteen. When I try to be sincere, to express only what I have really felt, I am frightened at seeing how little my impressions of the greatest writers accord with traditional judgments, and I hesitate to tell all my thought.

In the frank and intimate record Montaigne set down on paper in the privacy of his library in the Château Montaigne, he observed, first of all, that his opinions were subject to change—not his fundamental opinions, perhaps, but those opinions to which bigots give so much weight. He found inconsistencies within himself. He made the great discovery that life is a living thing; that living is an adventure the outcome of which is happily uncertain.

Michel Eyquem had a vanity: let us forgive him for it. He was not of the nobility, but he wished to convey the impression that he was, that he might explode the pretensions of the nobility with better grace. He added "de Montaigne" to his name and he wrote that his ancestors had occupied the château for many generations, whereas his great-grandfather had purchased the estate in 1477 and had never exercised the right to the name "de Montaigne," nor had Montaigne's father, Pierre Eyquem. This estate was in Périgord not far from the flourishing commercial city of Bordeaux, where Pierre Eyquem was a merchant of wines as well as a landed proprietor.

Pierre Eyquem was of middle-class French stock, with an admixture of British blood. As a young man he had served as a soldier in Italy under Francis I, and in his thirty-third year had married Antoinette de Lopez, a daughter of a Jewish family, whose ancestors had been driven out of Spain and had embraced the Protestant faith. (It was usual for Jews to avoid persecution either by becoming converts to Catholicism or by becoming Huguenots.) There were nine (or it may have been eleven) children born of this marriage, of which Michel was the eldest. Michel was born at the château at high noon on February 28, 1533.

Pierre Eyquem was in every way a remarkable father. An uneducated man himself, he had definite ideas about the proper training and instruction of his children. He wished them to be close to the soil, to learn peasant ways and be, in all things, humane in their feelings. He gave Michel a peasant godfather and godmother, and had him suckled at the breast of a peasant woman. He had ideas about the "conditioning" of children which should interest the Behaviorist psychologists of our time. He forbade corporal punishment and enforced the rule that his children should be taught by gentle persuasion and not by threats, severe discipline, or anything which would shock the nervous system. Pierre arranged that his children should be awakened by the sound of music, he "being of the opinion it did trouble and disturb the brains of children suddenly to wake them in the morning, and to snatch them violently and over hastily from sleep." Among his other activities (he was once mayor of Bordeaux) Pierre Eyquem conducted an employment agency and a labor exchange, and through this agency he brought to the château as instructor to his children a German tutor who knew no French but was learned in Latin. Pierre made it a rule that everybody in the household, the servants included, should learn Latin from the German tutor and forbade the use of French before the children until they should have reached six years of age. Mother and father, cook and gardener, nurse and page, dutifully learned Latin.

When at the age of six Michel Eyquem was sent away to the College of Guienne at Bordeaux, he already knew Latin literature and spoke a kind of Latin better than he spoke French. He tells us, however, that he was dull and backward as a child, a dreamer who was never much in danger of mischief because he did nothing whatever. "For, though I was of a strong and healthful constitution, and of a disposition tolerably sweet and tractable; yet I was withal so heavy, idle, and indisposed that they could not rouse me from this stupidity to any exercise or recreation nor get me out to play." He envied the ability of other children to excel in athletics but not to the point of emulating them; the only thing he enjoyed in the nature of exercise was horseback riding.

His father wanted him to be a lawyer and that was the profession in which he was educated. And at the age of twenty-one he had served out an apprenticeship in Toulouse, after leaving school at the age of thirteen, and his father purchased him a magistracy under the system then prevailing. In the following year he accompanied his father, then mayor of Bordeaux, to Paris to plead for the restoration of the privileges of the city which had been abrogated by the king after the salt tax uprising.

Next year he began the practice of law in Bordeaux, but a more important thing happened to him: he met and became the friend of Étienne de la Boëtie, a brilliant young lawyer, for whom he formed a strong attachment which lasted until Boëtie's death six years later while still in his thirties. At this period of his life Montaigne was somewhat dissipated and self-indulgent. He has given us an astonishingly frank account of himself and of his self-indulgences of these years of sowing wild oats. He was bored by his work as a magistrate. But he was of good address, charming in his manner, and a few years later we hear of him as a man respected and admired by the rival monarchs, Henry III and Henry of Navarre, and learn that he was entrusted with various diplomatic missions between the rival factions. He is strangely silent about these years of his life; but he emerged from them with a particular attachment for Henry of Navarre.

Meanwhile Boëtie died, leaving Montaigne his fine library. And at the age of thirty-three Montaigne married François de la Cassaigne, a woman of a middle-class family, who brought to him a considerable dowry. She proved to be a perfect mate for him, for she was efficient, cautious, and capable: she managed his affairs for him on the estate, which he would surely have let go to the dogs, because he had no business or monetary sense, no knowledge of farming: he was negligent and forgetful; he could not read his own handwriting two days after he had written something; and he was utterly helpless in practical affairs. Of marriage he has written, "Marriage hath for its share, usefulness, justice, honour, and constancy—a flat pleasure but a universal one. Love is founded upon delight alone, and giveth it, truly, of a kind more poignant, more caressive, more vital . . . A man doth not marry for himself, whatever people say; he marries quite as much, for his posterity and his family."

He was not over-faithful to his wife; but his temperament was not very sanguine and he seems to have caused her no distress. From all accounts his marriage was a happy one. "Every strange woman," he writes, "seems to us a comely woman; and every man knows by experience that the continual sight of one another cannot give the pleasure which comes of taking and leaving by fits and starts. As for me, these interruptions fill me with a fresh love towards my family, and restore me in pleasanter fashion to the groove of my home. . . . The fact that happy marriage is so rare is a sign of its value. When we fashion it finely and take it the right way, there is no nobler institution in society."

In this he was following the custom of the good French bourgeois. Six children, all girls, were born of the union, only one of whom reached maturity. In 1568 his father died, leaving him the château and the estate. He spent two years in Paris seeking a high appointment in court; but the most fanatical of religious wars—the war between Catholicism and Protestantism—was brewing at that time and he, being of a peaceable nature, hating all forms of cruelty and intolerance, gave up public life in disgust and retired to his château. In 1572 occurred the dreadful Massacre of St. Bartholomew's Day. Montaigne refused to become embroiled with either side and it was in that year that he determined upon the task which was to occupy him the rest of his life—that of setting down from day to day his comments on what he read and on the things that interested him. In the library of the château he had Latin mottoes from the classics inscribed upon the beams and the walls of his study, such as, "I determine nothing; I do not comprehend things; I suspend judgment; I examine"—"The human race is too greedy of fables"—"Men are tormented by their opinions of things; not by the things themselves."

Beginning first as a mere commentator upon the works he read, he developed a tendency to examine himself, to write about his contacts with the peasants and tradespeople; to set down his impressions of life; and lastly to study carefully and accurately his own nature, making a clinical report of his conduct, his feelings, his ideas. In 1580 he published the first two volumes of these *Essays*. He sent a copy to Henry III, and decided to travel. He made a tour of Switzerland, Germany, and Italy. On this trip he kept a diary of the things which interested him. In Bologna he saw a priest attempt to exorcise a devil from a melancholy man, and when Montaigne questioned the priest, he said he had relieved a woman of an unusually large devil only the day before. Montaigne sets down all the priest told him. He witnessed a circumcision and described the ceremony in detail. He encountered, during Lent, a group of Flagellants, men, women, boys, and girls, whipping themselves until their bodies were raw and bloody, but apparently without pain. He was received everywhere as a man of high estate and was entertained by cardinals and magistrates. The fame of his *Essays* had preceded him and he was asked by the ecclesiastical authorities to remove certain passages they considered inimical to the Church; whereupon he made changes but only to emphasize the matter objected to.

Nevertheless he conformed always outwardly with Church observances, putting up votive tablets for himself, his wife and daughter at the shrine of Loretto. He was particularly interested in the courtesans and houses of prostitution in Rome and Venice, and he visited many of them, carefully noting down what he saw. He was also suffering from the stone at this time and sought the baths and cures, to no avail.

On his return to France he was elected Mayor of Bordeaux, the office his father had held before him. He made an excellent mayor, instituting many reforms. He was on such intimate terms with Henry of Navarre that, when the latter succeeded to the throne, he twice visited Montaigne at his château. During the plague of 1587 Montaigne absented himself from the city and remained on his estate, an act which has brought severe censure upon him by some commentators and which caused charges of neglect of duty to be lodged against him.

He was tired of political life, anyhow, and he probably welcomed the opportunity to be relieved of his post. He had found two devoted disciples in Pierre Charron, an eminent ecclesiastic, and in Mademoiselle Marie de Gournay, a German woman, whom he spoke of as his adopted daughter and who may have been his mistress. It was to Mademoiselle de Gournay that he left the work of editing and revising his unpublished *Essays*.

While he was in Paris superintending the publication of a new edition of the *Essays,* he was thrown into prison on trumped up charges by the Catholic League, but was released within eight hours on the order of Catherine de Medici. On his way home he attended the States General at Blois, but left in time to escape the assassination of the Duc de Guise. He died on September 13, 1592, after long months of pain, from stone. Toward his last years he wrote much about death. But he had a brave attitude toward dissolution:

> Few men die in the opinion that it is their last hour, and there is nothing wherein the flattery of hope does more to delude us. It never ceases to whisper in our ears, others may have been much sicker without dying; my condition is not so desperate as it is thought, and at the worst, God has done some miracles. Which happens by reason that we set too much value upon ourselves. It seems as if the universality of things were in some measure to suffer by our dissolution, and that it did commiserate our condition. For as much as our depraved sight represents things to itself after the same manner, and that we are of opinion they stand in as much need of us as we do of them; like people at sea, to whom mountains, fields, cities, heaven and earth are tossed at the same rate they are.

The greatest single work of Montaigne is the *Apology of Raimond Sebond*. It is a long sustained work of irony; on the surface a vindication of Catholic orthodoxy and in reality an assault upon every conviction, Catholic or Protestant, upon which faith is based. It is the bitterest satire he ever penned, and it was inspired by the fanatical fratricide between Catholics and Huguenots, which within a few years had cost eight hundred thousand lives, left nine towns razed to the ground, two hundred and fifty villages burned, and had turned the whole countryside of France into a shambles. Montaigne's château was twice invaded, but he kept his temper and his counsel and nothing was harmed.

Much ink has since been spilled in argument as to whether Montaigne should have done this or that, whether he should not have espoused a cause and declared himself in the momentous religious and political uprisings of the day. But his eternal question, *"Que sçay je?"* ("What know I?") is the answer. As J. M. Robertson says in his admirable introduction to the Oxford University Press edition of the *Essays of Montaigne,* translated by Trechmann, "The human wisdom of Montaigne had entered into the life-blood of France and of the world." Plutarch nourished Montaigne, and the genius of Shakespeare fed upon the genius of Plutarch and Montaigne. The quarrel between Huguenot and Catholic has long been dead now: the essays of Montaigne are eternal. With sublime audacity that swart little man, who has described himself so perfectly and minutely to us, has given us all reason to face life with more courage and assurance.

On Learning to Read

By LEE WILSON DODD

Lee Wilson Dodd, who died May 16, 1933, of a heart attack, had turned to literature after practicing law for five years. Not only a teacher (Bread Loaf Writers' Conference and Sarah Lawrence College), he was also poet, playwright, and novelist (SPEED, THE CHANGELINGS, PALS FIRST, THE BOOK OF SUSAN). Next autumn, according to a report in TIME, he was to have succeeded Professor George Pierce Baker as active instructor of playwriting in the famed Department of Drama at Yale.

FOR the past twelve months or so I have been engaged, at two summer schools and a junior college, in "teaching literature." What precisely have I been teaching, and what benefits, if any, may my pupils have been deriving from the experiment? Experiment I must call it, for I have had neither the formal and severe training of professional scholarship nor any instruction in the science—if it be a science—of pedagogy. I came to these jobs as a man who had spent much of his life in reading and writing—as a "literary man." To minute, exhaustive knowledge of world literature I could not pretend. Such were and are my disqualifications. What compensating gifts may my employers have hopefully supposed me to be bringing with me?

They must have argued, I presume, that a lifetime devoted to literary pursuits could not, culturally, have been spent wholly in vain. Be it far from me to question this assumption! After all, if a man has written verse, novels, plays, essays, short stories, book reviews, and so forth, for thirty or more years, he is entitled to the benefit of the doubt; he may well have picked up some notions as to the differences between good writing

---

From *The Atlantic Monthly*, July, 1932. Used by permission of the author and *The Atlantic Monthly*.

and bad, and if he has put in most of his spare moments in reading he ought at least to have gained a bowing acquaintance with a number of satisfactory authors. It is only fair to add that the one advantage I claimed for myself over many (by no means all) teachers of literature was a really fanatic love for well-written books. This love, I suggested, being white-hot and ineradicable, could hardly fail to communicate a few sparks of its secret fire to my students.

Has it done so? In this cynical, debunking age, I know perfectly what answer the ungentle reader is expecting, and I am not at all sorry to disappoint him.

Yes, I believe that it has done so. Not, certainly, to all, and perhaps not extravagantly to any who were unmarked from their cradles by the bite of the Bookworm. But a year of teaching, or of teaching at, literature has convinced me, somewhat to my own surprise, that literature can indeed be taught. A desire to read, and to read good books, can at least be stimulated even in more or less obdurate youthful breasts.

Heaven forbid that I should now imagine myself, unaided and untrained, to have discovered some new and revolutionary technic for "teaching literature!" What little I have accomplished has doubtless been far better accomplished many times before by professional teachers. I have had one or two masters myself in past years who brought to their classrooms not only scholarship but a winning humor, humanity, and grace. Remembering them, I blush for my present temerity. However, one can do only what one can. What is it that I have at least been trying—and trying very hard—to do?

Briefly, I have been trying to teach my students *how to read*.

The fine art of reading, I quickly and painfully discovered, is in no little danger of being lost. Most of the students, I found, were quite unaware that reading is anything more than a mechanical acquirement. It seldom occurred to them that the great books of the world will not unbosom themselves to slovenly, incurious, inartistic readers. The page of a great book does not differ mechanically from the page of a worthless book —it is merely a sheet of paper with some black, odd-looking specks on it. It remains that, or is transformed into wisdom, beauty, joy. But this transformation depends finally upon the reader—upon the reader's ability *to read*.

A printed poem, for example, is very like the printed score of a musical composition. The poem itself does not exist for you until you have correctly and artistically performed and interpreted it. With a poem, this performance, this interpretation, is usually a solitary joy, a purely mental re-creation from the printed page. It need not be so. The poem may be performed and interpreted for others, may be read aloud. Comparatively few of us, however, even if we are fond of poetry, can bear to listen to a poem thus recited or read aloud. Why? For a number of reasons, but for one chiefly: the reading aloud, nine times in ten, is wretchedly done. Not many people these days can read prose aloud acceptably; as for verse—! The mere presence of meter before its readers seems to reduce them to a condition of imbecility. They either gabble and stutter through it with no apparent awareness either of its natural movement or of its meaning, or they monotonously chant it in a somnolent singsong, or, worse still, they smother it in all the affected graces and overblown sentiment of professional "elocution." Our poets themselves suffer from this general artistic paralysis, and when they attempt to read out their own compositions they present the horrid spectacle of infanticides publicly butchering their children.

Now, obviously enough, if one cannot read a poem aloud without destroying it, this must partly be due to one's inability to read it to one's self. Partly, I say, because the self-consciousness of unaccustomed public performance, even if the public be only a single suffering friend, tends to exaggerate all one's errors of technic or taste. Nevertheless, if you can read a poem to yourself with pleasure, you should at least be a little better able to read it to others without giving them positive pain; and, if you cannot, the odds are that you have never, in any significant sense of the word, *read* that particular poem.

For what does reading—what I should like to call *re-creative* reading—imply? Many difficult things. A book might well be written—if sensitively written—to enumerate, analyze, discuss them. Such a book would necessarily have much to say of the delicate functions of rhythm (in heightening yet controlling emotion, in regulating emphasis, and so forth), much of the root meanings and sky-branching connotations (suggestive emotional overtones) of words, much of language as logic and of language as representation—of language as architecture, as line and mass, as color, as music. And the lurking presence of an often extremely subtle irony in almost all first-rate writing would have to be pointed out as a quality too frequently missed by the indifferent, unalert reader. We need, in short, a new rhetoric, not to teach good writing, which can hardly be taught, but to teach good reading, which can far more certainly be taught. Why readers go wrong is the underlying question to be dealt with; yet clearly, in a brief paper, I cannot deal with it here. Two widely differing illustrations of the process of going wrong may, however, be given.

A girl student—a lively and lightly sophisticated young modernist—was protesting against my cruelty. "I can't do it!" she almost wailed. "I simply can't read stodgy old-fashioned stories like that! They bore me so. Aren't you ever going to give me something to read that I don't have to begin by hating?"

She had been assigned *The Vicar of Wakefield,* and we had met for a first conference upon it.

I might, fairly enough, have reminded her that since she had herself elected "A Survey of English Literature," she could hardly expect me not to try, at least, to interest her in certain of the established classics. We were at the time supposed to be "surveying" the eighteenth century. But why waste one's breath? I held out the forbidding volume and asked her to read me the opening paragraph. She gave me a single desolated glance, sighed, accepted the book, and hurriedly and indifferently began as follows:

" 'I was ever 'v the opinion that the hones' man—' "

"Oh, wait, please," I said. "Just read what's there. Don't add or subtract anything."

"I don't understand."

"You put in a word, removed several letters, and subtracted a comma."

Her impatient little wriggle was very expressive.

"Begin again," I suggested. "Take it more slowly."

She began again, with an exaggerated dragging of each syllable:

"'I .. was .. ev-er .. of .. the .. opinion .. that—'"

"You've repeated two fatal mistakes in seven words," I interrupted.

"You're just trying to get my goat!" she snapped.

"Yes. I am. And now that I've got it—"

"You haven't! You can't make me like this book by being angry. It's a stupid, silly book—and just because people used to be dull enough to like it—"

"Some people are still dull enough to like it. I am, for one."

"I don't believe you really like it. You just think you ought to."

"Oh, no," I said. "There's no 'ought' about it. I'll admit I haven't much respect for the plot of this story. I'll admit the melodramatic coincidences toward the end of it are rather silly. But they're not important. No one ever rereads *The Vicar of Wakefield* for its plot."

"I can't imagine reading it again!"

"I've read most of it a number of times," I said.

"Oh, you have to—because you're a teacher."

"No, I'm not that kind of teacher—and I've a fairly good memory. I like turning back to it now and then for the pure joy of appreciation."

"What is there to appreciate?"

"A good deal. For one thing, Goldsmith's deceptive simplicity. Whenever he's being particularly deep and subtle, he pretends he is merely being naïve. That's called irony, you know—or perhaps you don't; but it is. Only, Goldsmith's irony has a quite special flavor. There's nothing harsh or ill-tempered about it. He has a secret process by which he blends irony with sympathy and charm—

and the secret, worse luck, appears to have died with him."

"I don't see what you mean." She was a little worried, however. "I just thought he was—sort of formal and silly and awfully sentimental."

"Yes. That's because you haven't read the book yet."

"Oh! I did read it. I told you I would, and it nearly killed me—but I honestly did!"

"My dear girl," I said, "suppose I asked you to play a sonata by Mozart for me—and you rattled away at the notes, missing perhaps a third of them, without timing or expression, because you had decided in advance that Mozart's music was silly and old-fashioned and you had no use for it."

"But I love Mozart!"

"Exactly. And I love Goldsmith. So you can imagine how I feel when I ask you to play me some Goldsmith—and you promptly murder him."

"Well—I'm sorry. I didn't know you felt that way. I don't see how you *can!*"

"And I don't see how so bright a girl as you can occasionally be so obtuse. But, of course, girls in general aren't very quick at detecting irony."

"I thought irony was saying one thing and meaning another."

"So, roughly, it is."

"But Goldsmith's so deadly *plain!*"

"Is he? Let me read you this first paragraph—slowly. It shouldn't be read too slowly; the movement is *Adagio ma non troppo*. But Goldsmith is devilish sly. Until you're familiar with him you have to watch him, or you'll miss something delightful every few words." And I reached for the book and began, abominably enough, underlining each lurking point for her.

As I concluded the first page my pupil was actually blushing.

"Please don't go on!" she begged. "I simply didn't realize he was being as cagy as that. I never felt like such an idiot in my life!"

She jumped to her feet and held out her hand. "I'll really *read* it for you this time," she said.

Another student came to me flushed with a great discovery. She had been reading for the first time the lyrics of William Blake.

"They're the lovelist things I ever read!" she exclaimed. "They're poetry—the real thing! I don't see why you've had us poke through all that Pope and Gray and Cowper and stuff. The minute you read Blake you realize all that sort of thing isn't poetry at all."

"Well," I replied, "that's splendid. It's a wonderful gift to be able to distinguish true poetry from sham poetry at a glance."

"You just *feel* the difference at once," she said.

"Read me one of the lyrics you like best," I suggested.

She opened the book.

"I like all of them! . . . Well, of course, there's 'Tiger, Tiger.'"

"Yes. Read me that."

She did so, with a breathless, happy excitement. "It just thrills me!" she added.

"Why?"

"It's so vivid! It makes you see and understand a tiger as you never have before. It makes you feel that he's the most magnificent thing in the world."

"Rather terrifying, though?"

"That's part of it—that's why it's so exciting. It's so—suggestive!"

"What does the tiger suggest to you?"

"Oh—strength and swiftness and fire and—"

"Yes—?"

"But the main thing is—it works you all up so. When I read it the first time I just wanted to jump up and yell!"

"And do you think that's why Blake wrote the poem? Because he'd seen a tiger—or had imagined one so completely that he had to exclaim how magnificent and beautiful and terrifying it was?"

"I .. yes .. I suppose so. That's why it's *real* poetry—he was so excited himself."

"I see. It hasn't occurred to you, then, that the poem may mean something more than that—something quite definite that Blake wanted to say to you?"

A shade of disappointment crossed her face.

"You see," I continued relentlessly, "Blake wasn't the sort of man who just got vaguely, however gloriously, excited over tigers and lambs and things. He was a very positive, pugnacious man. He thought he had seized the hidden truth about pretty much everything by direct intuition or inspiration. He thought human reason was of the Devil, but that the poetic imagination was of God. He identified his imagination with Truth, with God himself. In short, he was as pure an example of the seer, of the convinced mystic, as you will find anywhere. His visions to him are reality—the one possible Reality. So you may be certain that through his Tiger he is expressing what he believes to be one aspect of Eternal Truth . . . and you haven't really *read* that poem until you have read it as he intended it."

She looked more disappointed than before, and even a little alarmed.

"But I've read the poem over and over! I know it by heart. And I don't see how you can tell just what he *meant* by it."

"You can't," I explained, "unless you have studied all of Blake's poems and prose writings and designs very closely, in order to discover what he intends by the *symbols* he uses. Like most mystics, Blake was a symbolist, and he had built up a whole system of symbolism. Moreover, he uses these symbols to express as exactly as he can all his ideas about life, death, and eternity. A symbol is nothing but a figure of speech which is used to stand for an idea—and with Blake a given symbol stands invariably for a given idea. Now it happens that the Tiger is one of Blake's fixed symbols; and I repeat that you may know Blake's poem by heart, but you haven't really *read* it until you have discovered what Blake meant by his Tiger—discovered, that is, what he himself was excited about."

"Oh, good Lord," said the girl, "but that takes all the poetry out of it!"

"Which isn't my fault, you see, but Blake's—if it's anybody's. Besides, Blake would violently have disagreed with you. Poetry, to Blake, was the expression of Eternal Truth."

"Oh . . . How can I find out . . . What *did* he mean by the Tiger?"

"He meant the wrath of God," I said. "Just as by the Lamb he meant always the love of God."

"Oh . . . I wish you hadn't spoiled it for me!" she wailed. "It doesn't seem nearly so wonderful any more. It takes the poetry out of it."

"Why? By adding a meaning?"

"Yes—no—oh, I don't know," she said. "I guess I just like to feel things sort of vaguely and get excited about them."

"In other words, my dear girl, you are still a complete romantic. You like one *kind* of poetry, and so proclaim it to be the only kind there is. There are lots of supposed critics, even nowadays, who completely agree with you."

She brightened a little at this.

"Well, anyway," she said, "it's awfully interesting—and I'm going to think it over." And she left me with a little puckered frown between her eyes. I was glad of that frown. It didn't worry me that she should feel, temporarily, that I had spoiled something precious for her. I hoped, indeed, that it might lead her to take one more courageous step in the always difficult re-creative process of learning to read.

These two illustrations of faulty reading—or, preferably, of *non*-reading—have perhaps been given at too great length, for in themselves they are far from exhausting the subject. Yet they do, I think, bring out two very general, opposite, and disastrous tendencies. Both these girls were students of more than average intelligence. Both, in the usual phrase, were "fond of reading." Neither had ever been taught, or had discovered for herself, how to read.

The failure of the first student with *The Vicar of Wakefield* was due to a very common contemporary prejudice. I have discovered that at least a third of my students, if not a good half of them, approach the masterpieces of former generations truculently, with obvious chips on disdainful shoulders; for our young people, it appears, are instinctive and convinced believers in progress. Today, they assume, is necessarily better, more enlightened, than yesterday. At least I know not how else to interpret the widespread assumption that the best of our new books are necessarily superior to any written, or that could conceivably have been written, in the darker ages of the past.

The argument (seldom precisely formulated) would seem to run as follows: We know more than our ancestors; therefore we write better than our ancestors. So why waste time on inferior productions? The study of literature should rationally be confined to the best, which is clearly contemporary literature. Q. E. D.

That there are possibly a few dropped stitches in the fabric of this argument never seems to occur to them. It is not my purpose for the present to point these out. I am here concerned only with the effect of this attitude upon many promising students—upon their mere ability to *read*.

If you approach a book, any book, with rooted suspicion and bored indifference, the chances of your being able to read that book, re-creatively, are extremely small. To begin with, you will already have abandoned a first principle of good reading— namely, fair-mindedness, a desire to give the author before you a square deal. In other words, you must grant him your complete attention. You must really listen to what he has to say. If, having done so, you find what he has to say false, or dull, or his manner of saying it awkward or meretricious, you may excuse yourself and leave him. But until you have heard him with attention you have not really heard him, and any judgment you may pronounce must necessarily be unfair.

My first student, then, had not been courteously fair-minded to Goldsmith; she had not listened to him; her mind had been elsewhere while her eyes merely fulfilled an appointed task. Now Goldsmith always speaks quietly, politely, with a minimum of emphasis; he is too well bred to solicit attention; he assumes that his readers are equally well bred. This is evidently a dangerous assumption in a period of clamor, public posturing, and impervious ballyhoo.

As for the second student, her inability to read William Blake did not spring (Heaven knows) from lack of attention. She is the type of student, by no means uncommon, for whom reading is always an emotional debauch. If an author thrills her, she asks no more of him; the immediate esthetic thrill is for her the beginning and end of art. To have been made to *feel* something—even if one is hardly aware what it is one has felt or why one has felt it—is enough. Intellectual curiosity, understanding, remain in abeyance. The cheek flushes, the heart beats faster, and the miracle has been accomplished—even if the revolutionary thinker and mystic, Blake, be transformed thereby into a spineless romantic and purveyor of golden gush to schoolgirls.

But the particular error is not the point. Twenty more might as easily have been illustrated and commented upon. The point, in the end, is but this, that a catholic appreciation of the better books of the world depends upon our ability to *read* them, and that reading is an art in itself—an art to be studied as other arts are studied and, within the limits of a given personality, more or less perfectly acquired. Teachers of literature are—if they are anything useful—teachers of reading. Such at least is my present conviction. It is almost the first and last duty of a teacher of literature to master the art of reading himself, and to help, by any means in his power, his students to master it. Our existence as teachers of literature is justified only so far as we are able to teach our pupils how to read.

Practice What You Teach

By JAMES WEBER LINN

James Weber Linn is Professor of English at Chicago. He also writes a column for THE CHICAGO DAILY TIMES.

TWO men sat and chatted in a Pullman, on a crack train speeding over the flat lands of the Middle West. They seemed to be of an age somewhere between forty and fifty-five, that indeterminable period in the lives of the alert and successful during which the appearance remains unaltered almost for decades. They were well, if quietly, dressed; they might have been business men on the way to a convention. That, in fact, is what they were; only their business was education, and the convention was a meeting of the Modern Language Association of America, where one was to read a paper on Balzac, and the other was to listen, to observe, and possibly to select a new assistant professor. They were old acquaintances, classmates in a large Eastern college, and colleagues in a still larger Western university, in which one was a dean and the other a professor in the department of Romance languages.

The dean was by way of being an authority on Pope; the professor was indubitably an authority on nineteenth-century French literature. Both had published books on their subjects. The dean's book on Pope had brought him, in royalties, something more than two hundred dollars; the professor's textbook on the history of French literature twice as many thousands. The professor smoked cigarettes by habit and preference, the dean a large cigar. They were, of course, talking shop, but the talk had taken a direction unusual among scholars, even though the scholars were teachers also.

From *The Saturday Evening Post*, March 26, 1932. Reprinted by permission of the author and *The Saturday Evening Post*.

"I hear," remarked the professor cheerfully, "that the new system of undergraduate teaching at the University of Chicago is not going very well."

"It's too soon to say," replied the dean. "It isn't new, exactly. Wisconsin tried it on a smaller scale, and has just given it up. And what is more, it isn't teaching, as you call it; it is just a process of educational manufacturing without bookkeeping. And finally, it can't fail. It is a blessed thought in our business, Bob, that no system of education, if persisted in, can in the long run fail to educate."

"That was John Manly's wise crack," commented the professor. "And I must say I don't agree with him. I think our whole system of undergraduate education in the American college has failed, and will continue to fail as long as we persist in it. And just for that reason I welcomed the Chicago plan, and hope they make something out of it."

"Well," said the dean, "so do I. But it doesn't seem to me that even Chicago has gone to the root of the matter. Of course, I don't agree with you that our undergraduate education is a failure. I do go so far as to admit that it has one very grave defect. And I don't think the Chicago plan touches this defect."

"Lack of standards?"

"Not exactly. Confusion of standards. We don't know what we want, and we don't care what the boys and girls want."

"What they want," remarked the professor with a grin, "if by 'want' you mean 'wish,' as I suppose you do, is a good time. What they need is discipline and more discipline. I don't mean moral discipline. I see no advantage, and innumerable disadvantages, in concern with their conduct. I mean intellectual discipline. We try to make them think, but we don't force them into thinking straight. Therefore they leave us intellectually as immature as they come to us, except as four more years of age have given them a bit more judgment perhaps."

"Rot," replied the dean, knocking the ash from his cigar. "The fault, dear Bob, is in ourselves and not in lack of discipline that our undergraduates remain underlings. We are manufacturers who have neither any clear idea of what we can use in the way of raw materials, nor any definite conception of what we want to produce. No business man would put up a factory without first deciding whether he wished to make surgical instruments, locomotives, or golf clubs. But we do just that. We do not even, as Edward Lear said, 'churn salt water violently in the hope that it will turn into butter, which it seldom or never does.' No, we churn we know not what, in the hope that it will turn into something of value to our contemporary civilization. And what a tribute to American youth is the fact that it frequently does!"

"American youth!" said the professor. "I am sick of American youth. In my observation, about one-tenth of it has the brains and ambition to think at all. The women are more 'conscientious,' as the phrase goes, than the men, and so they get slightly higher marks; but they are stupider than the men, if anything. Eighty per cent of my students don't really know enough to pound sand down a rat hole, and don't want to."

"A French rat hole, you mean," commented the dean. "Why should they want to, Bob?" He looked out of the window. The train was sweeping through a little city in Ohio. There were vistas of business streets, smeared with dirty snow—for this was in the Christmas holidays—and cinematographic films of warmly clothed men, women and children going about their affairs beside buildings not ugly perhaps, but certainly not distinguished for architectural beauty or for repose of spirit. "I don't know the name of this place, but I have no question that half of its inhabitants under twenty are either in some college somewhere or planning to go to one. Some of them will undoubtedly sit in your classroom one of these days. Ask yourself, my dear boy, why anybody brought up in Main Street should take a passionate interest in French poetry, even including the *Chanson de Roland*—which is, by the way, rather dull reading."

"As dull," inquired the professor caustically, "as Pope?"

"I think so," replied the dean. "And certainly I do not expect one-tenth of our undergraduates to take an interest in

Pope. Not a real interest; not the sort of interest that rouses them to thought. Remember your Emerson. 'What is the hardest task in the world? To think. From thinking we blench and withdraw on this side and on that.' Yes, even you and I, even when our own subjects are involved, often blench and withdraw from thinking; and yet you expect these young Main Streeters to indulge in it eagerly, upon matters which not only have never concerned them in the past but cannot possibly concern them in the future. The wonder is that a tenth of them do, not that 90 per cent refuse to do so."

"They ought not to be in college at all," commented the professor.

"Ought not? Then why are they there? Why, my dear fellow, we go out into the highways and hedges and compel them to come in. We even offer them scholarships."

"To the one-tenth," cut in the professor.

"Did you never hear of scholarships for all-around accomplishment? Did you never hear of athletic scholarships? Did you never hear of college employment associations, which are organized for providing boys and girls not book-learned enough to win prizes with jobs that will enable them to stay in college? I say we compel, or seek to compel, and seek to encourage the compulsion by public opinion, half of these young Main Streeters to attend our colleges, and especially our state universities. That is exactly what I mean when I say that as educational manufacturers we do not know what we want in the way of raw material. At our own university we admit every boy or girl who can present a certificate of graduation from any high school. Harvard admits without examination only boys from the top seventh of the graduating classes from the public schools—and then only under special circumstances. And yet we and Harvard seek to develop exactly the same product in four years—an educated young man. And what is more, we know so little of the relation of high marks in the school classrooms to ambition, and even to brains, that I venture to suspect if you were teaching at Harvard instead of where you are, you would still be complaining that not more than one-tenth of your students had the brains and ambition to pound sand down a French rat hole. One-tenth of the top seventh!"

"I admit," said the professor, "that our own undergraduates, outside the classroom, impress me quite as favorably as do undergraduates at Harvard; at least those I have known."

"Maybe," said the dean with a smile as he took a fresh cigar, "that belief proceeds merely from your loyalty, which is, Bob, one of your most admirable characteristics, even when it leads you to the insistence that Tom, Dick, and Harry could profit by reading the *Chanson de Roland*."

"Or Pope," remarked the professor.

"Or Pope, as you say. But heaven forbid I should make comparisons among our college youth. They are the American mine-run, and we must certainly love them, for we have made so many of them."

"Heaven forbid, as you say," interjected the professor, "that I should love them."

"Ah, Bob, but you do, outside the classroom. Haven't you just been standing up for them to me, when you thought I was comparing our own unfavorably with those elsewhere? Yes, you love them, and that is why I can't understand why you treat them so abominably."

"I treat them abominably?"

"Yes, you, and all the rest of us. We underestimate them; we misunderstand them; we herd them here and there for our own convenience; outside the classroom we treat them as if they were all children, and inside the classroom we treat them as if they were all candidates for the doctorate. We take pay for teaching them, and spend most of our time on the study of subjects in which they are not only not interested but in which they are incompetent to take an interest."

"What do you mean?"

"I mean research. You are about to read a paper which everybody will admire and a few will even enjoy. It will enhance your reputation among your colleagues; by enhancing your reputation it will even increase your market value, and may result in the raising of your salary. No detail of your work on that paper will ever directly affect your teaching in French 102, will it?"

"No," said the professor honestly, though he saw the trend of the cross-examination.

"Then may I ask," said the dean, "how much time and particularly how much intellectual effort you have put in, during the past three months, on French 102, compared to what you have put in on that paper?"

"We-ell——" began the professor.

"Yes," objected the dean, "but in the end it is not well. Your students, dumb as 80 percent of them may be, know that you are more interested in Balzac than you are in them. Do you expect them to share your interest in Balzac, and particularly in the narrow and technical aspects of that voluble gentleman that you have been concerning yourself with? If you do, you are a vain dreamer, and unjust into the bargain. Theoretically, you are paid a salary ——"

"If you can call it that; a plumber wouldn't."

"You are paid a salary to teach, as a plumber is paid to plumb. What would you say of a plumber who spent five hours of the eight he was supposed to be working in your bathroom on an intensive study of the system of drains installed by Tutenkhamun in ancient Akhetaton?"

"Did he, really?" demanded the professor with more interest than he had hitherto shown in any of the dean's remarks.

"Bob," said the dean deliberately, "you are hopeless. You are worse; you are typical. Almost I begin to believe you have no human curiosity at all, only a restless, deep-seated, passionate intellectual curiosity. Do you really imagine that 80 percent of our young Main Streeters are like you in that, or that they ought to be like you? I think you do. I think in that you are typical of most of our colleagues. You think the primary purpose of our undergraduate colleges is to develop scholarship. You perceive that almost all your pupils disagree with you. And therefore, as you remarked a while ago, you think our whole system of undergraduate education in the American college has failed. At times I go along with you in thinking that college education is a failure. But I do not agree with you on the reason for thinking so."

"What," asked the professor, "is your idea of the purpose of our colleges?"

"I think our main difficulty is our failure to recognize that we have two sorts of young men and women to deal with, and that the vast majority of these young men and women— you put it at 80 percent a moment ago—are not interested in scholarship, and cannot be made to take an interest in it."

"What are they interested in?"

"When they come to college? In themselves only—which is the natural, if not the normal, interest."

"And when they leave college?" asked the professor.

"Many of them leave with their interest unchanged. In that lies our failure."

"But you say that they cannot be made to take an interest in scholarship."

"Not only so," replied the dean, "but I am glad of it. An interest in scholarship is ennobling, but it is also narrowing. An interest in scholarship is like an interest in making money—a bad thing if unaccompanied by other interests. For the 80 percent our hope should be to provide a finer culture, to give an increased knowledge of 'the best that has been said and thought in the world,' to make more and more of our young Barbarians and our young Philistines into 'children of light,' as Matthew Arnold phrased it. Parenthetically, what do you know about Arnold?"

"I know," said the professor, "that he was a side-whiskered, old-fashioned Victorian poet, who spent most of his life reading the papers of school children and writing essays on French essayists in which he praised all the wrong things."

"And I know," countered the dean, "that he was the most intelligent critic of society among the Victorians, and that if we made his theory of education—which was also the theory of Newman, the priest, and Huxley, the scientist—the theory of our own college education for the 80 percent, we should soon cease to hear so much talk of our failure as educators."

"Do you mean to imply," demanded the professor, "that Arnold and Huxley agreed on what should constitute a liberal education?"

"They differed widely," said the dean, "in their estimates of what studies a liberal education should include. But their differences are purely incidental. We are all agreed today that philosophy—which includes religion—literature, classic and contemporary, the fine arts and science are all elements of culture. But we are not all agreed that our primary purpose so far as the 80 percent are concerned is not to interest them in scholarship but to provide them with a finer culture. Perhaps I exaggerate our timidity when I say that we do not dare to agree on this."

"Why not?"

"Because if we once agreed on it, we should have to change, not our methods of instruction but our instructors; we should have to devise new ways of getting instructors; in our state universities we should have to offend many a taxpayer, and in our privately endowed colleges many a noble benefactor; and that would be a wrench. I think we college administrators do not wish to have to decide on the primary purpose of our institutions of higher learning. I think we prefer to muddle along. Although the colleges are complained of, they continue to flourish and to provide a sufficiently agreeable existence for many thousands of men and women who could hardly earn as much, in as pleasant company, in any other way as by teaching, and why should these teachers risk having to go to work? What other profession is so noncompetitive? In what other profession is incompetence for and inattention to the job rewarded by permanence of tenure achieved by attention to recreation?"

"Come now, Pete," objected the professor, slightly annoyed. "Do you call my research recreation?"

"For you, certainly," declared the dean. "You know I was not speaking of you when I was speaking of teachers generally, for in spite of your research you are a good teacher, or would be if you permitted yourself to be. But I do call your research recreation; as recreational for you as your golf, and no more related to your teaching than your golf is to giving me tips on the game. Still, if we agreed on the real duty of the colleges to the 80 percent of the undergraduates, we should not have to get rid of you. We should have to get rid of perhaps 80 percent of our present staff of teachers; or at least, transfer them to training schools for the candidates for the doctoral degrees. We should have, in other words, to pull them off the bodies of the undergraduates, whom they have got down at present and are sitting on with placidity varied by an occasional fit of sadistic pinchings and worryings."

"I should say that most of our colleagues were very fair scholars," commented the professor.

"And very fair teachers?" asked the dean.

"I don't know anything about them as teachers, but ——"

"Exactly," interrupted the dean, with more bitterness in his voice than he had shown hitherto. "You don't know anything about them as teachers, and you don't care; and they don't care, and why should they? In the first place, they know that however well or however poorly they may teach, it will make little difference in their careers; and in the second place, they couldn't teach well if they wanted to, most of them, because they know too much."

"You mean too little?"

"Too much about too little. Bob, where do we in the colleges get our teachers from? Out of what group? I'm going down now, as you know, to look over a couple of men that are highly recommended to us. Both of them were Phi Beta Kappa; both of them took their doctors' degrees *cum laude,* one at Columbia and one at Chicago; both of them have had years of experience in teaching; both of them are going to read papers day after tomorrow. If I find that one of them knows how to mix a cocktail and drink it like a gentleman, and not like a hungry orphan in a candy shop, and the other does not, I shall certainly pick the one that does. He will be the nearer to what I want, that I can get; but even he will not be very near."

"How do you know?" asked the professor.

"Because he was a Phi Beta Kappa, and took his doctor's degree *cum laude,*" answered the dean, "and because, like you, he has presumably spent five out of the eight hours a day he might have been giving to his teaching in the past three months in preparing the paper he is to read the day after tomorrow. Because, in other words, he will be strictly representative of the 10 percent of undergraduates who, according to you, 'have the brains and ambition to think at all,' and strictly unrepresentative of the 80 percent of young Main Streeters who will be his pupils. He will not understand them, and they, in consequence, will not understand him. He will not like them, and they, in consequence, will not like him. He will, in the classroom, despise them, and they, in consequence, outside the classroom, will not reflect for two minutes a day on what he has been saying to them. He will be able, he will be zealous, but he will be narrow in the range of his own interests and cheerfully contemptuous of interests not his own. His world will have been the world of the library, as, if he were in another department, it would have been the world of the laboratory; and he will quite honestly deny the truth of Robert Louis Stevenson's dictum that 'books are a mighty bloodless substitute for life.' "

"Then why take him at all?" suggested the professor.

"Because, as things are," replied the dean, "he will be the best I can get. For the 10 percent of potential scholars in his classes, he will be highly fit. He will be, I hope, the kind of man to whom young people who find scholarship, research, really attractive will turn as naturally as sunflowers to the sun. He will, I believe, indirectly and influentially, as well as directly and personally, 'widen the circle of truth,' as we all love to say in our commencement speeches. But what can he do for the great mass of our undergraduates today, who not only have no interest in real scholarship but are quite incapable of it?

"Men of his group and type are actually uneasy in the presence of 80 percent of undergraduates you speak of. They look upon the facile, wide-ranging, perfectly normal emotionalism of young people as insincere; some of them even regard it as abnormal and dangerous. Having themselves been concentratedly industrious almost to the breaking point, they are inclined to sneer at the activities of youth as not only misdirected but vapid. You think not? Well, let me ask you. Haven't you a boy in French 102 this semester named Zimmerman?"

"Zimmerman? Wait a minute. W. Zimmerman. A big ox? The sort that every now and then goes to sleep in the classroom?"

"Yes, that's Bill. I gather you don't think much of him?"

"He comes and he recites. He might scrape through with a C. What about him?"

"Has he any business in college?"

"Hardly, I should say. He is lazy, not particularly interested, and, if I remember, was reported to me as having written only four thousand words for a term paper when I asked for five."

"Bill worked all summer with a construction gang. He is getting up at 5:30 now every morning to deliver papers. He is also trying to get together a group of small boys for instruction in games next spring and summer, if he is lucky. He played a pretty fair game of football until his shoulder was hurt. No, I shouldn't call Bill lazy or uninterested—at least in life. But I agree that he has no place in your classroom. Or, to put it the other way round, even you, Bob, have no place, with your present ideas, as teacher of such a boy. And yet Bill is quite surely representative of 80 percent of our undergraduates."

"If I am not fit," began the professor, "to teach human oxen, male or female ——"

"Not, as I say, because you do not know enough, but because you know too much. Not because you are unsympathetic, but because you are too narrowly sympathetic. Scholarship, Bob, is a jealous mistress. She demands pure passion in her worship. Once she attaches a courtier, she will not let him go. He must live and die in her service alone. The rewards of that service are great in peace and content with the employment, but the limitations are strict. It decreases sympathy with society; it compels irritation with Bill Zimmerman; it makes the teaching of Bill a bore. Yet we asked Bill to come to college; in his freshman year he even had a scholarship. We shall give him a degree some day; and when he is an alumnus, and making money, we shall ask him to give some of it to us, for the salaries of whoever are to teach his sons and daughters when they come in their turn. Don't you think, Bob, that Bill is entitled to teaching by somebody who is glad to have him about? Don't you think he is entitled to teaching by somebody who is primarily interested in Zimmerman and not in research?"

"I think," said the professor a little angrily, "that you are trying to classify me among the fish. I may be cold-blooded, but I swim to the surface of life occasionally."

"I said ten minutes ago," insisted the dean, "that I did not mean you when I spoke of the general run of college teachers. It was only because you insisted on making the matter personal that I illustrated with Bill Zimmerman. We'll pass Bill; and I hope you will, too, because if you don't, he will be ineligible for basket ball, and that would be more of a college calamity than if either of us here should break a leg. Among the students, I mean. Bill was the captain of his high-school basketball team when we awarded him a freshman scholarship. I don't say that his captaincy had anything to do with the scholarship, but I suspect that Bill thought at the time that we expected him to play in college, and that we hoped he would be eligible."

"Bah!" said the professor. "Never mind Zimmerman. What I should like to ask is, if we are to have college teachers primarily interested in the masses and in their general culture, how are we to get them?"

"I can't imagine," said the dean. "At present, we are moving in the other direction. In many colleges, only men and women badged with the symbol of primary interest in research are permitted to teach at all; and everywhere the men and women not so badged are whispered down by the formal educationalists."

"Look here, Pete," interrupted the professor triumphantly. "Whom do you remember of our teachers back in Willherst? Hoppy, and Phillips, and Winchester, and Suddard, eh? Well, weren't they great scholars? At least Hoppy was, and Winchester."

"And Phillips wasn't, nor Suddard," laughed the dean. "Great men if you like, but not scholars. Remember the nights in Suddard's rooms when he read us *Almayer's Folly,* and how Phillips used to go over and adjust the curtain just so, and then tell his classes the ghost story, just about the same time every year? And even Winchester—did you know, even when you were a senior, that Winchester was a great scholar? Not a bit of it. You knew that he could read the ballad of *Sir Patrick Spens* so that you could see the Scotch ladies combing their hair and waiting, waiting, but you didn't know that old Winny had dug up two entirely new versions of *Barbara Allen* among the Tennessee mountaineers, and you wouldn't have given a damn if you had known, except as a human-interest story—now, would you?"

"I don't suppose I should," admitted the professor. "But he was a great teacher because he was a great scholar."

"Nonsense," declared the dean. "Any really great mind transcends the limits of its instinctive interests. Socrates as a teacher would have been at home in the mind even of a born salesman, even of a baby vamp. I don't suppose Mark Hopkins cared much what sort of student sat at the other end of his log; he could match that student's interests whatever they might be. But there are few minds with any such quality of universality. And what I am trying to talk, Bob, is college business, not idealism."

"Well, then, if you aren't going to do anything about it, what are you going to do about it?"

"I wish," admitted the dean, "I knew. What we want are not brilliant students but independent thinkers; men who are genuinely interested in the best that has been said and thought in the world, not exclusively interested in little bits of it here and there; men who are all the more interested in the normal undergraduate because they know themselves to be far from unusual; men who understand the 80 percent as the 80 percent understand one another, but who have more to give to the young than the young have to give one another, and are better trained in communication. I think perhaps that once we made such men and women welcome as teachers in our colleges, we should find more of them turning to the profession. Good teachers are not born; they are made; but they are not made, except in rare instances, out of the raw material of which scholars are made. In every college there are scores and scores of undergraduates who are planning to go into the law, into newspaper work, into advertising, into manufacturing, into salesmanship, who would be of more social value as teachers of undergraduates. As things are, they never think of becoming teachers—though a few of them become coaches in sports— because they do not dream that success in college teaching is open to them. As of course, at present, it isn't.

"If I should say to Bill Zimmerman now, 'Why don't you teach?' he would pop his eyes open, and say, 'Dean, I never got but one A in my life,' or 'Wouldn't I have to get a Ph.D. or something like that?' And of course I'd have to answer, 'That is so.' But I don't know that it has to stay so. I don't know any real reason why we should not begin to realize that scholars are fit only to inspire potential scholarship, and that for by far the larger number of our undergraduates, no matter what our educational system is, teachers must be recruited and trained and rewarded who are not scholarly but merely intelligent and humane. And I do know that we are selling the greater number of our undergraduates gold bricks today. Fortunately, the boys and girls have such a pleasant time outside the classroom that they don't much care what goes on in it, and, fortunately, their parents are blinded to the situation by their memories of the Hoppys, and Phillipses, and Winchesters, and Suddards they once knew. Heaven is my witness that they never see any of those who teach their children in the colleges today, except occasionally at banquets, and then they don't talk to us; we talk to them, and there is great safety in loquacity."

"If that is so," replied the professor, yawning, "I should feel never safer in my life. . . . What shall we have for dinner, Pete?"

"Duck soup," replied the dean amiably. "We live on it, Bob."

Seabury Versus Cicero

By HEYWOOD BROUN

Heywood Broun was born in Brooklyn, New York, December 7, 1888. He has been a newspaper man all his life, beginning as a reporter on The Morning Telegraph *(New York). He has successively been on the staff of* The New York Tribune *and* The New York World. *Since 1928 his views have been expressed for the Scripps-Howard newspapers. Mr. Broun now writes his daily column, "It Seems To Me," for* The New York World-Telegram.

THE subject of the symposium was "Is education keeping step with the changing times?" I haven't been around where education was going on for a long time. All I hear about it is from my son, who reports that Horace Mann would have won the basketball game if the referee hadn't given them a couple of raw decisions. This leaves education about where it was when I quit it.

But the symposium was conducted before the parents' association of my old alma mater. Naturally, I wanted to show the principal and the rest that I had gone out into the world with a general inclination to do the institution credit. Unfortunately, I forgot practically all I had planned to say.

The reason for that was that I found myself in such violent disagreement with one of the speakers. I often find myself in violent disagreement with people. But not frequently enough. There never was an age in which there was so much stuff said and done with which there should be disagreement. But being in opposition to something never inspires me with the tongues of angels. I more or less foam at the mouth and remain inarticulate.

The declaration which unbalanced me was that we should return to the modes of the Middle Ages. At that time a thing called "authority" or "excellence" existed in education. In other words, you started for a goal, and when you arrived you remarked, "Here's where I get off." And upon alighting you could sit down and rest yourself for the remainder of your natural existence.

I don't believe that. I think the trouble with most human progress is that the traveler picks himself some Grand Central Station. That's a mistake, because if he doesn't get there it is tragic, and if he does that is also tragic.

I have known certain fine flaming fighters who went out to win an objective, and when they succeeded it ruined them for life. They immediately became armchair reactionaries. I have in mind specifically certain stalwart champions of the suffrage for women. They got it, and after that they felt that anything more was unnecessary. Those who pointed that the ballot had not completely solved the feminist problem were stigmatized as impatient radicals who didn't know when they were well off.

Least of all should there be a terminus in the process of education. But that notion is fostered by our academic customs. The colleges hand a sheepskin to an impressionable young man and tell him that he is a Bachelor of Arts. That gives him the impression that in some way he is through and that he need never admit one other new idea into his head.

We even speak of certain institutions for the inculcation of culture into young women as "finishing schools," as if graduation carried with it the sanctity of finality. But I wouldn't call it a sanctity. It should more properly be a stigma. I cannot think of any branch of learning in which men should be encouraged to share a mourners' row with Alexander and weep because there are no more worlds to conquer.

It is true that the Bachelor may return to his university to become a Master of Arts or a Doctor of Philosophy, but even then he is a fool if he regards himself as finished. Einstein still looks through telescopes in search of some star which may lie a little beyond the farthest.

And yet I think that what is called "higher education" has done great damage to schools which are termed "secondary." In the private high schools, at any rate, the very valuable time of the pupils is too largely taken up with fitting them for college entrance requirements. In this changing world it is quite possible that many of these boys and girls won't go to college. And I can think of no more inadequate preparation for life than an equipment to pass certain examinations which you are never going to take.

It seems to me that all schools should from the very beginning undertake to fit the scholars for life. I have never been for the dead languages they taught me, in spite of the fact that I didn't learn very much about them. I am even less for the dead literature with which I was encumbered.

In my second year of high school I had to read *Silas Marner*. I had to read it because Yale or Harvard or Princeton might be interested in what I thought about it. And this still seems to me a singularly morbid curiosity. I have never held any dinner table enthralled by recounting the plot. The book did not make me a better boy or a more useful citizen.

I'm certainly for more utilitarianism in our schools. I'd have my son know Seabury instead of Cicero.

Canine Primary

By ROBERT LITTELL

Robert Littell was at one time literary editor of THE NEW
REPUBLIC. *Later he became dramatic critic and columnist
for* THE NEW YORK WORLD. *At present he is doing free-lance
writing in New York City. He is the author of* READ AMERICA
FIRST.

OF COURSE I wanted my dog to have all the advantages of modern psychological pedagogy, so I
entered him at the John Dewey Day Dog School, an
institution said to be conducted under the auspices of Teachers'
College. To be sure, he would meet the sons of more famous
dogs at one of those church boarding-schools, but I want my
dog to be non-sectarian. Also, he is a mongrel, and the patrician
dogs might make fun of him. I call him Nero after the well-
known violinist. I am sure he is gifted in some direction, and it
might as well be music.

"This is Nero," I said to the principal of Day Dog, "and I
should like him to learn how to beg, give his paw, play dead,
fetch a ball, point a bird, walk on his hind legs, carry a newspaper in his mouth, and lie down when I say *couche-toi*. And
when I say *couche-toi* I mean *couche-toi*. I love my dog, but
I want him to be versatile, and obedient."

"Progressive canine pedagogics," answered the principal,
twiddling the Phi Beta Kappa key on his watch chain, "have
arrived at the conclusion that there is no place in the curriculum for modern languages until close to the age of adolescence,
let us say eighteen months. And as for your other requests,"
he added, smiling with indulgent pity, "we cynologists of the
new school believe in the fundamental approach. We do not

From *The New Republic,* December 7, 1932. Used by permission of the
author and *The New Republic*.

44

teach formal subjects, such as begging and carrying newspapers, for some time. We begin by studying the dog's reactions until we understand his personality. We try to rehabilitate the dog's emotional attitudes, which are nearly always warped by faulty home environment. We attempt to bring out the suppressed traits of his character. A dog, if left alone with a number of objects, will choose that which most appeals to him. . . ."

"Chew?" I interrupted timidly.

"No, choose. Our tests have selected a list of eleven hundred objects which appeal to one side or another of dog nature. Our teachers show the dogs how to play with those objects. For correct play habits are the foundation of character. Upon that foundation the normal dog builds with amazing rapidity. He learns to adapt himself to unusual situations and to the society of other dogs. He learns to abandon moping, day dreaming and isolationist or antisocial conduct. And he graduates, if we have been successful and if the dog's owner co-operates, a complete, well-rounded, psychically integrated and physically homogeneous dog."

"What does he know?" I asked.

The principal looked at me scornfully. "Knowledge is secondary," he said, "the main thing is to unfold the tiny buds of dog personality."

Then he showed me through the school. In one room a group of puppies were tearing shoes apart with their teeth. In another, full of older dogs, I saw a teacher crawling on all fours, holding a ball in her mouth and growling.

"At first," explained the principal, "the teachers have to talk to the dogs in very simple language." In a third room some of the dogs were chasing each other around, others were gnawing bones, scratching themselves and barking.

"Recess?" I questioned.

"Not at all," said the principal, rather acidly, "these dogs are learning to integrate their personalities."

So I left Nero, who whined pitifully as I went, at the Day Dog School. He came back wagging his tail, so I supposed everything was going splendidly. A few days later I received a letter from the school. "Little Nero," it said, "is an introvert. We have had a faculty meeting about him, and it seems best that his vitality should be built up by drinking extra milk in the middle of the morning." Enclosed was a bill for ten dollars for the milk, which I paid. Some weeks went by, weeks during which I was absorbed by the affairs of the world of men. Nero seemed quite as happy and lively as ever, but otherwise I could not notice any change in his play habits or personality, and he destroyed slippers, barked at strangers, slept on brocade sofas, just as before. Although I was very busy I called up the principal. "Nero," he said, "is becoming gradually externalized. His teacher considers him much less self-centered. The dogs in his class are now studying dog biscuit. The classroom is full of samples of the materials that go into dog biscuit, the walls are hung with maps showing where dog biscuit is made. By observing familiar objects and tracing them back to their component sources do we lead the plastic canine mind out of Narcissism into the wonders of the objective universe."

The next day Nero refused to eat any dog biscuit and was caught munching a first edition of the poems of Edna St. Vincent Millay. The influence of the school had begun to tell. Already Nero was beginning to decide things for himself, or, in the words of a pamphlet on primary canine mentality lent me by the principal, to "opt."

Nero's first monthly report, while not brilliant, was satisfactory. "Nero," it said, "is adapting himself rapidly to the group, and is barking with greater self-confidence, but lacks co-operative spirit and is more than normally destructive of materials." Enclosed was a bill for thirteen pairs of shoes, which I thought rather high, but a footnote explained that Nero vastly preferred new shoes to old, and that the zest of novelty was a highly important educative factor. I was tempted to write back that Nero had just finished a home-study course in hook rugs, and enclose a bill for the rugs, but I hate arguing with people who know so much about psychology and so many long words. And anyhow Nero seemed very happy.

I have never received so many letters as I did from that Day

Dog School since the time when in a moment of ghoulish curiosity I answered an advertisement for the Cliffview Mausoleum. First it was Owner's Week. "Next week is Owner's Week," wrote Nero's teacher, "and every owner will give his dog something for the dog to take back to school and present to the School Museum. It is suggested that the gift should be either fruit, flowers or something illustrating the Industrial Revolution in America." Then it was Woodchuck Week. "Your dog," said the mimeographed letter, "has been digging on his own initiative, along with other primary dogs, a deep hole in the Nature Study Yard. He will soon get to the bottom, which is concrete. He expects to find something at the bottom when he gets there. If he doesn't find anything he will be disappointed and disillusioned, a hole-complex may form in his mind and he will tend to indulge in fantasies rather than action. The teachers and the older dogs think that it is imperative that every dog should find a woodchuck at the bottom of his hole. Unfortunately our woodchuck fund is exhausted. Won't you please send a live woodchuck to reach the school not later than Thursday?"

Then there was a bill for bus fare for taking all the preprimary dogs on an expedition to the George Washington Bridge. Then another monthly report. "Nero is much more social-minded than when he came to Day Dog, and coordinates well for his age. He is already becoming an independent little mechanism. However, he is a highly sensitive dog, and cannot bear reproof. Perhaps this is because he is not admonished sufficiently at home. May we ask his owner to co-operate with us. Do not whip or slap Nero, but when he misbehaves show him what he has done and explain why it was a mistake. Reason with him as much as possible. . . . Scratching: excellent; Music: only fair."

Well, he can't be perfect. I would be the last person to wish for a regimented, under-individualized dog. And he is certainly making progress. The class has just been studying primitive wolf life. The wolf was the ancestor of the dog, and many dogs have wolflike traits. It seems quite logical for them to study, through lantern slides and samples in little bowls, how wolves lived and what wolves ate. And wolf folkways are as good an approach as any to an understanding of our complicated civilization. One should study wolves imaginatively, from the inside. All the dogs are asked to pretend that they are wolves. If some of them develop howls or take to biting visitors, that's only the seamy side of a very beautiful and understanding educational carpet. On the whole I am satisfied with Day Dog. Nero lacks concentration, but is full of self-expression and curiosity. And curiosity, they say, is the mother of wisdom.

And yet somehow I am sorry that Nero has not learned how to give his paw, or stand on his hind legs, or balance a piece of sugar on his nose. He can't do any of the normal useful dog tricks. He jumps all over people, his voice is shrill, and he talks all the time. When I say *"couche-toi"* to him he barks and runs around the room. Yet of course I would not want to have these things driven into him at the expense of a budding, blossoming, vital personality.

The principal of Day Dog says that the basic methodology of canine education could probably quite successfully be applied to children (though unfortunately no one has thought of doing so), but not to lizards. Lizards, it appears, have no personalities or emotional content worth integrating.

I Get a Colt to Break In

By LINCOLN STEFFENS

Lincoln Steffens has spent his life as a journalist. In 1892, after an unsuccessful search both in American and European Universities for a wholly satisfactory system of ethics, Mr. Steffens began his career as a journalist. Today, after receiving a Pulitzer Prize for his autobiography, Mr. Steffens is still a journalist reporting fearlessly his special investigations of political corruption.

COLONEL CARTER gave me a colt. I had my pony, and my father meanwhile had bought a pair of black carriage horses and a cow, all of which I had to attend to when we had no "man." And servants were hard to get and to keep in those days; the women married, and the men soon quit service to seize opportunities always opening. My hands were pretty full, and so was the stable. But Colonel Carter seemed to think that he had promised me a horse. He had not; I would have known it if he had. No matter. He thought he had, and maybe he did promise himself to give me one. That was enough. The kind of man that led immigrant trains across the continent and delivered them safe, sound, and together where he promised would keep his word. One day he drove over from Stockton, leading a two-year-old which he brought to our front door and turned over to me as mine. Such a horse!

She was a cream-colored mare with a black forelock, mane, and tail and a black stripe along the middle of her back. Tall, slender, high-spirited, I thought then—I think now that she was the most beautiful of horses. Colonel Carter had bred and reared her with me and my uses in mind. She was a careful cross of a mustang mare and a thoroughbred stallion, with the stamina of the wild horse and the speed and grace of the racer. And she had a sense of fun. As Colonel Carter got down out of his buggy and went up to her, she snorted, reared, flung her head high in the air, and, coming down beside him, tucked her nose affectionately under his arm.

"I have handled her a lot," he said. "She is as kind as a kitten, but she is as sensitive as a lady. You can spoil her by one mistake. If you ever lose your temper, if you ever abuse her, she will be ruined forever. And she is unbroken. I might have had her broken to ride for you, but I didn't want to. I want you to do it. I have taught her to lead, as you see; had to, to get her over here. But here she is, an unbroken colt; yours. You take and you break her. You're only a boy, but if you break this colt right, you'll be a man—a young man, but a man. And I'll tell you how."

Now, out west, as everyone knows, they break in a horse by riding out to him in his wild state, lassoing, throwing, and saddling him; then they let him up, frightened and shocked, with a yelling broncho-buster astride of him. The wild beast bucks, the cowboy drives his spurs into him, and off they go, jumping, kicking, rearing, falling, till by the weight of the man, the lash, and the rowels, the horse is broken—in body and spirit. This was not the way I was to break my colt.

"You must break her to ride without her ever knowing it," Colonel Carter said. "You feed and you clean her—you; not the stable man. You lead her out to water and to walk. You put her on a long rope and let her play, calling her to you and gently pulling on the rope. Then you turn her loose in the grass lot there and, when she has romped till tired, call her. If she won't come, leave her. When she wants water or food, she will run to your call, and you will pet and feed and care for her." He went on for half an hour, advising me in great detail how to proceed. I wanted to begin right away. He laughed. He let me lead her around to the stable, water her, and put her in the stable and feed her.

There I saw my pony. My father, sisters, and Colonel Carter saw me stop and look at my pony.

"What'll you do with him?" one of my sisters asked. I was bewildered for a moment. What should I do with the little red horse? I decided at once.

"You can have him," I said to my sisters.

"No," said Colonel Carter, "not yet. You can give your sisters the pony by and by, but you'll need him till you have taught the colt to carry you and a saddle—months; and you must not hurry. You must learn patience, and you will if you give the colt time to learn it, too. Patience and control. You can't control a young horse unless you can control yourself. Can you shoot?" he asked suddenly.

I couldn't. I had a gun and I had used it some, but it was a rifle, and I could not bring down with it such game as there was around Sacramento—birds and hares. Colonel Carter looked at my father, and I caught the look. So did my father. I soon had a shotgun. But at the time Colonel Carter turned to me and said:

"Can't shoot straight, eh? Do you know what that means? That means that you can't control a gun, and that means that you can't control yourself, your eye, your hands, your nerves. You are wriggling now. I tell you that a good shot is always a good man. He may be a 'bad man' too, but he is quiet, strong, steady in speech, gait, and mind. No matter, though. If you break in this colt right, if you teach her her paces, she will teach you to shoot and be quiet."

He went off downtown with my father, and I started away with my colt. I fed, I led, I cleaned her, gently, as if she were made of glass; she was playful and willing, a delight. When Colonel Carter came home with my father for supper, he questioned me.

"You should not have worked her today," he said. "She has come all the way from Stockton and must be tired. Yes, yes, she would not show her fatigue; too fine for that, and too young to be wise. You have got to think for her, consider her as you would your sisters."

Sisters! I thought; I had never considered my sisters. I did not say that, but Colonel Carter laughed and nodded to my sisters. It was just as if he had read my thought. But he went on to draw on my imagination a centaur; the colt as a horse's body—me, a boy, as the head and brains of one united creature. I liked that. I would be that. I and the colt: a centaur.

After Colonel Carter was gone home I went to work on my new horse. The old one, the pony, I used only for business: to go to fires, to see my friends, run errands, and go hunting with my new shotgun. But the game that had all my attention was the breaking in of the colt, the beautiful cream-colored mare, who soon knew me—and my pockets. I carried sugar to reward her when she did right, and she discovered where I carried it; so did the pony, and when I was busy they would push their noses into my pockets, both of which were torn down a good deal of the time. But the colt learned. I taught her to run around a circle, turn and go the other way at a signal. My sisters helped me. I held the long rope and the whip (for signaling), while one of the girls led the colt; it was hard work for them, but they took it in turns. One would lead the colt round and round till I snapped the whip; then she would turn, turning the colt, till the colt did it all by herself. And she was very quick. She shook hands with each of her four feet. She let us run under her, back and forth. She was slow only to carry me. Following Colonel Carter's instructions, I began by laying my arm or a surcingle over her back. If she trembled, I drew it slowly off. When she could abide it, I tried buckling it, tighter and tighter. I laid over her, too, a blanket, folded at first, then open, and, at last, I slipped up on her myself, sat there a second, and as she trembled, slid off. My sisters held her for me, and when I could get up and sit there a moment or two, I tied her at a block, and we, my sisters and I, made a procession of mounting and dismounting. She soon got used to this and would let us slide off over her rump, but it was a long, long time before she would carry me.

That we practiced by leading her along a high curb where I could get on as she walked, ride a few steps, and then, as she felt me and crouched, slip off. She never did learn to carry a girl on her back; my sisters had to lead her while I rode. This was not purposeful. I don't know just how it happened, but I do remember the first time I rode on my colt all the way round the lot and how, when I put one of the girls up, she refused to repeat. She shuddered, shook and frightened them off.

While we were breaking in the colt a circus came to town. The ring was across the street from our house. Wonderful! I lived in that circus for a week. I saw the show but once, but I marked the horse-trainers, and in the mornings when they were not too busy I told them about my colt, showed her to them, and asked them how to train her to do circus tricks. With their hints I taught the colt to stand up on her hind legs, kneel, lie down, and balance on a small box. This last was easier than it looked. I put her first on a low big box and taught her to turn on it; then got a little smaller box upon which she repeated what she did on the big one. By and by we had her so that she would step up on a high box so small that her four feet were almost touching, and there also she would turn.

The circus man gave me one hint that was worth all the other tricks put together. "You catch her doing something of herself that looks good," he said, "and then you keep her at it." It was thus that I taught her to bow to people. The first day I rode her out on to the streets was a proud one for me and for the colt, too, apparently. She did not walk, she danced; perhaps she was excited, nervous; anyhow I liked the way she threw up her head, champed at the bit, and went dancing, prancing down the street. Everybody stopped to watch us, and so, when she began to sober down, I picked her up again with heel and rein, saying, "Here's people, Lady," and she would show off to my delight. By constant repetition I had her so trained that she would single-foot, head down, along a country road till we came to a house or a group of people. Then I'd say, "People, Lady," and up would go her head, and her feet would dance.

But the trick that set the town talking was her bowing to any one I spoke to. "Lennie Steffens' horse bows to you," people said, and she did. I never told how it was done; by ac

53

cident. Dogs used to run out at us and the colt enjoyed it; she kicked at them sometimes with both hind hoofs. I joined her in the game, and being able to look behind more conveniently than she could, I watched the dogs until they were in range, then gave the colt a signal to kick. "Kick, gal," I'd say, and tap her ribs with my heel. We used to get dogs together that way; the colt would kick them over and over and leave them yelping in the road. Well, one day when I met a girl I knew I lifted my hat, probably muttered a "Good day," and I must have touched the colt with my heel. Anyway, she dropped her head and kicked—not much; there was no dog near, so she had responded to my unexpected signal by what looked like a bow. I caught the idea and kept her at it. Whenever I wanted to bow to a girl or anyone else, instead of saying "Good day," I muttered "Kick, gal," spurred her lightly, and—the whole centaur bowed and was covered with glory and conceit.

Yes, conceit. I was full of it, and the colt was quite as bad. One day my chum Hjalmar came into town on his Black Bess, blanketed. She had had a great fistule cut out of her shoulder and had to be kept warm. I expected to see her weak and dull, but no, the good old mare was champing and dancing, like my colt.

"What is it makes her so?" I asked, and Hjalmar said he didn't know, but he thought she was proud of the blanket. A great idea. I had a gaudy horse blanket. I put it on the colt and I could hardly hold her. We rode down the main street together, both horses and both boys, so full of vanity that everybody stopped to smile. We thought they admired, and maybe they did. But some boys on the street gave us another angle. They, too, stopped and looked, and as we passed, one of them said, "Think you're hell, don't you?"

Spoilsport!

We did, as a matter of fact; we thought we were hell. The recognition of it dashed us for a moment; not for long, and the horses paid no heed. We pranced, the black and the yellow, all the way down J Street, up K Street, and agreed that we'd do it again, often. Only, I said, we wouldn't use blankets. If the horses were proud of a blanket, they'd be proud of anything unusually conspicuous. We tried a flower next time. I fixed a big rose on my colt's bridle just under her ear and it was great—she pranced downtown with her head turned, literally, to show off her flower. We had to change the decoration from time to time, put on a ribbon, or a bell, or a feather, but, really, it was not necessary for my horse. Old Black Bess needed an incentive to act up, but all I had to do to my horse was to pick up the reins, touch her with my heel, and say, "People"; she would dance from one side of the street to the other, asking to be admired. As she was. As we were.

I would ride down to my father's store, jump off my prancing colt in the middle of the street, and run up into the shop. The colt, free, would stop short, turn, and follow me right up on the sidewalk, unless I bade her wait. If any one approached her while I was gone, she would snort, rear, and strike. No stranger could get near her. She became a frightened, frightening animal, and yet when I came into sight she would run to me, put her head down, and as I straddled her neck, she would throw up her head and pitch me into my seat, facing backwards, of course. I whirled around right, and off we'd go, the vainest boy and the proudest horse in the State.

"Hey, give me a ride, will you?" some boy would ask.

"Sure," I'd say, and jump down and watch that boy try to catch and mount my colt. He couldn't. Once a cowboy wanted to try her, and he caught her; he dodged her forefeet, grabbed the reins, and in one spring was on her back. I never did that again. My colt reared, then bucked, and, as the cowboy kept his seat, she shuddered, sank to the ground, and rolled over. He slipped aside and would have risen with her, but I was alarmed and begged him not to. She got up at my touch and followed me so close that she stepped on my heel and hurt me. The cowboy saw the point.

"If I were you, kid," he said, "I'd never let anybody mount that colt. She's too good."

That, I think, was the only mistake I made in the rearing

of Colonel Carter's gift-horse. My father differed from me. He discovered another error or sin, and thrashed me for it. My practice was to work hard on a trick, privately, and when it was perfect, let him see it. I would have the horse out in our vacant lot doing it as he came home to supper. One evening, as he approached the house, I was standing, whip in hand, while the colt, quite free, was stepping carefully over the bodies of a lot of girls, all my sisters and all their girl friends. (Grace Gallatin, later Mrs. Thompson-Seton, was among them.) My father did not express the admiration I expected; he was frightened and furious. "Stop that," he called, and he came running around into the lot, took the whip, and lashed me with it. I tried to explain; the girls tried to help me explain.

I had seen in the circus a horse that stepped thus over a row of prostrate clowns. It looked dangerous for the clowns, but the trainer had told me how to do it. You begin with logs, laid out a certain distance apart; the horse walks over them under your lead, and whenever he touches one you rebuke him. By and by he will learn to step with such care that he never trips. Then you substitute clowns. I had no clowns, but I did get logs, and with the girls helping, we taught the colt to step over the obstacles even at a trot. Walking, she touched nothing. All ready thus with the logs, I had my sisters lie down in the grass, and again and again the colt stepped over them. None was ever touched. My father would not listen to any of this; he just walloped me, and when he was tired or satisfied and I was in tears, I blubbered a short excuse: "They were only girls." And he whipped me some more.

My father was not given to whipping; he did it very seldom, but he did it hard when he did it at all. My mother was just the opposite. She did not whip me, but she often smacked me, and she had a most annoying habit of thumping me on the head with her thimbled finger. This I resented more than my father's thoroughgoing thrashings, and I can tell why now. I would be playing Napoleon and as I was reviewing my Old Guard, she would crack my skull with that thimble. No doubt I was in the way; it took a lot of furniture and sisters to repre-

sent properly a victorious army; and you might think as my
mother did that a thimble is a small weapon. But imagine
Napoleon at the height of his power, the ruler of the world on
parade, getting a sharp rap on his crown from a woman's
thimble. No. My father's way was more appropriate. It was
hard. "I'll attend to you in the morning," he would say, and I
lay awake wondering which of my crimes he had discovered.
I know what it is to be sentenced to be shot at sunrise. And it
hurt, in the morning, when he was not angry but very fresh
and strong. But you see, he walloped me in my own person;
he never humiliated Napoleon or my knighthood, as my mother
did. And I learned something from his discipline, something
useful.

I learned what tyranny is and the pain of being misunderstood and wronged, or, if you please, understood and set right;
they are pretty much the same. He and most parents and
teachers do not break in their boys as carefully as I broke in
my colt. They haven't the time that I had, and they have not
some other incentives I had. I saw this that day when I rubbed
my sore legs. He had to explain to my indignant mother what
had happened. When he told it his way, I gave my version:
how long and cautiously I had been teaching my horse to
walk over logs and girls. And having shown how sure I was of
myself and the colt, while my mother was boring into his
silence with one of her reproachful looks, I said something that
hit my father hard.

"I taught the colt that trick, I have taught her all that you
see she knows, without whipping her. I have never struck her;
not once. Colonel Carter said I mustn't, and I haven't."

And my mother, backing me up, gave him a rap: "There,"
she said, "I told you so." He walked off, looking like a thimble-
rapped Napoleon.

What College Did to My Religion

By PHILIP E. WENTWORTH

Philip E. Wentworth was born in the Middle West. He entered Harvard in 1924 with the notion of preparing himself for the ministry. He gave up the idea before he was graduated from the University. Since 1928 Mr. Wentworth has been engaged in educational work.

TO SAY that college does something to the average student's religion is to state a truth which will be conceded by anyone who has given the matter a moment's thought. Nine young men and women out of every ten who will receive their degrees this June would probably admit, if they were called to testify, that education has acted as a poison to their faith. In many instances the virus generated by the reasoning processes induces only a mild distemper of skepticism, but in others it works like an acid, eating its way into the bump of credulity until in the end this estimable organ is completely corroded. Devout parents and clergymen have frequently observed this phenomenon and deplored it. When they discuss it, however, as they often do, they betray a common failure to understand the intellectual chemistry which has produced this wholesale apostasy of the younger generation.

In these pages I propose to show how higher education reacts upon faith by describing my own religious crisis just as it occurred while I was in college. At the time, I had good reason to sift my doubts with unusual care. When I entered Harvard in the fall of 1924, I was not only a Christian, I was also an avowed candidate for the ministry. Then for four years I underwent a process of mental readjustment which shook my little world to its foundations. Through it all only one thing was clear to me: if I could reconcile religion with intelligence, I knew that I could go on into my chosen career fortified by the experience; if I could not, every consideration of honor would compel me to make other plans. In the end I gave up the ministry.

Because my crisis was so acute, I know what fundamental questions underlie the intellectual reorientation which has become an inevitable part of the college curriculum for every thinking student. From my own experience I can demonstrate why it is that education so often spells the end of orthodoxy.

The environment in which I grew up was that of the typical middle-class American home just after the turn of the century. Queen Victoria had been dead five years when I came into the world, but her spirit lived on and was the tutelary genius of my childhood and youth.

I was born a good Presbyterian, and, fittingly enough, pre-destination played an important rôle in my early life. Both of my parents were gentle, unaffected, devoted Christians, and my father was an elder in the church. We lived in a small city of the Middle West, on the fringe of what H. L. Mencken calls "the Bible Belt." Long before I could be aware of it myself, the double accident of parentage and geography had shaped me for the service of God.

Our neighborhood was made up of families like mine. All social life was centered in the church and its activities. Our minister, who was an intimate friend of the family, was an upright old Scotsman, a living monument to all the Christian virtues. He had served our parish almost as long as anybody could remember, and his never-failing kindliness and charity made him universally beloved.

My earliest distinct recollection is of family prayers. This was a regular feature of our daily life. After supper we would retire to the library, where my father, with wife and children gathered about him, would read a chapter from the Scriptures.

Psalms and *Proverbs* were his favorite books, and he repeated them so often that I soon knew them by heart. After the reading came prayers, during which each little event of the day would be rehearsed and we would give thanks to God for all the good things we had enjoyed.

It was natural that a child brought up in such a home should early come to think of the God who ruled over it, whose presence was so imminently felt in every department of daily life, as one of his most intimate acquaintances. He was very real, this God of my childhood; as real as my father, and in fact quite like him. There was nothing sinister about Him, nothing to incite fear—except, of course, when I disobeyed Him. He was merely the head of the world as my father was head of our household. The ways of both were often inscrutable to me, but I never doubted their ultimate wisdom and their concern for my own good.

By the time I came to the age of reason the system under which I had grown up had implanted in my mind certain clear ideas about the universe and my place in it. The world was created by God as a laboratory for testing human beings. In the Bible He had revealed His commandments, which were distinct, direct, and admitted of no argument. Obedience to these injunctions was virtue, disobedience sin. The one meant honor and happiness and life everlasting; the other was the way of shame and disgrace in this world, and led to eternal torments in the world to come.

God, however, was more than a moralist. He was also an engineer. The world which He had fashioned was not an automatic mechanism. It had been set going in the beginning by its Creator, and He, like a good mechanic, had been tinkering with it ever since. The forces that moved it were direct manifestations of His power. "The heavens declare the glory of God; and the firmament sheweth his handywork." If He could save men from their sins, He could also protect them against accidents, diseases, and the shafts of their enemies. Faith and good works, then, were not only the way of the soul's salvation, they were also the best kind of insurance against the stings of fortune while one lived.

These religious concepts were laid down in the Scriptures and were supported by a kind of evidence in everyday life. God was constantly being moved by the prayers of the just to repeat in our day the miracles He had performed in ancient times. Everyone who had eyes could see it for himself. Did not our pastor often intercede for the recovery of the sick, and did they not usually get well? Did he not pray every Sunday that the President of the United States would be given wisdom to lead the affairs of the nation, and was not our prosperity the manifest answer? It was all very simple and all very right, and surely the way of the transgressor was hard.

But, you say, these were the ideas of a child. True, and the child got them from his parents, who shared them item by item with the neighbors, who held the same beliefs in common with one hundred million other people in all the Middletowns of America.

It would hardly be possible to exaggerate the importance of a wonder-working God in this Christian scheme of things which I took for granted with the air I breathed. Innumerable stories from the Bible, moreover, indicate that such a Deity was also taken for granted by every one of the Scriptural heroes from Adam down to John of Patmos. Through all the centuries of religious history this idea has persisted, which would seem to indicate that a God who kicks over the traces of natural law and upsets the normal sequence of cause and effect occupies an important place—if not, indeed, the central place—in Christian cosmology.

I am well aware that in certain churches today even the clergy are disposed to pass lightly over the miracles. This tendency, however, is wholly confined to the more liberal churches, whose communicants are sophisticated people. Such parishes are not really representative of Christianity, for the obvious reason that their members are not representative of the rank and file of humanity. Sophisticated folk, if they go to church at all, tend to do it as a matter of form and fashion; they are moved by no strong convictions.

To find the original God of Christianity still resplendent

in all His glory, still hurling His thunderbolts and making no concessions to rationalism, one should go preferably to a Roman Catholic Church—to the shrine, say, of Sainte Anne de Beaupré or Our Lady of Lourdes. There one comes into the awful presence of a real God, who heals the sick, gives sight to the blind, makes the crippled walk, rewards the just, damns the wicked, and in all the vicissitudes of life is able to give tangible evidence of His power in answer to prayer. And the same Deity, less colorful, perhaps, but no less real, will be found among the Baptists, the Lutherans, the Methodists, the Congregationalists, the Presbyterians, and every other sect of Protestantism.

This was the God of my childhood. And He still reigns in undimmed majesty over the lives of millions, whose supplications continue to move Him just as effectively as they did in the days of Abraham. Here, for example, is a testimonial taken from the *Chicago Tribune* of August 28 last:

> The steeple of the Presbyterian Theological Seminary, at 2330 North Halsted Street, was struck by lightning and set afire. One hundred and seventy-five theological students, residents of a near-by dormitory, rushed into the street in a downpour of rain to help the firemen fight the blaze. Dr. John Timothy Stone, president of the Seminary, heard the crash when the steeple was struck. He rushed out into the storm and called upon the students who were helping to fight the blaze to pray. Dr. Stone and his students knelt on the rain-soaked grass and offered a prayer for the safety of the building. The firemen were unable to get into the steeple, and by the time they had raised a fire tower and trained a hose on the fire an hour later the rain had put out the blaze.

It is hardly necessary to point out that Dr. Stone's action was entirely consistent with his beliefs as a good Presbyterian. In his moment of danger he did what every religious man or woman does instinctively under similar circumstances: he appealed to the wonder-working God who presides over the

Christian universe. And I dare say the good Doctor has already used the incident to point the moral in some stirring sermon.

I emphasize the importance of this God of magic because He is the source of most of the difficulties with which the churches now find themselves beset. They cannot give Him up and remain Christian; they cannot keep Him and retain the loyalty of educated people. It is a critical dilemma indeed. I was soon to face it in my own life, but at the time of which I write I had no suspicion that it existed.

I arrived at the age of eighteen comfortably adjusted to the Christian universe in which all things work together for good to them that love God. The example set by my family, and indeed by the entire community in which we lived, convinced me of the truth and justice of the divine plan. As I began to think seriously of what I should do with my life, everything pointed to the ministry as the ideal solution. Christian living was the way of happiness. And what better use could any man make of his powers than to devote them to the propagation of truth, so that others who had been denied it might be led to share its beneficent effects? The decision hardly called for conscious effort.

So in due course I went before the Presbytery of the church, where, to the delight of my parents, I was accepted as a candidate for the ministry. The church to which we belonged published a little quarterly, and the next issue carried my picture with this word of explanation: "Philip E. Wentworth, who came before Presbytery last spring, will start his college work this fall preparatory to entering the Christian ministry."

The question was: What college? Without going into the detailed considerations that influenced my judgment in this matter, suffice it to say that I finally settled upon Harvard. My father was not a college graduate, but he was bent on giving me the advantages of formal education which he had lacked, and he was satisfied to leave the choice to me. But I met unexpected resistance when I sought the advice of our pastor.

He was uneasy when he learned that I was thinking of going to Harvard. Of course it was a fine university, but the Unitarians had smirched it. He reminded me that the Unitarian Church was the only Protestant denomination from which transfers of membership were not freely accepted by the Presbyterians. Before a Unitarian could be welcomed into our communion he had to be closely examined, for the title of his sect was a denial of the Trinity. Harvard, the minister said, had been the Sorbonne of Unitarianism, and I should run a grave risk of learning false doctrine if I went there.

Instead of flying in the face of Providence, I should do better, he said, to consider his own college. It was a small institution in Missouri, founded and supervised by the synod of our church. It had educated many eminent Presbyterian ministers. I could go there knowing that I should be safe from all the insidious temptations of rationalism.

He urged me eloquently, but I stood my ground. When I went before Presbytery I had sworn allegiance to truth, and I did not think it would prove to be as frail a vessel as the good dominie's counsel implied. I suspected that it might turn out, on closer acquaintance, to be a little too broad to fit into any narrow creed. I was not primarily interested in dogma anyhow. Sufficient unto the seminary would be the evils thereof. First, I would widen my general knowledge. Then, even if it should be necessary to modify some of my doctrines, I felt certain that the fundamental verities of religion would remain impregnable.

So to Harvard I went. On a September evening in 1924, I called to say good-by to the old minister, who, throughout his long friendship with the family, had been almost a second father to me. In the quiet of his study he knelt beside me and offered up a fervent petition to God to make me diligent in the pursuit of truth. Dear, faithful soul! Within a year he was dead and was spared the pain of learning that his parting prayer was being answered—in a sense the irony of which he could never have understood.

Before I went to college I was thoroughly at home in a universe which revolved about the central figure of an omnipotent Deity. In Cambridge I was suddenly plunged into another world. I found myself breathing a wholly different atmosphere. My teachers spoke a new language; their words were familiar enough, but the import of them was strange to me. It was essentially a difference in attitude and point of view.

The change was first brought home to me in the study of history. To my mind the rise of Christianity out of the ashes of imperial Rome had seemed the material evidence of a transcendental truth—a revelation of the hand of God at work in the affairs of men. Not so to my professors. All events in history were manifestations of cause and effect operating upon the natural level. The institutions of society evolved according to orderly processes. Religion was itself subject to these processes. I shall never forget one lecture which traced the evolution of God—from the fierce, bloodthirsty Yahweh, tribal Deity of a few Semitic nomads, through successive stages until He finally emerged in the New Testament as the gentle, merciful, forgiving Father of all mankind.

In the course of time the impact of new knowledge, and especially knowledge of science and the scientific method, wrought great havoc with my original ideas. All things, it seemed, were subject to the laws of nature. This concept supplied my mind with a wholly new pattern into which my religious beliefs refused to fit. In such an orderly universe there seemed to be no place for a wonder-working God. He would be an outlaw, unthinkable and impossible. The bottom dropped out of my world, and I wrestled with myself in a futile attempt to patch it up.

What, then, about morals? Without an omnipotent Deity to reward virtue and punish evil, was "the good life" only an illusion? I could not believe it, yet I could think of no satisfactory answer. Life had lost its meaning. I was desolate.

Perhaps, though, I could still rehabilitate God by setting Him up as the First Cause—the moving power behind natural law. But there was small comfort in this thought. A God who had created the world and then left it to govern itself by natural law had hedged Himself about by barriers through which even He could not break. Prayers could not move Him. Though He might exist, He could not be of service to man. Obviously such a God would be too remote, too inaccessible, for the purposes of religion.

I saw, too, that the Modernists were troubled by these same difficulties. In their haste to strike up a compromise with the intellectuals, they were trying hard to make a self-respecting Deity out of the nebulous What-Is-It of Eddington and Millikan. It seemed to me that they had fallen between two stools. I studied philosophy and read further about this First Cause. Then I began to marvel at the disingenuousness of the human mind when, unable to imagine how the world began, but demanding some explanation of the inexplicable, it can arbitrarily select three letters from the alphabet and call *g-o-d* an answer. I preferred to think that we know more about such matters when we admit we know nothing than when we resort to such palpable self-deception.

While I was debating these problems so basic to my religious beliefs, the controversy between Fundamentalists and Modernists was coming to a head, and the impending Scopes trial in Tennessee was shocking the conscience of thoughtful men everywhere. These events helped to clarify my thinking. I saw that the battle had been joined between religion and intelligence. Was faith, then, simply a defense of ignorance, a substitute for thinking?

In the summer of 1925, I followed the proceedings at Dayton with intense interest, and one aspect of the dispute over evolution struck me particularly. Learned scientists and liberal clergymen were brought to testify for the defense. Their evidence was not admitted at the trial, as I recall it, but all of them gave out statements to the press, and they were unanimous in saying that there was no real conflict between religion and science. This struck me as a downright evasion of the issue. The quarrel was not between religion and science in the abstract. The pious legislators of Tennessee had taken it upon themselves to protect one specific and clearly stated postulate of Christianity against the equally concrete and definite theory of evolution. What was the conflict here?

The controversy raged, as everyone knows, over the first chapter of *Genesis*. Now why should religious folk set such store by that text? In explaining how the world was created in six days, the story of *Genesis* clearly established God in the central conning tower of the universe and conferred upon Him the omnipotent powers He needed to control the mechanism. Thus it affirmed the first great postulate of Christianity: An all-powerful God rules over the world of His creation. But that is not all. From this premise is derived a corollary of the first importance to religion: Man is dependent for his safety in this world and his salvation in the next upon the God who made him.

Here, then, is the religious significance of the Biblical story of creation. The lawmakers of Tennessee maintained, therefore, that the story was fundamental to Christianity, and in this it would appear that they were better theologians (however tenuous their claim to greatness in the law) than the liberal clergymen who tried to refute them. For the Christian religion rests in large part upon the foundation of those assumptions laid down in the first chapter of *Genesis*.[1] The moral code is directly derived from the special relationship there established between God and man.

Now what happens to this nicely rationalized system of religious beliefs when scientific notions are superimposed upon them? The God of Christianity becomes enclosed in a circle of natural law from which He cannot escape. He is deprived of His freedom to interfere with the normal sequence of cause and effect. He is no longer able to play the rôle of Cosmic Policeman, meting out vengeance and punishment of evildoers and offering protection and rewards to the just. The elaborate sanctions which religion has built up to enforce its code vanish into thin air.

---

[1] If this statement is challenged on the ground that it ignores the immense contribution of Jesus, I answer that Jesus would have been impossible without the God who first makes His appearance in *Genesis*. Without such a God, it is obvious that there could never have been a Son of God.—AUTHOR

Thus, in the field of action, a conflict of primary importance is set up between Christianity and scientific ideas. Mystic rites, sacrifice, supplication, and prayer are typical modes of religious behavior, and they are conditioned by religious beliefs. People who have oriented themselves to a scientific universe go about their affairs in other ways. Dr. John Timothy Stone and the firemen approached their common problem differently.

Having reached these conclusions, I realized that if I was to continue to believe in the good life I should have to look beyond the teachings of orthodoxy for my reasons. The supernatural had become meaningless. No longer able to lean upon the gods, I must learn to stand alone.

It so happened that I stayed in the East each summer vacation and had not been home since I first entered Harvard as a freshman. Meanwhile, I had written innumerable letters to my parents, acquainting them with all the successive changes which my ideas had undergone. They were sorely troubled. At first they contented themselves with giving me well-intentioned advice to pray and read my Bible constantly. If I did this, my doubts would surely pass, for God was testing me and would not desert me if I proved steadfast. When at last, toward the end of my sophomore year, I wrote them that prayer had lost its meaning, they concluded that they would have to take heroic measures to save me from myself. I received a long letter from my father.

He was now convinced, he said, that my going to Harvard had been a ghastly mistake. Two years of it threatened to destroy the faith which had been instilled into me from birth. If I continued in my present course, he could never forgive himself for failing to heed the advice of our old pastor, who had foreseen exactly what had happened to me. "For what shall it profit a man, if he shall gain the whole world, and lose his own soul?" He was convinced, therefore, that it would be best for me to plan on not returning to Cambridge in the fall. If I preferred, he would be willing to let me do nothing at all the next year; I could stay at home and get my bearings anew. After that I could make a fresh start and go on with my studies at the Presbyterian college in Missouri, which he had now concluded was the proper place for me. Of course I was no longer a child to be governed wholly by others; I should have to make my own decisions and take the consequences. But in this important matter he urged me to consider well and be guided by his maturer judgment.

Needless to say, this letter was very disturbing to me. I could understand and sympathize with my father's feelings. But, much as I regretted to displease him, I could not ruthlessly suppress my own convictions. I wrote him to this effect and begged him to allow me to complete the studies which I had begun. I had seen enough of a progressive university and its methods of stimulating students to think for themselves to know that I should never be able to bear the hothouse environment of a denominational college. After the interchange of several letters my father finally capitulated, although he said it went sorely against his conscience.

That third year at Harvard was much less distressing to my peace of mind than the first two had been. The uncertainties which new knowledge had bred no longer paralyzed me. Other certainties began to take form as I set about building up a tenable philosophy of my own. By the end of my junior year these ideas had begun to shake down and adjust themselves to the new pattern which my mind had accepted.

It was now out of the question for me to entertain any hope that I might be able to reconcile my new philosophy of life with those religious assumptions which I had formerly taken for granted. I could not become a Christian minister. Instead, I found myself strongly attracted toward an academic career. But I was still enrolled as a candidate for holy orders, and it was incumbent upon me to notify Presbytery of my withdrawal.

Back home our old pastor was dead, and a younger man who had formerly assisted him had taken his place. So to him I wrote, in April 1927, outlining the change in my beliefs just as I have explained it here, and asking him to lay the matter before Presbytery. Within a few days I received his answer.

His letter was cordial and tolerant, but it demonstrated so conclusively the impotence of the Church to deal with, or even to understand, the problem of my generation that I shall quote it in full.

April 16, 1927

MY DEAR PHILIP,

Your father has frequently talked with me about your difficulties. I was therefore not unprepared for your letter, although the Philip who speaks in these pages is an altogether different Philip from the one who left us less than three years ago.

I need not tell you how sorry I am that you have had to go through this crisis. Most of us, some time or other in our college lives, have had to face the very problems that are yours. If a man thinks at all, such questions are bound to torment him sooner or later. Knowing you as I do, I am sure that you have been honest in facing them. Still, it is the way a man answers that really matters; his doubts may always either make him or break him.

I shall not attempt to debate the points which you have raised. You ought to know already how faith can move such mountains of doubt as the unguided reason may build up. There is only one thought that I should like to place before you. As you have been looking at the fact of Christianity from the point of view of a personal God, have you been absolutely fair in seeking the proof on both sides? By that I mean, have you been reading your Bible, praying, and trying to believe, or have you just taken the external view that it cannot be so, and tried to prove *that* by your thought and reading? Not one of us could keep his faith in any vital matter if he listened only to those who argue against it. Religion isn't a question of logic or reason, although there is a logic in it and a man has to have a reason for the faith that is within him.

However, I am not going to harass you with a sermon. I want you to know that whatever you do and wherever you go I still count you one of my true friends. Whether it means anything to you or not, I am going to pray for God's blessing upon you, that He may lead you out into the fullest life. You are still numbered here as one of ours, and always will be. If at any time I can serve you in any way, you have only to let me know. And be assured of this—that with my hand goes my heart.

Yours faithfully, etc.

There is something very touching in the manifest sincerity of such an appeal. But what good is it to urge a man to pray when the whole system of religious conceptions has lost its validity for him?

In 1928 I took my degree from Harvard. Four years have now elapsed since then, and my ideas have undergone no important modification. Subsequent studies have confirmed me in the point of view which I have indicated here, and I remain irretrievably lost to religion. This is a source of permanent chagrin to my family. The years have tended to cover over the wound, to the extent that we never discuss the difference in our opinions; but underneath the tacit acceptance of our disagreement I know that my parents nurse a secret hurt too deep for time to heal. In their prayers and meditations I am sure that while they live they will not cease to plead with their God for my redemption.

Thus it will appear from my little history that we members of the skeptical younger generation are a problem. It is an inevitable consequence of America's generous passion for education. Thousands of young men and women go to college each year from homes more or less like mine, to return changed beyond recognition in all their ideas. And a few thoughtful appraisers of our social trends, men like James Truslow Adams and Walter Lippmann, who are not believers themselves, seem to agree with clergymen and the more devout parents in thinking that the transformation is not always a change for the better.

In this they are probably right. College not only may, but

often does, deprive a student of his religious convictions without giving him anything to take their place. Christianity, after all, is a composite of two elements: one purports to explain the nature of the world and man's relationship to the God who rules over it; the other prescribes a course of conduct the sanctions of which are derived from this relationship. The really serious dangers of skepticism become apparent when a student rejects the supernatural part of his religion and concludes that there are no valid reasons left for decent conduct. Robbed of standards, he is likely to adopt the easy ethics of business, which permit a man to do almost anything so long as it leads to success in money-making. This commercial point of view is rapidly becoming the real philosophy of the nation, as Mr. Adams brilliantly demonstrates in *The Epic of America*.

If a life of pure acquisitiveness becomes the ideal of college students, they can find reasons to justify themselves in some of the new theories of psychology. These doctrines tend to glorify the illimitable expansion of the ego as "self-expression," and create in uncritical minds the notion that it is foolish, even harmful to health, to try to suppress one's desires—a favorite dogma of Freud and the psychoanalysts. In this connection it seems to me very strange that, despite our cult of science, we have not yet grasped the full import of the new knowledge that has come to us from the laboratory. The usefulness of the physical sciences is measured by the power they have given mankind to control the forces of nature. Control is the essence of scientific purpose. But the new psychology, calling itself a science, has supplemented the decay of religion to rob us of control over *human* nature—that is, over our appetites.

One solution of this dilemma may lie in the creation of a philosophy which, without calling upon the supernatural, will reassert the effectiveness of the human will as an instrument for governing the desires and impulses. Then it will be possible to restore to good odor the essentially *human* values of life which lift us above the level of mere animal instinct. The system of ethics which would be enforced by such a philosophy would not be strikingly different in many particulars from the moral code of Christianity, but the reasons for obeying it would be found wholly in the satisfactions of the good life itself, not in the promise of reward or punishment after death.

But only a congenital optimist could bring himself to believe that a mere system of ethics, however satisfying to the intellect, could ever take the place of religion among the masses. Most men and women are incapable of sustained self-control. Greed, pride, lust are too much for them. They can be held to the path of duty only by some power outside themselves—some higher authority which is able to generate repressive fears stronger than their native passions. Over vast multitudes the Church has for centuries enforced an external discipline of precisely this kind.

When religion begins to lose its hold upon the minds of men, as it is now doing with us, a peculiar thing happens. The Church is driven by its own weakness to shift its social responsibilities to other shoulders. Now there is only one other institution strong enough to take on new burdens in such an emergency, and it is an institution which, like the Church, has always been engaged in forcing a measure of parental control upon men who either would not or could not control themselves. This is the State. As religion becomes inoperative, governments are overworked.

In America at the present moment there is ample evidence that this peculiar dislocation of function has already reached an acute stage. The ineffectiveness of Christianity as a social force is revealed, on the one hand, in an outbreak of crime the seriousness of which is common knowledge; and the government has not yet been able to devise satisfactory measures for dealing with it. The Church, on the other hand, aware of its weakness, aware that it can no longer command obedience to its teachings by the time-honored method of invoking the wrath of God, is led to lean more and more heavily upon the State, borrowing secular support for purely religious injunctions. The sad plight of Christianity in Tennessee, which has had to call upon the law for official protection against evolution, is a symbol of spiritual decadence. National prohibition is another sign of the same thing writ large. Thus for some years the churches have been abdicating in their own field and putting their faith in legal restraints.

It is no accident, then, that the groups which are demanding ever more stringent laws to regulate our private lives are identical, almost to a man, with the religious groups in the population. It makes no difference whether they are Protestants clamoring for stricter enforcement of prohibition or Catholics agitating for stricter legislation regarding the dissemination of birth-control information. In both instances increasing pressure is being brought to bear upon government to take over the practical functions of religion—and for the obvious reason that religion, in its decay, is no longer able to do its work in the world.

Though I am an apostate, I must admit, therefore, that it gives me no satisfaction to realize what a large company of young men and women now share the label with me. But I see no help for it. The Church has lost its power to move us. Its conceptions seem as unreal to my generation as the gods of ancient Greece.

The breakdown of Christianity is particularly unfortunate in America, where our educators are so busy building new dormitories and thinking up new systems of instruction that they do not see how urgently the situation calls upon them to redefine the purposes for which their pedagogical machinery exists. In so far as the colleges destroy religious faith without substituting a vital philosophy to take its place, they are turning loose upon the world young barbarians who have been freed from the discipline of the Church before they have learned how to discipline themselves. Perhaps this was what one of my least orthodox Harvard professors had in mind when he once said: "There are only a few men in the world who have earned the right *not* to be Christians."

Universities and Religious Indifference

By BERNARD IDDINGS BELL

Bernard Iddings Bell was born in 1886. Dr. Bell has spent his life in the Church, particularly in the Church as it touches the college or university. He has in turn been college preacher at Princeton, Yale, Williams, Wellesley, Vassar, Harvard, the University of Chicago, Amherst, Wells, Cornell, and Columbia. From 1917-1919 he was aide to the Senior Chaplain of the Great Lakes Naval Training Station. Since 1919 he has been Warden of Saint Stephen's College, Annandale-on-Hudson. Among his books are RIGHT AND WRONG AFTER THE WAR *(1918), and* BEYOND AGNOSTICISM—A BOOK FOR TIRED MECHANISTS *(1929).*

O NE OF the most serious charges brought against the typical American university of the moment is that its graduates are, for the most part, either antagonistic to religion or else, more commonly, indifferent to it. There seems to be no doubt that the facts bear out the allegation. Occasionally this undoubted irreligion becomes vocal, as in the case of the man who lately wrote for *The Atlantic Monthly* the account of what happened to his faith while he was at Harvard.[1] But more often religion is simply ignored. It is quite true that students talk a great deal about it, rather strangely much if it be as dead a thing as they commonly insist. "Bull sessions" turn to it as the most usual alternative to talk about sex. But this chatter is for the most part vague

Copyright September, 1932, by *The Atlantic Monthly;* copyright 1932 by Bernard Iddings Bell. Used by permission of the author and *The Atlantic Monthly.*

[1] "What College Did to My Religion," by Philip E. Wentworth. See page 58.

and uninformed, and gets nowhere. Probably that is why it makes such an excellent subject for those interminable bickerings which undergraduates substitute for intelligent conversation.

But religion as a subject for serious intellectual concern enjoys no vogue among the great majority in university halls. It is rarely a subject for serious study, and the students are conspicuously absent from worship. Systematic spiritual culture they almost never undertake. Most of them appear to be ignorant that there is such a thing. Expected attendance at chapel is for the most part gone, nor has voluntary association with religious bodies taken its place. University alumni are not commonly to be found among those who support, by personal activity or otherwise, the religious bodies of America. These are facts, to be faced by honest men.

It is, to be sure, quite possible to maintain that these things are the necessary result of modern enlightenment; that to believe in God and to adore Him are incompatible with scientific ways of thinking; that religion is merely a curious survival of primitive superstition. If anyone desires to explain things that way, it is permitted him; but to most thinking people such a contention seems somehow too simple to be quite true. For countless generations man has sought to approach Truth by way of three experiences: the scientific, which has to do with what the senses may show; the artistic, which reveals truth and beauty through creative activity; and the religious, which consists of intuitions of personality. It seems an odd thing that all of a sudden man should have found out that the first of these (plus a tolerated, though not much respected, use of the second) is valid, while the third, equally instinctive to mankind, equally venerable, and equally a part of racial experience, has become absurd.

There are those who remember, with more than a little distress, how the Middle Ages ignored one of the modes of experience, the scientific, to its great deprivation. Bowing religion out, as of no possible validity, seems also a little supercilious, and dangerous. An experience attested by all the ages probably has something to it. That it may safely be ignored or laughed at, by any individual or culture, would seem to need some proving. If it is to be abandoned, the forsaking of it should be a last resort, not something to be accepted with nonchalance and gayety, in the typical undergraduate manner.

— As a matter of fact, modern scientific thought does not prevent a belief in God or the practice of religion, not by a very great deal. Nor are the greatest leaders of science the ones who despise the faith. Newton was a convinced Christian. Laplace, Laënnec, and Pasteur were faithful Roman Catholics. Dalton was a devout Friend. Galvani was a Franciscan tertiary. Ampère sympathetically and regularly read Thomas à Kempis. Faraday was a lay preacher, and J. C. Maxwell a Presbyterian elder. Romanes and Claude Bernard reasoned their way into Christianity. Lister died a faithful communicant. Fabre was a mystic, who said that atheism was a mania. Kelvin saw no incompatibility between his science and a faithful and regular worship of God. One could multiply such examples. Even Darwin was a theist, as may be seen by anyone who reads the last paragraph of the *Origin of Species*.

All of these men are now dead; but it is notorious that many of their successors of the moment are so anxious to promote the consideration of spiritual values that they all too frequently tumble into print, some of them exhibiting more zeal than knowledge in profession of faith in that which passes scientific knowing. As for philosophy, it is not merely such men as Maritain and Wust and Streeter and Hocking who are in revolt against mechanomorphism. The thing is clean gone out of fashion, except in American undergraduate colleges. It will hardly do, in the face of the facts, to explain collegiate indifference to religion on the ground of intellectual necessity. It is not modern thought that is to blame.

Nor is it, perhaps, the individual undergraduate who is altogether at fault. Youth is always conformist, more so than childhood or middle age. The undergraduate hates to be eccentric, or even to seem so. Half of the problems of college education are conditioned by this undergraduate prejudice against originality or independence of thought. The college student therefore reflects, quite naturally and understandably, the current notion that only those things are important which advance worldly position. Our generation ignores religion as far as possible, because to do so enables men and women to avoid interference with impulses engendered by cupidity. Contemporary civilization is largely built upon the basic idea that the world may become any man's oyster. It is the *Zeitgeist* which impels our students to a profound reverence for acquisitiveness.

Not that the universities fail to assist in this. More than a little they help to debase their undergraduates: by an all too eager surrender to the popular opinion that an educated man is merely one who can do and get things; by an overemphasis on expansion in numbers and extravagance in building and ballyhoo generally; by the making of men into bachelors and masters of arts when they happen to be merely technicians, and doctors of philosophy for most unphilosophical achievements; by a fawning upon potential benefactors, regardless of whether or not they are men and women of any discrimination. The universities, too, have been swimming with the tide.

It is not merely religion from consideration of which undergraduates are distracted by such unacademic antics. All thought about ultimates suffers together. Philosophy is disparaged. Even science itself has come to appear to the student eye not so much a method of arriving at truth as a means to an end, which end is the larger production of things and the mightier accumulation of cash. All true scholarship is injured by greed; but religion suffers most. Science can be exploited, and is therefore to be respected. Religion does not pay, and therefore may safely be ignored—in fact, had better be ignored. That is the simple and ugly explanation of a large part of student loss of faith in God and spiritual culture.

For all this *let us blame the mores;* but let us also fault the universities for a passive and profitable surrender to *the mores.* There is something cancerous in higher education as we have it in America. Perhaps the tissue has become diseased from too rapid growth and too rich food. Possibly a diet of depression will not hurt, although one has a slight misgiving that in the course of the next few years it will be the cultural rather than the applied side of scholarship that will suffer most. It may be that some major surgery is a bit overdue.

The degradation of university ideals does not, however, fully explain the religious indifference of undergraduates. Sometimes it is those very students who are most in revolt against the current immorality, off campus and on (that ethics which defines the good life in terms of possessions and pleasure), who are least concerned with spiritual experience. They know what they hate and despise, but they are not aware that religion is as rebellious as they. It is not too much to venture a guess that one thing which is wrong is that American universities fail to inform their students about the nature of the spiritual enterprise. Many of them have no faculties of theology at all; and where such faculties do exist they are commonly isolated from undergraduate teaching and from vital contact with colleagues in other fields of knowledge. It has come to pass that theology is looked upon as a professional subject. Nothing could be more unfortunate for balanced thought.

Religion is as basic a discipline as science, and as reputable intellectually. Yet it is possible for a student in almost any of our leading universities to read for his primary degree, and his advanced degrees, without gaining even a suspicion of that fact. Consequently, we have such astonishing attitudes of mind as that of the young Harvard man to whose *Atlantic Monthly* article reference has been made. He seems to be reasonably intelligent, not at all incapable of understanding religion. The trouble is that he apparently has no knowledge of what religion is. He has outgrown a crude and semi-magical concept of God, such as a child may properly hold, with no realization that grown men mean by religion something both more delicate and more complex. As a lad he was a Presbyterian. As a man he knows nothing of the profound and penetrating studies of religion made by the Scottish theologians, or by such American Presbyterians as Dr. Buttrick and Dr. Coffin and Dr. W. A. Brown, to take only three outstanding examples. He scorns the devotions conducted at the shrine of Sainte Anne de Beaupré, which are for persons of childlike mind; but he ignores the magnificent work of modern Roman Catholic thinkers. The man is ignorant—and he ought not to be. His university should have brought him into contact with religious thinkers comparable to those whom he has met with in the fields of science, history, and art.

The mystical side of experience and its contribution to an understanding of the universe are not commonly regarded by American universities as necessary fields of undergraduate study. Religion has next to no place in their curricula, or in their other official activities. This is, or ought to be, a matter of common knowledge, but an instance in point may be cited.

In 1925, at Harvard, the Student Council appointed a committee to look into and report upon certain aspects of education at that university from the undergraduate point of view. This was done, and the findings of the student committee were published in the *Harvard Advocate* for April, 1926. Among other things, the report recommended that a new kind of required course be made available which would include the study, not merely of philosophy, but also of religion. It stated: "It becomes urgently necessary that the college teach the business of life in all its aspects"; and again: "The committee recommends the innovation of including the philosophy of Christianity in the work of the course. This suggestion is not made in a missonary or crusading spirit, but is dictated as a remedy for the prevailing ignorance concerning so important a subject."

The committee of students made many excellent suggestions, and almost all of them have subsequently been adopted by Harvard College, including the one mentioned. It is only fair to observe, however, that the college authorities acted upon this specific recommendation in such a manner as to defeat, in large measure, what appears to have been the primary object of the Student Council in sponsoring it. The new course has, indeed, been added to the curriculum, but it is only a half course, and, instead of being required for a degree, it is optional and actually limited to two hundred students. Under these conditions it is obvious that the very students who most need the instruction which the new course offers will be the last to avail themselves of it.

This half-hearted acceptance by the college authorities of the suggestion which the student committee appears to have considered most important stands in strange contrast to their complete adoption of other suggestions of far less moment which were advanced in the same report. The Student Council committee went on to ask, for example, that the overgrown college be divided into smaller units, and this has subsequently been effected on a grand scale, at the cost of more than twelve million dollars. Such is the confusion of values in American universities.

It is unjust, perhaps, to single out Harvard. It is safe to say that most of our universities have been even less alert to their responsibilities in this direction, with the exception of parts of Columbia and the University of Chicago, where Dean Shailer Mathews has persuaded the authorities at least partially to face this fundamental problem. It is a too common custom in American universities to expend millions on brick and mortar while, in matters vitally important in their bearing upon education, faculty action lags behind common need and student demand.

Under such circumstances, it is hardly reasonable to expect that students should know much of anything about religion. This neglect of a great segment of knowledge is partly due to the example set by our state-supported institutions, which are compelled by law to eliminate from official consideration any serious study of the spiritual life; but it is also caused by a feeling on the part of those who direct our educational policies that religion is a non-intellectual and relatively unimportant activity of the human race. Such a position, in the light of human history, is more than a little absurd. The search for

God has always been one of man's chief concerns. The race has known that there were some things which it could find out only by scientific observation, others discoverable only by creative activity, and still others—and these the deepest and most subtle—to be mastered only by that seeking of ultimate Reality in personal terms which is religion. To ignore any of these basic human disciplines is dangerous, but to ignore religion is apt to be the most harmful of all. The cultivation of science without religion will always become pregnant with the sort of cynicism which once brought Greek thinking to a despairing close, from which the reintroduction of religion alone revived it. It is this very sort of cynicism which increasingly characterizes the intellectual life of the twentieth century. For the health of human thought, religious experience needs consideration by our universities.

The words "religious experience" seem better to use here than the word "religion," because that word "religion" is apt to be divorced from experience and given a derivative meaning. Religion is not itself a philosophy of religion, a formulation of religion, an organization of religion. Dogma, while immensely important, is actually a generalization of religious experience. Ecclesiastical organization is significant only because it is an attempt to preserve opportunities for religious experience. Religion is a way of living in terms of contact with Reality, personally conceived. If we do not give to men a knowledge of the technic involved in religious experience, we deprive them of part of their birthright.

There are many people to whom such statements as these will have no meaning whatever. Their minds are closed; they are fantastic and fanatic in their intellectual lopsidedness. There is no use discussing with such persons the place of religion in an educational program. But there are many, increasingly more, who will realize the truth of what has been said. Among them will be found not merely church people but many who have no connection with any church; not merely ecclesiastical enthusiasts, but also poets, philosophers, nonbehavioristic psychologists, and a good many of the most eminent scientists; people who see life without bias, who realize that religion is not magic, not merely morality, but rather a seeking for what the mind cannot otherwise grasp. Perhaps we may hope for a day when such persons may determine the policies of our American institutions of higher learning.

The World of Babbitt's Son:
1942

By HENRY HAZLITT

Although only thirty-eight years old, Henry Hazlitt has won authoritative positions in the fields of finance and literature. Mr. Hazlitt has been financial editor of THE NEW YORK EVENING MAIL, *editorial writer on* THE NEW YORK HERALD *and on* THE SUN, *and literary editor of* THE SUN. *He is now literary editor of* THE NATION.

THE temptation to speculate upon the kind of physical and economic world that most of us will be living in ten years from now is too great to be put aside. Compared, at all events, with the efforts of men like Jeans and Eddington and Haldane to tell us what conditions on earth will be like when the sun begins to cool, such prophecy seems as narrowly practical and immediate as that of a clothing manufacturer making his plans for next spring. For at least five out of every six of us (future death rates have proved to be very accurately predictable) ten years from now means *our* world, not that of our remoter descendants.

Perhaps our conjectures will seem more plausible if we pretend not to be predicting at all, but merely to be recalling. So let us assume that it is a late Friday afternoon in the summer of 1942, and that we are seeing the world through the eyes—though not altogether through the mind—of Theodore Roosevelt Babbitt, son of George F. Babbitt. Ted, you will recall, was about eighteen years old in 1922, and his marriage to Eunice Littlefield was the last act in the book. He is about

From *Scribner's Magazine*, May, 1932; copyright, 1932, by Charles Scribner's Sons. Reprinted by permission of the author and *Scribner's Magazine*.

thirty-eight now, himself the father of a seventeen-year-old daughter and a son of twelve. But Eunice and Myra are now traveling in Europe, and young Herbie is at a boy's camp in Maine, so this Friday afternoon we happen to find Ted in his private airplane, going about a hundred and eighty miles an hour on his way from Zenith for a week-end visit to Brent Dodsworth (Sam's son), who is now living on Long Island.

Ted has done pretty well in the electrical-equipment business, otherwise he could not afford to sport a Packard plane in addition to a Cadillac car. Private planes are still comparatively rare; there are only a little more than a million of them in the country, as compared with more than thirty million automobiles, and Ted himself did not buy one until the motor had been silenced, and the device perfected in 1938 that enabled planes to rise and land vertically.

Ted is looking down on the countryside. It is not altogether an attractive picture. It is covered with fine broad concrete roads, but it has been virtually swept bare of trees where the roads have been laid down, and planted with telephone posts instead.

For the most part it is an even uglier countryside than it was in 1932. There is not much to boast of in most of the architecture. Many of the older houses are in the fake Tudor style that broke out over the country in the late twenties and early thirties. But there have been some improvements. Most of the filling stations have been taken over by the great oil companies; there are fewer of them than there were a decade ago, and they are individually much more attractive. The greater part of them are built in concrete, without decoration of any kind, but some of the newer ones are in chromium and glass. And in 1936 a serious movement began, which has since been growing, to plant rows of trees along all the automobile highways. The trees so far planted are still rather small, unfortunately, and can hardly be seen at all from the height at which Ted is flying. But the factories are almost uniformly more attractive, and one very great gain has been the total abolition in some of the States of advertising signboards. And between Zenith and

New York there are already two or three of the new "garden cities," thoughtfully planned and spaciously laid out, full of trees and parks, made up of dwellings and business structures of a harmonious architecture. To be sure, these cities have been made possible only by methods which Ted has often denounced as communistic—but he has to admit that he admires them.

Ted's own interests are practical rather than esthetic, and what fascinates him much more than the garden cities are these new metal houses produced by mass-production methods along the lines suggested more than a decade ago by Buckminster Fuller, which have just begun to make their appearance in the last year or two. Young Dodsworth had telephoned Ted that he was living in one of these, and though Ted had seen the exact duplicate of it (the eight-room model of the General Homes Corporation), he was curious to find how it felt to spend the week-end in one.

Now he is nearing New York City, and slows down. (It has been possible for the last two or three years to go as slowly as you want in an airplane.) Ted has not been in or over New York for nearly two months now, and he is constantly excited by the changes there. The traffic conditions are still unspeakably bad; indeed, they are much worse than they have ever been, and even Ted doesn't understand how any one can want to live there. (Of course the traffic congestion in Zenith is much worse too.) Up to 1939 there had been no legal height limit to office buildings, and their mad erection, stimulated by real-estate values and puerile pride in height records, had gone on. In spite of the elementary mathematics of the situation, the connection between high buildings and congestion was for years either ignored or denied. A child of six might have been expected to understand that if you doubled the average building height in a city you doubled the population that it housed and hence you doubled the congestion on the same street area, but the real-estate interests and the structural-steel interests, by the most energetic propaganda against this idea, had successfully fought the popular recognition of its truth for years, and even when they were no longer able to do that, they were able, for a few years, to bring various sorts of pressure on politicians to prevent any ordinance limiting building height from being adopted. But finally, in 1939, a measure had been adopted limiting the height of new buildings to twenty stories. This has done nothing so far to cure the congestion; it cannot, of course, begin to have any effect in that direction until the older skyscrapers become obsolescent and are torn down. Meanwhile the erection of twenty-story buildings where twelve-, ten- and four-story buildings have been before is not helping matters.

Ted prefers to look for one of these new open or "aerated" city blocks, several of which have been erected in the last year. Instead of a solid wall of buildings facing the street on all four sides, the block is composed of a series of detached X-shaped buildings (except that the cross is at right angles) each twenty stories in height. From Ted's view, looking directly down, one of these blocks seems to be composed of a double row of X's or turned plus signs:

$$X \quad X \quad X \quad X \quad X \quad X$$
$$X \quad X \quad X \quad X \quad X \quad X$$

This allows the free play of light and air on every side of each building. As the rear of each building can be seen by pedestrians on the street behind it, and as the sides can also be seen, each building is of course finished on all sides, instead of consisting, like so many of the older structures, of an elaborate and expensive façade, and sides and rear of cheap brick. Between the buildings are footpaths, permitting pedestrians to walk directly through the block at any point. The rest of the open area between buildings is planted with grass, flowers, and trees, most of which, of course, can be seen from the street, and are equally pleasant from an airplane view. Since the airplane has become popular, too, the new buildings have been paying more attention to the appearance of their roofs. These are flat, surrounded by chromium steel railings, and paved with attractive colored tilings. The roofs are used a great deal by sunbathers, many of whom are nude, and though Ted always finds the sight of pretty girl sunbathers—on roofs or beaches—

a very pleasant one, he is too accustomed to the spectacle to become excited by it.

But Ted has to be getting on, so that he can find Brent's place when it is still light. He finds it with little difficulty, and Brent shows him through it with great pride.

It is an odd place for Ted's eye to become accustomed to, and looks from the outside like a hexagonal steel-and-glass tent raised slightly from the ground on a thick hollow steel pole.

"Yes," says Brent, in reply to Ted's observation to this effect, "in fact the house is put up pretty much the way you would put up a tent. The General Homes Corporation deliver the parts of this 1942 model house and have one of their assembly crews erect it in two or three days. First they actually *bore* a hole in the ground; then they sink the central supporting shaft into it, and then they *hang* the house from the shaft."

"Gosh!" says Ted in admiration.

"You see," Brent goes on (he is, incidentally, an officer in General Homes), "suppose for some reason a man should become dissatisfied with the location his house was on. Suppose the neighborhood should begin to run down, or suppose he should have to take a job out at Toledo. Well, if he had an old-fashioned house, he'd have to try to sell it; he'd probably have it on his hands a long time and then sacrifice it. But with this house, he can just 'phone General Homes, and within a week we'll dismantle it, transport it, and have it erected again on the new site. All he has to worry about is selling the land. At the end of ten years the house will still have a good trade-in value. It can be much more easily sold than the old-fashioned house because it can be transported to any site, because it conforms to standard specifications, and because our national reputation stands squarely behind it."

Ted felt uncomfortably that Brent was handing him an habitual sales talk, but nevertheless he was impressed. "What's this?" he asked, pointing to some brightly polished gadgets.

"The one on the left is the heating thermostat, and the one on the right the cooling thermostat: this house holds a temperature of 70, if you want, winter and summer."

"I have the same sort of thing at my house in Zenith," brags Ted.

"I know, but I bet it cost you four times as much. An old-fashioned individual-type house of the same quality as this couldn't be built for less than $20,000. This one sells for $6495 f.o.b. Detroit, and once the company can put this model into *real* quantity production, it will be able to sell it for $3000."

"Well, I tell you, Brent. This is a mighty swell house, and all that, but I should think you'd want something more—well, individual. I don't see how a man can take a lot of pride in a house that's just exactly like a hundred thousand others."

"Listen, Ted; you're pretty stuck on your Packard plane, now, aren't you?"

"You bet."

"And you're pretty proud of your Cadillac, aren't you?"

"Sure I am."

"Well, there are at least ten thousand duplicates of your Packard plane and several hundred thousand duplicates of your Cadillac."

"Yep; I never thought of that."

"Just because your dad was kidded a lot, Ted, you're afraid of the word 'standardization.' But there's nothing wrong with that at all, provided it's *good* standardization."

Ted and Brent sink into armchairs with their cocktails and begin to talk about the business situation, but we can hardly understand their conversation unless we know what has happened in the last ten years. The recovery from the panic of 1929–32 was a slow one. From the perspective of 1942 it has become clear that the depression was the result of two main causes. The first was the collapse of world commodities from the inflated war price-levels. For nearly a decade after the war these price-levels had stayed up, or had declined slowly and harmlessly—except for the sharp drop between the spring of 1920 and the spring of 1921—and the curious impression had become all but universal that commodity prices as a result of the war had reached a permanently higher level; but in 1929, 1930, and 1931 the decline had become a rout. There was of course nothing sacrosanct or particularly permanent about the price-level of 1913, but the record of prices after the Napoleonic Wars and our own Civil War should have indicated that prices, given time, manage after a war to return to somewhere near the levels they started from. The second cause for the depression was also connected with the war, but more indirectly. It lay in the almost insane post-war economic policies of Europe and the United States. As every one knows, the economic burden laid upon Germany had been more than could possibly be met, and the United States, while professing to wish to collect its war debts, had kept raising its tariff higher and higher to make it impossible for Europe to pay the debts in goods, the only possible ultimate medium. Imitation of, and retaliation against, the United States brought the erection of preposterous tariff walls everywhere, and choked the channels of world trade. None of these policies was modified until it had already brought disastrous consequences, and even then the modification never went far enough. There is no need here to rehearse at length the painful events during the period of readjustment—the wage reductions, strikes, riots by the unemployed, the collapse in rents, and the long series of receiverships, especially of important railroads. By the fall of 1933 most of this readjustment had been accomplished, and the recovery in 1934 was fairly rapid. The railroads were finally taken over by the government in 1935—for the most part to the relief of the railway security holders, who took a cut in nominal interest but most of whom, at least among the bondholders, were able to salvage their principal. The difference between the railroads under public and under private management was not so great as to remove discussion of the relative merits of the two systems: most business men complained that the roads were much more bureaucratically and less efficiently run than under private management, but they had to admit that freight rates were lower, as there was no longer any need for having an unnecessarily high general freight-rate level mainly for the purpose of keeping the less profitable roads going. The railroads, however, seemed to be growing relatively less important each year. Though they still carried the bulk of the heavy freight for long hauls, lighter freight for short hauls was more and more being carried by trucks, and in the last five years the roads had been losing passenger business rapidly to the airplane lines.

Public-utility companies had been falling more and more into government hands, but general attention was now focused, not on these, but on the great industrial companies. These had gone through one process of merger after another, or had formed trade associations which acted, for the most part, exactly as a single company would have acted. The Sherman anti-trust act remained on the books, but had virtually become a dead letter. First the oil and natural gas companies had been made almost exempt from its provisions: indeed, competing oil companies drilling wells in the same "pool" had been in many cases legally compelled to merge. Then, as other industries came to be controlled by single companies, or were bound together by tight trade associations, special government regulatory bodies, modeled after the Interstate Commerce Commission, had been appointed to control their practices, prices, and output; and these commissions for separate industries were in turn co-ordinated by a central commission, composed of the chairmen of each of the other commissions. Ted and Brent talk for a long time of how commission-infested the whole country has become, and of the enormous red tape and bureaucracy involved in the system, and they relate to each other various absurd errors made by the individual commissions and the co-ordinating commission. But the situation of private industry has become more and more confused. Mergers and the holding-company system have gone to the length where it has become almost impossible to trace the connection between the ultimate security holder and the individual property. In fact, most investors have their funds in the securities of investment trusts, which have their funds in the securities of holding companies, which have their funds in the securities of other holding companies, and so on. It has become more ridiculous than ever before to talk of any connection between the ultimate stockholder's "vote" and the actual policies of the underlying operating companies. The separation between management and ownership has become practically as great, in other words, in the industries that are not yet subject to commission control as in those that are.

The situation is confused in other directions. In 1934, for example, when it became clear that Russia, with its low-cost wheat, was driving the high-cost American wheat farmer out of business, and when the latter had finally seen through wheat tariffs and "price-stabilizing" Farm Boards, it was finally decided that nothing could save him but lower production costs. Taking its cue from Russia, our government formed a great harvesting machinery company, and proceeded to rent tractors and other agricultural equipment and services to farmers at cost. This had been highly successful, for the most part, but a protracted discussion was now going on in Congress on the question of whether this corporation should remain in the hands of the Federal Government or be sold to a private syndicate.

Compulsory unemployment insurance had finally been adopted in most of the States with the exception of those in the Southeast, and Statewide employment agencies had been created. Congress had passed a Constitutional amendment for Federal unemployment insurance, but this had not yet been ratified by the States. A few of the States, also, had adopted schools to take care of workers dropped from obsolescent and dying industries and to train them as workers in one of the growing industries. In these States no worker could receive unemployment benefits for more than three to six months without enrolling in one of the schools.

The country had not gone communist, but the possibility of its doing so was no longer small. As the Communist party had grown year by year, the Republicans and Democrats, recognizing that there was no difference between them, had merged into one Republican-Democratic party (usually referred to simply as the Republican party). The Republicans had been able to elect a President in 1940, but by a rather narrow popular margin. There was a possibility of a Communist majority in Congress after the 1942 elections, and the Communists were confident of electing a President in 1944. The Communist party was controlled, however, by moderates, and was not very different in its immediate aims from the old Socialist party—but the word Communism had acquired prestige and the word Socialism had lost it. Communism in Russia had been successful, in the sense that it had remained in power; but it had gradually come to look more and more like a combination of State and private capitalism.

This was not considered important, however, as the Communists continued to describe everything they did in orthodox Marxian phrases—just as organized Christianity had been able to pursue a Nietzschean policy with the aid of phrases taken from the Sermon on the Mount. (The Communists had also taken another idea from Christianity, or at least from Catholicism. They did not permit their own population to read volumes that were unfavorable to Communism either directly or by implication, but in order to answer capitalistic arguments they had formed a sort of Jesuit society, the members of which were not only permitted but encouraged to study heretical books with the purpose of confuting them.) American capitalism, on the other hand, had come to look more and more like State socialism, but in spite of the fact that this State socialism was growing yearly, our statesmen continued to describe our system as one of rugged individualism, and to point proudly to our steadfast adherence to Jeffersonian principles.

The economic problem that is now causing the greatest concern to the world, however, is that of the gold standard. A German chemist, using the advanced knowledge of the atom, succeeded two years ago in producing gold artificially at about the price of copper. Prices all over the world rose violently as the first of this gold came on the market; and the immediate effect threatened to be much the same as the after-war depreciation of the mark and other European currencies. It is now recognized everywhere that the gold standard is doomed. Individual nations, the United States included, have hurriedly adopted "compensated dollar" schemes similar to that long ago advocated by Irving Fisher, but these schemes have worked very badly, and an international conference has been called to meet in the autumn for some possible joint action.

To be sure, Ted and Brent do not talk of all these things; like you and I, they talk mainly of their immediate personal affairs, and especially of the shortcomings of their mutual friends, and even more especially of the shortcomings of Brent's second wife, Eva, who is now in Reno getting a divorce. Reno, to meet the competition of other cities, has had to cut the residence period down to one week. Some of the States have adopted more liberal divorce laws, but New York—though it has legalized birth control—has changed its divorce laws very little. But as divorce has become so easy to obtain in a number of Western cities, the pressure for more liberal divorce laws in the Eastern States has not been great.

"Yes," Brent is saying, "Eva's a fine girl; I haven't a thing against her, but she's too unsettled, always wanting to be on the go. I don't know, it doesn't seem to me that you can find many women now who like to stay at home a little. I wish there were more old-fashioned women like those of ten years ago."

"Trouble is today," agrees Ted, "every woman's got some career of her own. There's Myra, going to study to be a doctor. Every woman today wants to be a doctor, or a lawyer, or a politician, or to run a business——"

"Yes," adds Brent, "things are speeding up too much, too. Civilization's getting too complex. Ten years ago things were simple and quiet."

"But then, there're a lot of advantages," Ted reminds him. "What did people do with their evenings then? No television, for example."

"You're right," concedes Brent, "it's hard to imagine what people did without television. By the way, we don't want to miss the government's fine program tonight."

They turn on the machine, and a musical comedy is before their eyes. But they look at it only occasionally, and hardly seem to be listening to it. They go on with their own conversation. "Mark my word," says Ted solemnly as they sit drinking their highballs, "within two years prohibition will be repealed."

Lo, the Poor Introvert

By DOROTHY CANFIELD

*Dorothy Canfield was born in Kansas in 1879. She was edu-
cated in France and the United States. In 1907 she married
John R. Fisher and settled on one of the Canfield farms at
Arlington, Vermont. Her first novel* The Squirrel-Cage
*was writen in 1912. Mrs. Fisher has always been interested in
the education of children and worked intimately with Dr.
Montessori in adapting her instructional methods to American
children. During the war she conducted a Convalescent Home
for children in Southern France. Her best-known books are*
Hillsboro People *(1915),* The Bent Twig *(1915),* The Brim-
ming Cup *(1921),* Raw Material *(1923), and* Basque People
(1931).

WHO is that frightened biped, teetering unsteadily
forward on a tightrope over Niagara Falls, trying
to keep two balls in the air as he goes? He is you . . .
me . . . our poor race, born with single-track minds into the
traffic tangle of the world. We human beings piteously crave
black-and-white problems where one side is right and the other
side wrong. But here we are thrust into a world where both
sides are right and both sides wrong! We want stability more
than anything else, and we'd like to get it by leaning our whole
weight on something solid. But stability is to be had in this
world only by achieving some sort of balance between two opposing pulls. And this means that, no matter to which side humanity is leaning at any given moment, the only wise and
helpful advice to give it is to try to lean toward the opposite
direction.

But is not such advice—like most wise counsels—a waste of

breath? Has not humanity always ignored the excellent advice of philosophers, preachers, magazine-writers and gone
on leaning farther and farther to one side, until even the
majority could not help seeing that in another instant all
would be lost and, with a convulsive reflex of panic, righted
themselves and begun assiduously to lean just as much too
far the other way?

During what are now called the Dark Ages suppose that
someone had protested against the extent to which inward-
looking was being carried? Suppose that some sensible man
had seen that many of the people in hair-shirts trying to starve
themselves into seeing visions were on the wrong track? Would
he have been listened to if he had said that men with restless,
inquiring minds do not belong in hermits' cells any more than
race horses belong in an aquarium? If he had tried to persuade
a man with a genial liking for his fellows and a native gift
for bringing out the best in them that he was out of place
in a monastic order where solitary meditation is the rule,
would his advice have been followed? Would he have been
able to prevent even one loving mother from forcing her
practical, energetic little boy to lead a caricature of the contemplative life? Would it have diminished even by one turn
of the screw the pressure of public opinion remorselessly
clamping valuable human personalities into molds which broke
but could not shape them? Would it, do you suppose, have
saved even one naturally extravert mind from the miserable
hamstringing hypocrisy of trying to appear an introvert? Probably not. But nowadays we pride ourselves on our tolerance.
Might not a word of protest help to loosen the remorselessness
of the clamps now in favor? I wonder. It might—who knows—
loosen the screws by one turn.

For it is apparent, of course, that a tidal wave is now sweeping
around the globe in the opposite direction from that of the
Dark Ages. In Soviet Russia we see it rising to Bay-of-Fundy
violence. Less visibly, less dramatically, but none the less ir-
resistibly it is flooding up into every one of our small local
and personal inlets, homes, schools, playgrounds, teachers' con-

ventions, Rotary Clubs, committee meetings, churches. Everybody is carried along by it, young, old, mothers, fathers, educators, not to the wisely chosen destinations to which they think they are purposefully paddling their little crafts, but to the same sort of fatally one-sided excess which seems to us so incredible in the past. Open any popular treatise on the psychology of daily life (the modern equivalent of the *Stepping Heavenward* books, or the *Lives of the Saints,* or the *Family Physician*), and you will find listed as a dangerous symptom any liking in young or old to be occasionally alone and physically passive; as passive and idle, for example, as a certain seventeenth-century boy loafing under a tree from which presently a historic apple fell plump into the middle of his mind, widened to receptivity by silence and solitude.

Does a little tot on a playground sit down quietly by himself; there may be now a few, a very few ultra "progressive" schools where he is left in peace. But in almost all the others, the playground director, imagining perversities Freud never knew runs up with, "Come along, Buster! Don't mope in a corner. Be a good mixer!" Snap goes the tiny thread of thought; for Buster, like nine children out of ten, is helpless clay under the kneading and shaping of the older generation. Back he goes out of his morbid isolation into the milling pack, into the normality of group activity, perhaps to a wholesome healthy-minded mimic battle of bootlegger and hijacker.

Often enough such treatment is needed. I do not deny it. Vacant little blue eyes are frequently fixed on anything but trailing clouds of glory; active play is the safest of safety-valves for blowing off high-pressure exaggerated ideas and emotions. Yet something is wrong with the skillful yank given to the little boy by that well-trained playground director. Did she haul Buster back from dreamland because it was the best thing for him? No, she did not consider him at all, though if anybody had objected, she could have brought out plenty of catch phrases from her classroom notebooks to show that she had. (Only she never needs to, because nobody dreams of objecting.) What happened was this: bowed herself by the wind of prevailing fashion to the correct, active, group-minded angle, and looking around her to make sure that all her young charges were also correct, she perceived Buster's noncomforming little figure shockingly bent over in the opposite direction. Not because it was a good thing for him, but because it was a good thing for sacred conformity, she hastened to bend him right.

She was glowing with the same certainty of acting for the child's best interests that was felt in the Dark Ages by preceptors of the young who hushed up any signs of a dangerous questioning spirit, any impulse to improve the material present world, anything and everything except concentration on the getting into the desirable one of the two Hereafters. The same pleasant certainty of duty done must also have warmed the heart of the Roman adult of the good old "truly Roman" period who repressed in sensitive, imaginative little boys any tendency to preoccupation with the life of the spirit rather than with conquering lesser breeds of men abroad and putting over successful political deals at home. Each one of those educators, so different from one another, is entirely justified on the time-honored theory that a teacher's duty is to carry on the world as he finds it, to bring up the young as nearly as possible in the image of the past, and thus perpetuate unaltered the fine crystalline Kultur of the good old status quo.

Only it never is perpetuated unaltered. Once in so often it turns a complete somersault. Queer, with all the devoted efforts of each older generation to keep it unchanged! In our school history books the four centuries after the definite Fall of the Roman Empire are a sort of bog in which—let us confess it— most of us sink into the mud of ignorance, scrambling out into the air only when the substantial figure of Charlemagne heaves in sight. Why is that period harder than another for us to remember? There are as many memorizable dates and battles and jumbled-up history-book doings in it as in any other. Isn't it because the real event of those centuries was something that took place invisibly under the surface—a long obscure revolution in point of view? In that period European humanity stopped leaning to one side of its tight rope and, in a panic at having nearly fallen off, began to lean with all its might to the other side. On the mistaken principle, so firmly held by our deluded race, that if some is good, more is better, the leaning went, century after century, farther and farther towards what we now call (I know it is inaccurate jargon but you know what I mean) the introvert view of life, and away from the extravert which had been in style during the Roman period. Then came the inevitable realization, first by a minority and then by the majority, that the leaning to one side had again gone so far that only by another convulsive effort could we avoid falling off our tightrope. The Renaissance and the French Revolution are the names we give to the most dramatic episodes in that effort to right ourselves.

And now we are in the full enthusiasm of what might be called leaning to the Left rather than to the Right. Or were yesterday. When the electrician manipulating the spotlight in a theater slips a piece of the blue glass over the lens everybody on the stage is bathed in blue, no matter what the color of his skin. At present the light in which we are all bathed is red— a cheerful lively color, though a trifle monotonous when it is the only one. As it is. For it now floods every corner of the literate world. Our conscientious playground director certainly shares the reprobation felt by everybody at her boarding-house for the ideals of Soviet Russia. You would pain her— and to no purpose for she wouldn't believe a word you said— if you told her that in pouncing on Buster for being passive and solitary rather than active and group-minded she is proving that she is dyed to her bones with the contemporary philosophy of life which she holds in common with Stalin. She would in- form you that you did not know what you were talking about if you told her that she is skillfully marshaling the American children under her care, *left!* right! *left!* right! along the road filled by Soviet marchers, all the throng guided by a boldly printed signpost, reading, "To the Completely Extravert Life."

Till very recently few people doubted that that road was—at long last—the right one. We had found it, lying broad and unmistakable before us. Other generations had wandered back and forth across it, but our feet were set firmly on it. Ours is an extravert civilization. Ergo, an extravert civilization is the right kind to have.

I say that ours is an extravert civilization and by "our" I do not mean American. We have fallen into the habit of thinking of mass production, mass welfare work, mass government, co-operation, good fellowship, and widespread material comfort as our special contribution to the world's history. Our sense of proprietorship has been helped by the scoldings of visiting Europeans (generally out of sympathy with the majority at home) who have held us up as the authors of all that they disliked in the modern world. But if we look at what has been going on in Europe during the last half-century we see that they have been pushing us very hard in the same race, and that our seeming leadership has resulted chiefly from our having bigger numbers, wider territory within national boundaries, and fewer hampering prejudices from the past. But the goal has been the same. Occasionally (as in some of the cartels, in city government, for instance) Western Europe has sprinted out in front. We still have most bathtubs per capita, most miles of concrete roads, the most thorough averaging of individuality into broad mass effort.

But recently events have perceptibly slowed up the enthusiastic speed with which in English-speaking countries we were flinging ourselves forward over this road. Soviet Russia, still behind us in performance, has gone ahead of us in theory and, with disagreeable clarity, has written out the logical definition of a completely extravert life: that mass effort is human duty and all there is to human duty; that every part of every person's life without reservation belongs to the State (which is everybody working together for the common good); that individuality is, first, nonsense, a contradiction in terms, because the individual does not exist save as a member of a group; and second, treason to an ideal.

Now all the people living under what is called the Anglo-Saxon influence feel a chill of doubt when an ideal of theirs is clearly and articulately stated. Being an Anglo Saxon myself, I feel that this quality so mocked by logical Latins and Slavs has a cosmic value of which they do not dream and provides a method by which danger is glimpsed and avoided when blurting out the truth might frighten us into falling off our tightrope into the abyss. If you will allow a violent change of metaphor (well, to be honest, whether you allow it or not), I'd like to say that while all human beings, viewed from the perspective of history, look remarkably like the migrating lemmings of Norway, periodically seized by a tragic wanderlust that leads them into the ocean, if you examine them a little more closely you will notice that when the sound of breakers ahead begins to be audible the Anglo Saxons hesitate and shuffle their feet uneasily, instead of continuing to advance. I do not claim that this cautious role is a heroic or picturesque one. On the contrary it is probably due to prosaic, stuffy racial qualities. I merely point out that Slav and Latin lemmings may shout in exhilaration when they see their watery goal heaving and glittering before them, and plunge forward all the more heroically along the road laid out for them by logic, but that those of the human lemmings who speak English are rather given to guessing that something more serious than wet feet will happen to them if they proceed, and are apt to draw up beside the road in a crowd which is untidy, disorganized, and bewildered—but on dry land.

My purpose in writing this article will perhaps be clear if I say that I consider myself one English-speaking lemming calling out anxiously to others in the hurrying throng, "Don't you hear a noise like waves breaking on a cliff? I know, yes, I know! The road's laid out according to the latest rules. But I haven't any life-preserver. Nor you either. What do you say about working our way to the side to see if we can't find a path that looks as though it led somewhere else?"

Since keeping in step with our fellows is almost as necessary to us as eating, it takes more heroism than an ordinary person can muster to tear himself away from any crowd marching shoulder to shoulder, no matter where it is going. And I am an ordinary person. Perhaps I am doing no more than trying to locate some others with whom I can be in step. But even if I find them, it is not going to be easy for me, who am a natural extravert, to resist the contagion of the extravert creed, because there is in it (as in all creeds of course or they would not be creeds) so much truth. As most people go, most of the time, the extravert attitude is the one that works best.

What is that attitude? We mean by an extravert—do we not?—a person responsive mostly to stimuli from outside himself, concerned mostly with his relations to his fellow-men and with mastering with their help his material surroundings. Of course, by and large, that is the kind of person who survives and helps the race to continue living on a globe that has by no means any friendly interest in our survival. More than this, the extravert habits of group-activity are not only practically useful to the race but provide most of our satisfactions. As a rule, from the cave age down to the present, the human being who is actively "doing something" in company with others feels happier and more secure, is quieter in his mind, and hence in better health than the solitary brooding one. One gets tired of hearing the human race called herd animals. But this phrase is no less true because it is threadbare. The extravert ideal suits most of them most of the time. And though we have destroyed saber-toothed tigers and some other material difficulties, there is plenty left for extraverts to do. Society still needs organizing, waste places cry out for taming. We lag tragically behind our social dreams. We are still pioneers. We still need countless organizers and co-workers to man the ramparts of civilization.

To respond quickly, adequately, and masterfully to external stimuli, to arrange social relations intelligently and well—this is the herd ideal, this is the extravert way of life. It explains humanity pretty well. But consider what has been done by modern life in the matter of multiplying "external stimuli." The simple stationary routine of older times was lived always against the same landscape with the same group of well-known familiars. The slow wheeling of the seasons was the most marked change in outward circumstances. Under such conditions to be responsive to external stimuli presumably just kept a man's wits from wool-gathering. But now, with all of us coming and going everywhere and back all the time, associating for an instant or two with one set of people and darting on to another, the material background of life shifts around us all like a rapidly shaken kaleidoscope. The genuine extravert trying in these conditions to live up to the traditions of his temperament is brother to the chameleon tethered on the Scotch plaid shawl.

Then take that other life-work, beloved by extraverts, the arranging of social relations. To get them somewhere near right is a noble ideal. The only trouble with it is that it is not big enough. Part of humanity refuses to stay tucked up under its comfortable bedclothes. I do not refer only to the occasional personalities who are, so to speak, professionally non-extravert, the occasional poets and saints, and artists and dreamers and musicians. I make bold to say that some part of every one of us rebels against customs and conformity and cannot be satisfied with strictly social ideals, even the finest. Every one of us is troubled by dreams of abstract perfections beyond our power to realize, by moral codes from which our flesh recoils, towards which something in us that is not flesh yearns and aspires. A strict adherence to the orthodox theory of life now prevailing starves and smothers not only the occasional artistic or poetic or religious individual in whom introvert non-social tendencies are embodied, but also the poet or artist who would like to live in a corner of every human heart. The playground director may have been right in thinking that Buster, dreaming back there on the playground, was only a little lazy extravert. But on the other hand the truth may be that the child was moved at that moment to let a little light and air into the poet's corner of his personality. Perhaps all that was done by the young woman set by society to mold him was to slam shut the door of that corner and turn the key in the lock. She is not to blame. She was only doing her best to be virtuous and to make others virtuous according to the creed that is orthodox today and that has confounded in its anathema non-social with anti-social qualities.

Orthodoxy of all kinds in every period and place where it was powerful enough to do as it pleased has driven to madness or frustration valuable human beings whose personalities did not fit the prevailing style. Anybody can see this when he is not looking at his own orthodoxy. Any modern can tell you glibly about the frightful and unnecessary suffering inflicted on many normal, healthful people by the tyranny of the ascetic, solitary, inward-turned ideals of the Middle Ages. Just you try to tell him in return that acute and unnecessary suffering is now being inflicted on many normal and healthful human beings by the tyranny of the present idolatry of incessant, purposeful activity in groups, and he will instantly bring out the finest brand of hundred per cent pure Inquisitional conviction of righteousness as he says, "Oh, but don't you see, such people aren't normal. For their own good, they ought to be taught how to get their satisfactions in activity and in activity shared with others. All we are trying to do is to set them on the right road." If you try to show him how close the parallel is between his attachment to the accepted orthodoxy of today and that of the past to its prevailing ideals, you will just get called a bourgeois for your pains. This is the awful modern equivalent (borrowed from Russia) of the awful medieval statement that if you did not mend your ways you would go to hell—a threat now become a mere colorful ejaculation of impatience.

Looking back now, we can scarcely understand why in order to make it possible for St. Francis and his like to live happily the Middle Ages should have thought it necessary to make life a barren torment for Roger Bacon and his like. What did those ages think would be the harm in letting both varieties of human beings develop freely into their own kind of beauty, power, and usefulness? The answer to that question grins sardonically at us from our modern penalizing of the introvert temperament. How happily do we allow contemplative, impractical saints to live? We do not admit that a free, approved development of the St. Francis temperament would produce beauty, power, and usefulness because we admit as powerful, useful, and beautiful qualities only those which are produced by scientific minds like Roger Bacon's. It's perfectly simple, you see. Or, if we do not go so far as that, we demand, under penalty of social ostracism, that a race horse shall plow his acre every day before running a race, that a personality shall cultivate the social and extravert virtues first, and then, if it amuses him, add some introvert trimmings. You must have noticed the almost touchingly naïve notice posted up in substance all over Soviet Russia, "Wanted: Original thinkers and creative-minded seers in perfect conformity to our ideas. Large Reward offered to any who can qualify."

What is it that keeps an extravert, a well-mannered, practically useful, socially agreeable extravert, from being also a seer and a deep original thinker? Everything! Just everything. Why does not Einstein (our most amiable genius) win bridge prizes and go to dances? The very qualities which make the extravert a marvelous builder of society, an organizer of material problems, and an agreeable member of ordinary society prevent him from looking deeply into the causes and ultimate values of things and do not allow him to become broodingly aware of meanings hidden to the ordinary eye. Of course nobody would claim that a co-operator who is a good mixer or a busy captain of industry can never withdraw into himself and dream superhuman glimpses of abstract truth and beauty. No human being is ever born a pure type. There have been cases when a brooding recluse, blasted from his shell by some dramatic need, rushed out into the busy world, acted, organized, led, and created material order out of material chaos, as an extravert might do.

When we generalize and classify we are merely noting, as it were, the result of an election, with all the diverse elements in a character as candidates for votes. Occasionally the tendency towards outward- or inward-looking wins with a landslide of a majority. More often it is a bare plurality. Character is more fluid than our generalizations about it. But it is a grave error to think it more fluid than it is. There is no such thing as the hundred per cent extravert of the reverse; yet character, malleable enough among the young within certain hereditary limits, crystallizes through habit. The active and the social and the contemplative life cannot be lived equally well by any one person. One or the other atrophies as the years go by. Whatever his little holidays into solitude, the extravert remains a man of the crowd, who fits into the crowd, who likes the crowd and is liked by it, hence is necessarily limited to ideals and satisfactions that are not wholly beyond the crowd. There is nothing discreditable in this. Practical skill and material success are not wrong. The social virtues are fine ones. Most of us are fitted for the extravert attitude. It is the surest recipe by which to concoct an average contented life, useful to other people, satisfactory to oneself. My quarrel with Soviet Russia begins only when they assume that it is also the way to the highest excellence, and with the child psychologists and psycho-analysts only when they assume, as in the great majority of cases they do, that it is the one normal way of life for everybody—in short, only when adherence to group-life, to practical skills, to material success and the social virtues becomes a too powerful religion with a hell of its own.

When an introvert tries to keep out of the extravert way of life, active, practical, socially useful and agreeable, public opinion sends him to that hell. This usually turns him into a crank no matter what his native gifts or talents. And that helps no one. Cranks are dismal objects in any landscape. Especially depressing is what happens to the naturally solitary introvert, for whom the twentieth century provides no approved-of hermit's cell. The multiplicity of contacts with all sorts of human beings, made inevitable by modern facilities in transportation, are as intolerable to a man of such a temperament as prolonged immersion in an indecently crowded subway train. But since we, the majority, do not mind the usual contacts ourselves, we do not approve of his objection to them, and continue to insist, by tacit pressure of public opinion, that he shall stop being "queer." Some of such tyrannized-over introverts, the ordinary inarticulate ones, driven into a loathing of all humanity, find their only refuge in the insane asylums. Those few who have a gift for self-expression avoid a nervous breakdown by their pleasure in nauseating the rest of us by their Point-Counter-Pointish descriptions of how uncomfortable they are.

It is not impossible that the tiny bulwark of six hundred dollars' inherited income (together with the cranky, crabbed New England tradition of human oddities) saved for us both Emerson and Thoreau, as seers and geniuses rather than as futile embittered cranks. We cannot of course endow all the introverts with even tiny incomes, on the chance (a very small chance, to be honest) that they might turn out geniuses. But we might at no cash cost to us help them to be themselves, and hence much more valuable to everybody, by lightening the general condemnation of them, now almost unanimous. They are not interested in incomes anyhow. Beyond their bare needs, the only use of an income for them is as a shield between them and the disapproval of their fellows, which is for all us herd creatures, even for the lone-minded ones, a grim shadow over the sun. It would be comical indeed for us extraverts to say that "noblesse oblige" requires us to stand up for the rights of introverts. But if you leave off the "noblesse"—much too elegant wear for us plain homespun Marthas—there can be no doubt that something or other—decency perhaps—obliges us to lend a helping hand to personalities who are now penalized for possessing qualities of the utmost value to our race. (Yes, I know, they never turned over a hand for us back there in the Middle Ages when the gold medals were being hung on them. But that was their mistake. And anyhow let bygones be bygones.)

And there is one more thing we can do: fight to keep the choice open to our children. Remembering the terrific pressure toward uniformity always exerted by a prevailing creed, we can safely shelter and breathe upon any spark of originality without fear of pampering it. The gang needs no help from parents. Backed up with overwhelming public approval of successful group-activity as the only way of life, it is quite strong enough to rub off all eccentric knobs and corners it has wit enough to recognize. "Aw, the poor sap! He's taking *singing lessons!*" That's the way conformity to their ideal is secured. And to get average results it's a good enough way. In the majority of cases this kind of shaping and molding brings out those middling qualities that are, most likely, the strongest and most useful in the average little boy. But in the case of the unusual child, what tragic folly to allow a psycho-analyst to thrust your little boy or girl out into the gang if you have reason to believe that such rough-and-ready molding to the accepted pattern will leave an unhealed wound, a sense of exile, a burying forever of what is too precious for callous handling.

Of course there is a risk in letting your little boy grow up "different" in any way from all other little boys. Parents are notoriously cowards for their children. We are thrown into a panic by risk of any kind. And it is true that mediocrity is not only the natural way of life for most of us but the surest safe-guard against being hurt by our fellow-men. But for some personalities the effort to be mediocre hurts more even than being trampled under the hoofs of the herd. In moments of insight we suspect that conformity does not always pay even as a matter of earthly profit and loss, that Thoreau was more of a success than the man who kept the grocery store in Concord, and that Beethoven got a great deal more out of life than any of the young Viennese court officials who convulsed their circle with jokes about the crotchety, shabby, deaf crank of a musician.

Do you remember certain words written on this subject out of his wisdom by one of the most notorious of American cranks?

> "Underneath all, individuals!
>   I swear nothing is good to me now that ignores indi-
>   viduals.
>   The American compact is altogether with individuals,
>   The whole theory of the universe is directed to one single
>   individual—namely to *You*."

Vermont—a Way of Life

By WALTER HARD

According to the Survey Graphic, *Mr. Hard "lives in a village which has a winter population of 335 and swells to 1335 in summer when the tourists pour in. He owns Hard's Drug Store, which has been in the family since Civil War times." Mr. Hard writes poetry for the Vermont dailies.* Some Vermonters *and* Salt of Vermont *are two collections of his poems.*

TWO or three years ago when we said of a man, "Yes, he's making a living and that's about all," we meant he was really a failure. Now the man who is making a living is not a failure, he is looked upon by many thousands of his fellow-men as one of fortune's greatest favorites.

Generally speaking, the inhabitants of Vermont have always made a living—and that's about all. They did it during the so-called period of prosperity; they are doing it now. It is a kind of living which differs from that in the cities. It follows a more even line; a line without sharp rises and without deep depressions. During the high tide of prosperity which swept over much of the country, Vermont's way of living looked unambitious, smug, provincial, poor. Now it looks good to many people.

What makes it different?

An answer came this morning in a local paper. There was an advertisement which read like this:

> Wanted. To exchange a 2nd. hand Chevrolet Coach for a family cow. Exchange.

Let's look this man Exchange up. His case may be more or less

From the *Survey Graphic,* July, 1932. Reprinted by permission of the *Survey Graphic.*

typical. It may tell considerable about the way Vermonters live.

He was born on a mountain farm in Vermont thirty-five years ago. He grew up as every farm boy did, with responsibilities in the way of chores, from the time he was able to go about alone. By the time he was sixteen he was an important member of the family as a producer of the necessities of life. He never handled money because there was little of it used. He did handle tools and seeds and crops. He went to the school down the road two miles and learned to read, to write, to figure, and enough about the world to follow its life in the paper his father took. He went into the army with joy because of the chance to see life. He wasn't necessary at home. His father had fought in the Civil War. His great-grand-father on his mother's side had been one of the Green Mountain Boys. His two brothers, one a lawyer in Boston, the other working in New York, could not go to war. They had families. So Exchange kept up the family tradition and volunteered. While he was over-seas his father died suddenly and his mother and a young brother went to live near the Boston brother. The farm was sold to a lumber company and Exchange came home to find himself a capitalist to the extent of two thousand dollars, which represented his share of his father's estate.

His experiences in France had satisfied his desire to see the world. He wandered around visiting relatives, and then spent some weeks as near the old farm as he could get. He was attracted to the schoolhouse again, but it was nothing as prosaic as matters of education that attracted him this time. The same teacher was there as when he went away to war.

That was thirteen years ago. He bought a small place on the edge of a village of about 800 inhabitants. He bought the twenty-seven acres with a story-and-a-half house, two barns and a chicken house, all in good shape, for two thousand dollars. There was an apple orchard of fifty trees too, but it was badly run down, and there was an eight-acre wood lot. He paid twelve hundred dollars down, leaving the rest on mortgage. The next year he brought his bride there. In the twelve years since they have, beside rearing two boys, very much improved the buildings. They have cleaned up the orchard and grafted the old trees so they now pay a profit. They have also paid off the mortgage.

Exchange is handy with tools and has always had some carpenter work to do in the village and on neighboring farms. He and his wife have seen to it that some money is saved each month, no matter how little it may be. During the last few years up to the summer of 1931, he has had steady work carpentering for the two or three families who have bought summer places in the village. The high spot in his earnings was 1929 when he worked steadily for a year. Most of the mortgage was paid off that year and that year he bought the car.

Some years he and his family lived entirely on the products of his small farm. Every year they get the larger part of their living from it. There are hens, and Mrs. Exchange raises early chicks to sell as broilers to the summer families and perhaps to the storekeeper or the lawyer. She also sells eggs when the prices are good. When they are cheap she "puts them down" to use for cooking. She also cans enough fowl to allow at least a meal a week during the winter. Of course they raise all of their vegetables. Not only do they have fresh vegetables all summer but the surplus, canned, furnishes the winter supply. Now that the orchard is in bearing they get a cash income from it in addition to the apples they have to eat. They kept a cow up to the year of greatest prosperity when Exchange had a good offer for her, just at the time he found the milking a little too much in addition to his other work.

Now about that car. Of course they had wanted one for some time. They might have afforded it, but not by their standards. They waited until they had the cash and until the spending of it for a car would not curtail anything which was a real necessity. No installment buying for them. Exchange would buy a car "if he could get it right." Meaning he'd pay so much and no more. He finally bought a car, three years old, with little mileage on it. It had the wear but not the style. He paid $150 for it. His standing in the community was not affected in any way by the fact that it was not as late a model as some of his neighbors drove. It had no social bearing whatever.

That and a new kitchen range were his chief extravagances during his era of greatest prosperity. He banked the rest of his prosperity in a good savings bank.

Last year he had very little carpenter work and since fall he has had none. His cash income has almost ceased except for some wood sold during the winter. This was enough to pay for sugar and flour and for some warm coats for the growing boys.

So we get to the advertisement quoted in the beginning.

His cash income having largely stopped, he proceeds at once to get rid of the car which will run on nothing he can produce. It requires cash to buy gas and oil. He can get along without the car. He and his family may not want to get along without it, but they would be uncomfortable to ride around in something they could not afford. That is habit. It is also tradition. It is Vermont.

Not only does Exchange get rid of the cash-eater but he exchanges it for a producer—a producer of things which will further cut off his demand for cash. The family cow will cut butter from the grocer's bill and milk from the milkman's bill. She will also furnish fertilizer for the land.

It is evident that this man has never been very wealthy and that he never will be. But he will not be without food and shelter for himself and his family, given health and strength. Because there are so many Vermonters in like circumstances, more than elsewhere perhaps, one finds our present crisis much less noticeable.

Not only our small farmers who do other things when opportunity offers, but those who make a business of farming, have the same feeling of security as to home and food. They may get very slight money incomes, and they work hard, but they know they will not be ejected nor will they have to receive charity.

Here then is the fundamental difference between Exchange and his brother in the city. The latter works to get cash. With it he buys food and shelter. As soon as his cash income stops, no amount of effort on his part will make it possible for him to produce these necessities. The country dweller, on the other hand, just as Exchange did when the cash income stopped, can raise on the land what he needs to support life. Cash was not absolutely needed by Exchange. It is needed by his urban brother. While the city dweller unfortunately out of work and out of cash, watches his fuel gradually dwindle, he knows that he must either be cold or call for help. Exchange, however, takes his ax and goes to his woodlot. He gets a year's supply of fuel without spending a cent of cash except for a small tax, and he sells enough wood to much more than pay that. Of course he has a feeling of security which his brother in the city cannot know.

The dollar has played so little a part in the average Vermonter's life that he was not over-excited by the boom years. To be sure things were easier and there is probably a new rug in the parlor and a radio in the sitting-room. Savings bank deposits increased and better care went into some new garages. But there was no temptation to speculate in Wall Street. Their only speculation was on the crops and the weather which always afford enough outlet for the gambling spirit. During all of this period the general plane of living was changed very little. The old habits held fast and the giving up of some of the extras is not so hard now.

You remember that Exchange did not lose caste by buying an out-moded car. His wife was not snubbed at the Sewing Society nor did anyone speak of her "niggardly husband." This would be true in almost any village in Vermont. In the suburban community where Exchange's brother lives, all of his friends live in similar houses, drive cars that cost about the same amount, and have about the same incomes. If one gets a considerable increase in income and steps out with a better car, the rest feel bound to follow suit even to the point of uncomfortable stretching of the family budget. But in the country villages one's neighbors are people in various walks of life with incomes only alike in the fact that none of them are very large. Socially they are about as democratic as it is possible to be.

Of course the lawyer's house may be steam-heated and the doctor's wife may have "help," but none of them have servants. The few social distinctions are not based on ability to spend money. There is very little temptations to keep up with the Joneses.

It does seem as though the difference in surroundings must make some differences in feeling. Surrounded on all sides by things which man has built, all proclaiming the might of his genius and the power of his dollar, even to the highest pinnacle of his highest building, one must get to feel the omnipotence of money. When the money market is in a state of confusion and the business structure shows itself to be far from everlasting, in such surroundings one must feel that the bottom has dropped out of everything. But when one's outlook is on high mountains and deep valleys which have been ages in the making, whose changes are only those of the ordered seasons, man and his dollars seem less important in the scheme of things. When the market falls the countryman sees no sign of it on his landscape. These everlasting hills cannot fail to inspire confidence; to give strength.

It might seem that life in the Vermont hills was all work and no play. There is a contrast between the city and country idea of recreation, but there is no lack of it in either. Probably the countryman spends much less money on his amusements, and as that is one of the things which makes his position desirable just now, we might just see what he does for fun.

During the summer Exchange and his family are busy most of the time. The boys belong to the 4-H Club and always join in any outings they may have. Of course there is a daily swim in the creek on warm days, and some ball-playing in the early evening just before dark. Probably three or four times during the summer Exchange himself will knock off for a half-day to go to see the village ball-team play one of the neighboring towns. Many of the villages have their own teams. He will never fail to go to the County Fair in autumn, taking the family and making a day of it. Then he plays a second cornet in the Citizens Band, and he makes several excursions with it to near-by towns.

During the winter there are plenty of things to occupy the leisure time. Mrs. Exchange is head, this year, of the Parent-Teacher Association which meets fortnightly at the houses of the members. Her teaching experience makes her a valuable connection between teachers and parents. Then on the alternate weeks the Grange meets. There are frequent suppers at the church and a series of lectures and entertainments from a Lyceum Bureau, under the auspices of the Grange. To most of these things Mr. Exchange goes and sometimes the boys are allowed to attend. Then he has weekly band rehearsal and choir practice on Friday nights. The evenings at home he spends in reading the paper, his agricultural magazine, and probably a dozen books from the library during the course of the winter. Mrs. Exchange belongs to a magazine club and her reading is usually confined to the four magazines which come each month, and special articles and books which have to do with her Parent-Teacher Association work.

O yes, there are moving pictures once a week and the boys manage to get together enough money to go once in a while. Most of the entertainment, however, is home talent. For instance, the same paper which had the advertisement which we have used as a text, had an account of a series of tableaux, a Washington celebration, given in the town hall, in which the Exchange family all took part. The boys danced in the minuet. Their mother was Martha Custis, and Exchange himself played in the orchestra. The doctor, the lawyer, the merchant, farmers, laborers, mechanics—all classes and various members of their families were in the cast, and working with them and directing was a writer of international fame who happens to be their fellow townswoman. Just look over the players in the impromptu orchestra. A farmer; a college student, son of the rector; a barber; a laborer; an insurance agent; a hotel keeper; a truck driver; and a farmer's wife at the piano. And the leader, a regular resident of the village who happens to write symphonic music which is played by the best orchestras here and abroad. The highest priced seats were fifty cents. There are no ticket scalpers.

Usually after such a performance the floor is cleared and there is a dance. And there again you'll find all ages and all walks in life represented. Grandma may be sedately stepping the Portland Fancy in a set while opposite her grandson swings his best girl.

The fundamental difference between the city and country kind of recreation lies in the fact that the latter is largely the product of one's own efforts. It is not a matter of taking a few, and not so few at that, dollars, and going out to be amused. It requires a minimum of cash outlay and it derives much of its fun from the labor put into it. Of course some of the communities have permanent dramatic organizations which do serious work. They often have their own playhouse. As a rule, however, it is all just for fun, and it certainly is fun—the kind that re-creates.

Perhaps it would be unfair to leave out mention of schools, for in Vermont life education plays a very important part. Suffice it to say that Exchange and his wife are more interested in their boys' schooling than in anything else. They are ready to make any sacrifices to give them the best as far as the boys show a willingness to make good use of it. It would not be at all strange if one of the boys went to college. In fact his mother is saving some of her egg money each week with some such possibility in mind. Maybe the other one will go to agricultural high school and come back to the farm. They will have all the training the schools can give them and in addition they will have the invaluable education which comes from working with their parents in making their living. Each has things to do on the farm. Daily there is a demand for ability to meet new experiences which require initiative and self-reliance. These things they learn at home. Yes. There are educational facilities in Vermont, in school and outside too.

Of course not all Vermonters live just the life Exchange does. Many of them have more leisure, more comforts, more of the amenities of life. While the preponderance of life is rural, many live without any first-hand experience with the soil. Like their city brothers, they have to use cash as a medium.

But they have the same feeling of security because they know the soil can give them what they need just as it is giving it to the people all around them. They know they too could do it if their mode of life had to change.

If success is measured in tall buildings, mammoth factories, big business enterprises, or in dollars, perhaps the men of Vermont are unambitious. Many of her sons have gone away from her hills and done ambitious things. Perhaps that is her job in life: to produce men to go away from her hills. Certain it is this way of life, which for generations has been sustained by the land, gives a security, a serenity, a peace, which the fluctuations of the stock market can neither give nor take away.

Three Days to See

By HELEN KELLER

Helen Keller's life, with its struggles and accomplishments, is known to every American and to thousands of Europeans as well. Everybody should read her OPTIMISM, AN ESSAY (1903). *Coming from her unique exeprience, it is truly meaningful.* MY RELIGION (1927) *is logically a companion study.*

ALL of us have read thrilling stories in which the hero had only a limited and specified time to live. Sometimes it was as long as a year; sometimes as short as twenty-four hours. But always we were interested in discovering just how the doomed man chose to spend his last days or his last hours. I speak, of course, of free men who have a choice, not condemned criminals whose sphere of activities is strictly delimited.

Such stories set us thinking, wondering what we should do under similar circumstances. What events, what experiences, what associations should we crowd into those last hours as mortal beings? What happiness should we find in reviewing the past, what regrets?

Sometimes I have thought it would be an excellent rule to live each day as if we should die tomorrow. Such an attitude would emphasize sharply the values of life. We should live each day with a gentleness, a vigor, and a keenness of appreciation which are often lost when time stretches before us in the constant panorama of more days and months and years to come. There are those, of course, who would adopt the epicurean motto of "Eat, drink, and be merry," but most people would be chastened by the certainty of impending death.

In stories, the doomed hero is usually saved at the last minute

From *The Atlantic Monthly,* January, 1933. Used by permission of the author and *The Atlantic Monthly.*

by some stroke of fortune, but almost always his sense of values is changed. He becomes more appreciative of the meaning of life and its permanent spiritual values. It has often been noted that those who live, or have lived, in the shadow of death bring a mellow sweetness to everything they do.

Most of us, however, take life for granted. We know that one day we must die, but usually we picture that day as far in the future. When we are in buoyant health, death is all but unimaginable. We seldom think of it. The days stretch out in an endless vista. So we go about our petty tasks, hardly aware of our listless attitude toward life.

The same lethargy, I am afraid, characterizes the use of all our faculties and senses. Only the deaf appreciate hearing, only the blind realize the manifold blessings that lie in sight. Particularly does this observation apply to those who have lost sight and hearing in adult life. But those who have never suffered impairment of sight or hearing seldom make the fullest use of these blessed faculties. Their eyes and ears take in all sights and sounds hazily, without concentration and with little appreciation. It is the same old story of not being grateful for what we have until we lose it, of not being conscious of health until we are ill.

I have often thought it would be a blessing if each human being were stricken blind and deaf for a few days at some time during his early adult life. Darkness would make him more appreciative of sight; silence would teach him the joys of sound.

Now and then I have tested my seeing friends to discover what they see. Recently I was visited by a very good friend who had just returned from a long walk in the woods, and I asked her what she had observed. "Nothing in particular," she replied. I might have been incredulous had I not been accustomed to such responses, for long ago I became convinced that the seeing see little.

How was it possible, I asked myself, to walk for an hour through the woods and see nothing worthy of note? I who cannot see find hundreds of things to interest me through mere touch. I feel the delicate symmetry of a leaf. I pass my hands lovingly about the smooth skin of a silver birch, or the rough shaggy bark of a pine. In spring I touch the branches of trees hopefully in search of a bud, the first sign of awakening Nature after her winter's sleep. I feel the delightful, velvety texture of a flower, and discover its remarkable convolutions; and something of the miracle of Nature is revealed to me. Occasionally, if I am very fortunate, I place my hand gently on a small tree and feel the happy quiver of a bird in full song. I am delighted to have the cool waters of a brook rush through my open fingers. To me a lush carpet of pine needles or spongy grass is more welcome than the most luxurious Persian rug. To me the pageant of seasons is a thrilling and unending drama, the action of which streams through my finger tips.

At times my heart cries out with longing to see all these things. If I can get so much pleasure from mere touch, how much more beauty must be revealed by sight. Yet, those who have eyes apparently see little. The panorama of color and action which fills the world is taken for granted. It is human, perhaps, to appreciate little that which we have and to long for that which we have not, but it is a great pity that in the world of light the gift of sight is used only as a mere convenience rather than as a means of adding fullness to life.

If I were the president of a university I should establish a compulsory course in "How to Use Your Eyes." The professor would try to show his pupils how they could add joy to their lives by really seeing what passes unnoticed before them. He would try to awake their dormant and sluggish faculties.

Perhaps I can best illustrate by imagining what I should most like to see if I were given the use of my eyes, say, for just three days. And while I am imagining, suppose you, too, set your mind to work on the problem of how you would use your own eyes if you had only three more days to see. If with the oncoming darkness of the third night you knew that the sun would never rise for you again, how would you spend those three precious intervening days? What would you most want to let your gaze rest upon?

I, naturally, should want most to see the things which have become dear to me through my years of darkness. You, too, would want to let your eyes rest long on the things that have become dear to you so that you could take the memory of them with you into the night that loomed before you.

If, by some miracle, I were granted three seeing days, to be followed by a relapse into darkness, I should divide the period into three parts.

On the first day, I should want to see the people whose kindness and gentleness and companionship have made my life worth living. First I should like to gaze long upon the face of my dear teacher, Mrs. Anne Sullivan Macy, who came to me when I was a child and opened the outer world to me. I should want not merely to see the outline of her face, so that I could cherish it in my memory, but to study that face and find in it the living evidence of the sympathetic tenderness and patience with which she accomplished the difficult task of my education. I should like to see in her eyes that strength of character which has enabled her to stand firm in the face of difficulties, and that compassion for all humanity which she has revealed to me so often.

I do not know what it is to see into the heart of a friend through that "window of the soul," the eye. I can only "see" through my finger tips the outline of a face. I can detect laughter, sorrow, and many other obvious emotions. I know my friends from the feel of their faces. But I cannot really picture their personalities by touch. I know their personalities, of course, through other means, through the thoughts they express to me, through whatever of their actions are revealed to me. But I am denied that deeper understanding of them which I am sure would come through sight of them, through watching their reactions to various expressed thoughts and circumstances, through noting the immediate and fleeting reactions of their eyes and countenance.

Friends who are near to me I know well, because through the months and years they reveal themselves to me in all their phases; but of casual friends I have only an incomplete impression, an impression gained from a handclasp, from spoken words which I take from their lips with my finger tips, or which they tap into the palm of my hand.

How much easier, how much more staisfying it is for you who can see to grasp quickly the essential qualities of another person by watching the subtleties of expression, the quiver of a muscle, the flutter of a hand. But does it every occur to you to use your sight to see into the inner nature of a friend or acquaintance? Do not most of you seeing people grasp casually the outward features of a face and let it go at that?

For instance, can you describe accurately the faces of five good friends? Some of you can, but many cannot. As an experiment, I have questioned husbands of long standing about the color of their wives' eyes, and often they express embarrassed confusion and admit that they do not know. And, incidentally, it is a chronic complaint of wives that their husbands do not notice new dresses, new hats, and changes in household arrangements.

The eyes of seeing persons soon become accustomed to the routine of their surroundings, and they actually see only the startling and spectacular. But even in viewing the most spectacular sights the eyes are lazy. Court records reveal every day how inaccurately "eyewitnesses" see. A given event will be "seen" in several different ways by as many witnesses. Some see more than others, but few see everything that is within the range of their vision.

Oh, the things that I should see if I had the power of sight for just three days!

The first day would be a busy one. I should call to me all my dear friends and look long into their faces, imprinting upon my mind the outward evidences of the beauty that is within them. I should let my eyes rest, too, on the face of a baby, so that I could catch a vision of the eager, innocent beauty which precedes the individual's consciousness of the conflicts which life develops.

And I should like to look into the loyal, trusting eyes of my dogs—the grave, canny little Scottie, Darkie, and the stalwart, understanding Great Dane, Helga, whose warm, tender, and playful friendships are so comforting to me.

On that busy first day I should also view the small simple things of my home. I want to see the warm colors in the rugs under my feet, the pictures on the walls, the intimate trifles that transform a house into home. My eyes would rest respectfully on the books in raised type which I have read, but they would be more eagerly interested in the printed books which seeing people can read, for during the long night of my life the books I have read and those which have been read to me have built themselves into a great shining lighthouse, revealing to me the deepest channels of human life and the human spirit.

In the afternoon of that first seeing day, I should take a long walk in the woods and intoxicate my eyes on the beauties of the world of Nature, trying desperately to absorb in a few hours the vast splendor which is constantly unfolding itself to those who can see. On the way home from my woodland jaunt my path would lie near a farm so that I might see the patient horses ploughing in the field (perhaps I should see only a tractor!) and the serene content of men living close to the soil. And I should pray for the glory of a colorful sunset.

When dusk had fallen, I should experience the double delight of being able to see by artificial light, which the genius of man has created to extend the power of his sight when Nature decrees darkness.

In the night of that first day of sight, I should not be able to sleep, so full would be my mind of the memories of the day.

The next day—the second day of sight—I should arise with the dawn and see the thrilling miracle by which night is transformed into day. I should behold with awe the magnificent panorama of light with which the sun awakens the sleeping earth.

This day I should devote to a hasty glimpse of the world, past and present. I should want to see the pageant of man's progress, the kaleidoscope of the ages. How can so much be compressed into one day? Through the museums, of course. Often I have visited the New York Museum of Natural History to touch with my hands many of the objects there exhibited, but I have longed to see with my eyes the condensed history of the earth and its inhabitants displayed there—animals and the races of men pictured in their native environment; gigantic carcasses of dinosaurs and mastodons which roamed the earth long before man appeared, with his tiny stature and powerful brain, to conquer the animal kingdom; realistic presentations of the processes of evolution in animals, in man, and in the implements which man has used to fashion for himself a secure home on this planet; and a thousand and one other aspects of natural history.

I wonder how many readers of this article have viewed this panorama of the face of living things as pictured in that inspiring museum. Many, of course, have not had the opportunity, but I am sure that many who *have* had the opportunity have not made use of it. There, indeed, is a place to use your eyes. You who see can spend many frutiful days there, but I, with my imaginary three days of sight, could only take a hasty glimpse, and pass on.

My next stop would be the Metropolitan Museum of Art, for just as the Museum of Natural History reveals the material aspects of the world, so does the Metropolitan show the myriad facets of the human spirit. Throughout the history of humanity the urge to artistic expression has been almost as powerful as the urge for food, shelter, and procreation. And here, in the vast chambers of the Metropolitan Museum, is unfolded before me the spirit of Egypt, Greece, and Rome, as expressed in their art. I know well through my hands the sculptured gods and goddesses of the ancient Nile-land. I have felt copies of Parthenon friezes, and I have sensed the rhythmic beauty of charging Athenian warriors. Apollos and Venuses and the Winged Victory of Samothrace are friends of my finger tips. The gnarled, bearded features of Homer are dear to me, for he, too, knew blindness.

My hands have lingered upon the living marble of Roman sculpture as well as that of later generations. I have passed my hands over a plaster cast of Michelangelo's inspiring and heroic

Moses; I have sensed the power of Rodin; I have been awed by the devoted spirit of Gothic wood carving. These arts which can be touched have meaning for me, but even they were meant to be seen rather than felt, and I can only guess at the beauty which remains hidden from me. I can admire the simple lines of a Greek vase, but its figured decorations are lost to me.

So on this, my second day of sight, I should try to probe into the soul of man through his art. The things I knew through touch I should now see. More splendid still, the whole magnificent world of painting would be opened to me, from the Italian Primitives, with their serene religious devotion, to the Moderns, with their feverish visions. I should look deep into the canvases of Raphael, Leonardo da Vinci, Titian, Rembrandt. I should want to feast my eyes upon the warm colors of Veronese, study the mysteries of El Greco, catch a new vision of Nature from Corot. Oh, there is so much rich meaning and beauty in the art of the ages for you who have eyes to see!

Upon my short visit to this temple of art I should not be able to review a fraction of that great world of art which is open to you. I should be able to get only a superficial impression. Artists tell me that for a deep and true appreciation of art one must educate the eye. One must learn through experience to weigh the merits of line, of composition, of form and color. If I had eyes, how happily would I embark upon so fascinating a study! Yet I am told that, to many of you who have eyes to see, the world of art is a dark night, unexplored and unilluminated.

It would be with extreme reluctance that I should leave the Metropolitan Museum, which contains the key to beauty—a beauty so neglected. Seeing persons, however, do not need a Metropolitan to find this key to beauty. The same key lies waiting in smaller museums, and in books on the shelves of even small libraries. But naturally, in my limited time of imaginary sight, I should choose the place where the key unlocks the greatest treasures in the shortest time.

The evening of my second day of sight I should spend at a

theater or at the movies. Even now I often attend theatrical performances of all sorts, but the action of the play must be spelled into my hand by a companion. But how I should like to see with my own eyes the fascinating figure of Hamlet, or the gusty Falstaff amid colorful Elizabethan trappings! How I should like to follow each movement of the graceful Hamlet, each strut of the hearty Falstaff! And since I could see only one play, I should be confronted by a many-horned dilemma, for there are scores of plays I should want to see. You who have eyes can see any you like. How many of you, I wonder, when you gaze at a play, a movie, or any spectacle, realize and give thanks for the miracle of sight which enables you to enjoy its color, grace, and movement?

I cannot enjoy the beauty of rhythmic movement except in a sphere restricted to the touch of my hands. I can vision only dimly the grace of a Pavlowa, although I know something of the delight of rhythm, for often I can sense the beat of music as it vibrates through the floor. I can well imagine that cadenced motion must be one of the most pleasing sights in the world. I have been able to gather something of this by tracing with my fingers the lines in sculptured marble; if this static grace can be so lovely, how much more acute must be the thrill of seeing grace in motion.

One of my dearest memories is of the time when Joseph Jefferson allowed me to touch his face and hands as he went through some of the gestures and speeches of his beloved Rip Van Winkle. I was able to catch thus a meager glimpse of the world of drama, and I shall never forget the delight of that moment. But, oh, how much I must miss, and how much pleasure you seeing ones can derive from watching and hearing the interplay of speech and movement in the unfolding of a dramatic performance! If I could see only one play, I should know how to picture in my mind the action of a hundred plays which I have read or had transferred to me through the medium of the manual alphabet.

So, through the evening of my second imaginary day of sight, the great figures of dramatic literature would crowd sleep from my eyes.

The following morning, I should again greet the dawn, anxious to discover new delights, for I am sure that, for those who have eyes which really see, the dawn of each day must be a perpetually new revelation of beauty.

This, according to the terms of my imagined miracle, is to be my third and last day of sight. I shall have no time to waste in regrets or longings; there is too much to see. The first day I devoted to my friends, animate and inanimate. The second revealed to me the history of man and Nature. Today I shall spend in the workaday world of the present, amid the haunts of men going about the business of life. And where can one find so many activities and conditions of men as in New York? So the city becomes my destination.

I start from my home in the quiet little suburb of Forest Hills, Long Island. Here, surrounded by green lawns, trees, and flowers, are neat little houses, happy with the voices and movements of wives and children, havens of peaceful rest for men who toil in the city. I drive across the lacy structure of steel which spans the East River, and I get a new and startling vision of the power and ingenuity of the mind of man. Busy boats chug and scurry about the river—racy speed boats, stolid, snorting tugs. If I had long days of sight ahead, I should spend many of them watching the delightful activity upon the river.

I look ahead, and before me rise the fantastic towers of New York, a city that seems to have stepped from the pages of a fairy story. What an awe-inspiring sight, these glittering spires, these vast banks of stone and steel—structures such as the gods might build for themselves! This animated picture is a part of the lives of millions of people every day. How many, I wonder, give it so much as a second glance? Very few, I fear. Their eyes are blind to this magnificent sight because it is so familiar to them.

I hurry to the top of one of those gigantic structures, the Empire State Building, for there, a short time ago, I "saw" the city below through the eyes of my secretary. I am anxious to compare my fancy with reality. I am sure I should not be disappointed in the panorama spread out before me, for to me it would be a vision of another world.

Now I begin my rounds of the city. First, I stand at a busy corner, merely looking at people, trying by sight of them to understand something of their lives. I see smiles, and I am happy. I see serious determination, and I am proud. I see suffering, and I am compassionate.

I stroll down Fifth Avenue. I throw my eyes out of focus, so that I see no particular object but only a seething kaleidoscope of color. I am certain that the colors of women's dresses moving in a throng must be a gorgeous spectacle of which I should never tire. But perhaps if I had sight I should be like most other women—too interested in styles and the cut of individual dresses to give much attention to the splendor of color in the mass. And I am convinced, too, that I should become an inveterate window shopper, for it must be a delight to the eye to view the myriad articles of beauty on display.

From Fifth Avenue I make a tour of the city—to Park Avenue, to the slums, to factories, to parks where children play. I take a stay-at-home trip abroad by visiting the foreign quarters. Always my eyes are open wide to all the sights of both happiness and misery so that I may probe deep and add to my understanding of how people work and live. My heart is full of the images of people and things. My eye passes lightly over no single trifle; it strives to touch and hold closely each thing its gaze rests upon. Some sights are pleasant, filling the heart with happiness; but some are miserably pathetic. To these latter I do not shut my eyes, for they, too, are part of life. To close the eye on them is to close the heart and mind.

My third day of sight is drawing to an end. Perhaps there are many serious pursuits to which I should devote the few remaining hours, but I am afraid that on the evening of that last day I should again run away to the theater, to a hilariously funny play, so that I might appreciate the overtones of comedy in the human spirit.

At midnight my temporary respite from blindness would cease, and permanent night would close in on me again. Naturally in those three short days I should not have seen all I wanted to see. Only when darkness had again descended upon me should I realize how much I had left unseen. But my mind would be so crowded with glorious memories that I should have little time for regrets. Thereafter the touch of every object would bring a glowing memory of how that object looked.

Perhaps this short outline of how I should spend three days of sight does not agree with the program you would set for yourself if you knew that you were about to be stricken blind. I am, however, sure that if you actually faced that fate your eyes would open to things you had never seen before, storing up memories for the long night ahead. You would use your eyes as never before. Everything you saw would become dear to you. Your eyes would touch and embrace every object that came within your range of vision. Then, at last, you would really see, and a new world of beauty would open itself before you.

I who am blind can give one hint to those who see—one admonition to those who would make full use of the gift of sight: Use your eyes as if tomorrow you would be stricken blind. And the same method can be applied to the other senses. Hear the music of voices, the song of a bird, the mighty strains of an orchestra, as if you would be stricken deaf tomorrow. Touch each object you want to touch as if tomorrow your tactile sense would fail. Smell the perfume of flowers, taste with relish each morsel, as if tomorrow you could never smell and taste again. Make the most of every sense; glory in all the facets of pleasure and beauty which the world reveals to you through the several means of contact which Nature provides. But of all the senses, I am sure that sight must be the most delightful.

Galsworthy: An Estimate

By HENRY SEIDEL CANBY

In 1911, after having had charge of Freshman English at Yale, Dr. Canby was made assistant editor of THE YALE REVIEW *(cf. biographical notice under "Young Men in Politics"). In 1920 he was asked to edit "The Literary Review" of* THE NEW YORK EVENING POST. *In 1924 Dr. Canby, Christopher Morley, and William Rose Benét laid plans for* THE SATURDAY REVIEW OF LITERATURE. *One needs only to pick up a number of that useful and stimulating weekly to see how those plans have been fulfilled. Dr. Canby finds time for some lecturing at Yale in addition to editing his journal.*

THE British Empire, said Philip Guedalla at a recent dinner, is held together by the *Encyclopædia Britannica.* It holds together (I suppose that he meant) because the British have imposed their own outline of history upon the English-speaking world, so that the Irish Free State will have to get out an *Encyclopædia Celticana* before it becomes really free! And it may truly be said that England, the essential England, exists chiefly through, and in, men like John Galsworthy and their works.

I have heard Galsworthy called an idealist. I have heard him called a romanticist, and even a sentimentalist. None of these terms exactly fits. Like all great novelists he was a man in search of reality, and reality is not a simple term, like money, or fame, or craftsmanship. Someone said recently that perhaps the current loose talk of hard reality was misleading. It was not the hardships, the material failures, the envies and remorses of this time of trouble which were essential reality. They were only clouds passing over the moon. Reality was deeper. It was not intermittent trouble but human nature's daily food of love,

From *The Saturday Review of Literature,* March 18, 1933. Used by permission of the author.

friendship, felt happiness, or felt grief. The speaker cited Robert Frost as a man who had never swerved from the pursuit of such reality, regardless of external circumstance. I say the same of John Galsworthy. His novels and his plays have always dealt with what really mattered to an Englishman in the closing years of a great English period. In this sense John Galsworthy was a realist, a great realist.

I knew him well, not intimately, not from long association, but in circumstances far enough from the casual to let me write of him here with his personality rich and living in my memory. He was a gentleman—one thought of that first, always, with Galsworthy—sensitive, a little hesitant, but with rushes of strong feeling. He had the unshakable dignity of a man sure of his breeding who respects the rights of others and gets respect himself. I never saw him lose his temper but once, —when, in an international meeting, a Prussian who knew English perfectly heckled him in rapid German, with an evident purpose to take unfair advantage. Then he blazed out once, and gave up the chair as one gives way to an unmannerly child.

But this was but the surface of the man. More deeply considered, I find in him an English type, as distinctive as a manor house or an English garden. It is not the aggressive type of Englishman, arrogant, energetic, cool, which we call John Bull, but it is a type equally true to race and traceable in English history from long before the immigrations to America. He was the liberal, intellectual aristocrat, spiritual, sensitive, humanitarian, proud. England has always had such men, and they have been of her best. Spenser, I think, was one of them, and that poet-priest George Herbert, and (with a dose of snobbishness) Joseph Addison. Matthew Arnold was the schoolmaster phase of the type, Edward Fitzgerald its esthete, Horace Walpole its gossip. Nor have we lacked its strong racial manifestations here. Jonathan Edwards, in spite of the hysteria of his sermons, was the scholar-aristocrat who loves the human race, Jefferson had many of the attributes, and Emerson was perhaps the supreme example among English-speaking peoples of this

liberal and aristocratic intellectualism. Nor do I except Woodrow Wilson, whom Galsworthy himself trusted and admired.
These were men conscious of a code of behavior to which as
gentlemen they conformed, and this is their weakness in a
hard-boiled world, so that in politics it is only the shrewd ma-
neuverers like Jefferson who succeed. They are responsible, humane, and passionately in love with the possibilities of human
nature. In literature, they are the great reformers, for they are
not moved by jealousy, having been bred inside a tradition; they
are our best critics, for they wish to change not to destroy; and
their minds are set on those traits of good will and spiritual
satisfaction which they see still living beneath the frustrations
and warpings of the struggle for success.

Fine natures are finely moved. John Galsworthy came toward
the end of an age of possessiveness, when, in the words of
Tennyson, "proputty, proputty, proputty," thudded all over the
English-speaking world. Wealth was on the move from the
earliest 1800's onward. Land had been static in the eighteenth
century, and property had been felt as a right even more than
as an opportunity. With the opening of the colonies and the
beginning of industrialism, property became mobile. A continent was exploited, goods were multiplied. To the class that
merely owned, succeeded a class that acquired and possessed.
A middle class arose in England, conditioned in mind and emotions by the pursuit of property; it was the same class that made
America.

In England, the experiment was what the scientists call controlled and pure. The new bourgeois aristocracy took over the
code of the aristocrats who had owned by right, and subtly
modified it. They assumed responsibility, developed to a high
degree the character indispensable to a governing class in a
self-governing community, but began to invite the fatal karma
which pursues all men and women whose god is material success. England produced old James Forsyte, and the son of his
heart and will, Soames, in whose delineation Galsworthy's
powers reached their height; and the rebels Jolyon and
Irene; the conformist Annette; the by-products, Timothy

and the aunts; the wrecks and the frustrations, Val and Fleur.

But something was left behind by this new possessive class and lost, something crumbled, something rose like a heady fume dulling men and women, puzzling their hearts, and frustrating their desires, while their wills remained more powerful than ever. Responsibility to state and class they kept, and chivalry, and a sense of duty better than chivalry. Nevertheless this possessiveness, this submission to Things, the solid houses, the stocks and bonds, the responsibilities to property of the Forsytes, dimmed the sense of other gods whose altars grow cold only with peril to mankind. They neglected the Cyprian Venus, whose frustration and revenge Ashhurst deplored in that exquisite story, *The Apple Tree*—

> For mad is the heart of love,
> And gold the gleam of his wing;
> And all to the spell thereof
> Bend when he makes his spring.
> All life that is wild and young
> In mountain and wave and stream,
> All that of earth is sprung,
> Or breathes in the red sunbeam;
> Yea, and Mankind. O'er all a royal throne
> Cyprian, Cyprian, is thine alone!

They turned their backs upon the gods whose duty it is to see that the human heart stays human. Beauty, spirituality, love, even justice which the new possessive class had once demanded, were the victims of Things. Property had achieved a dulling of sensibility, a warping away from pleasure and the healthy satisfaction of the emotions, which the greed of the old aristocrats, and even the necessities of the poor, had never accomplished. Property made the Forsytes, and property chilled them. And yet these Forsytes in their own way were great. Beside them other racial types seemed lesser breeds without the law. They had the gift of character, the power of strength.

This was the puzzle of the nineteenth century, its challenge to an interpreter, which was like the challenge to the imagination of the young Shakespeare of the brilliant, full-blooded aristocrats of the Renaissance, with their gusto, their beauty, and their defiance of morality. A poet, a dramatist, a novelist was needed to attack this nineteenth century paradox, most of all a novelist, since the Forsytes were prose and their background all of England. An Englishman in England was at the heart of property; a liberal, a humanitarian, a "tender-minded" artist could sympathize and yet attack; an aristocrat could appreciate code and character; an idealist could discriminate where a satirist might only destroy. John Galsworthy was the man.

And indeed the story of Soames Forsyte is the story of man's spirit in the English nineteenth century, wrestling with property and thrown by it at the moment of apparent victory. It is the story of a defeated spirit (for Soames lost Irene and with Irene the possibility of love and a completed life)—of a defeated spirit rising wiser, stronger, more indomitable in character, making property his servant though he could not make it his friend, until at the conclusion of that extraordinary narrative Soames's very shortcomings have been turned into the steel and fiber of a man who knows what he wants and gets it, and what he cannot have and gives it up—a stoic, not to be envied, not to be loved, but certainly to be respected and approved.

This grasp upon the moral theme of England under industrialism is the key to John Galsworthy's superiority as a novelist of character to far cleverer men, such as Arnold Bennett and G. B. Shaw, to more worldly men and more widely experienced, such as H. G. Wells and Sinclair Lewis. Undeviatingly he pursues through this elaborate process of character building the rich results of tradition until Soames, eccentric and individualist that he is, becomes the symbol of whole shadowy generations of the English middle class. Unwaveringly he searches for the effect upon man of beauty neglected, and spirituality scorned by the religion of property. And yet, though the criticism in his novels is always against the tyranny of Things, his liberal mind admits, his aristocratic nature recognizes, a great character emerging, perhaps unexpectedly, from the havoc that accompanies a too material success. No propagandist could have done this. His *Forsyte Saga* is a tragi-comedy with a stoic ending, as was *The Tempest,* as was *Candide,* as was *Tess of the D'Urbervilles.*

Only in England I think could such books have been written. Proust's great study of an aristocracy decaying in the refinements of ultra-cerebration, belongs in a very different category. It is intensely French, and yet has no relationship with France at large in the century, not much indeed with Paris except as a background. The *Forsyte Saga* is intensely English, and quite as intensely upper and middle class, since to Galsworthy, humanitarian though he was, the lower classes were only shadows throwing into relief the responsible reality of his Forsyte world. And yet there is the character of a nation and of a race in the Saga. Narrow as its cross section, the type is there. It is a national study or it is nothing, whereas Proust has only the universal validity of a Racine—the actual existence of his cerebral Paris is of little importance; the psychology is all. Not so with the Forsytes. They are geological, and have in them the secrets of racial evolution. They are not all England, yet as they go, so goes England. Like Hardy's peasants and Shakespeare's Mercutios, Hotspurs, and Falstaffs, they are so racial that they can afford to be individualists.

All this explains, I think, Galsworthy's great reputation on the continent of Europe, where he was thought to be England's foremost novelist because in him and his were to be found the living explanations of what England was in the period of her dominating greatness. This explains the award to him of the Nobel prize, which never came to Hardy. His foreign readers also saw, as some of his compatriots have failed to see, that whatever were their faults of sentiment, diffuseness, and a reach beyond the author's grasp, the novels of Galsworthy were epic in their scope and had that broad stretch of significance which, since Balzac and the Russians, we have expected of fiction that deals with mores rather than manners. This explains also, I believe, his great vogue in America, but with a difference. For here unquestionably we, whose culture and training more than our blood, have owed so much to the English tradition—we read Galsworthy for news on a grand scale of the English character, so subtly like our own while so obviously different from it. The Forsytes are potentially Americans of the age of property who stayed at home, who never sailed for Plymouth and the Hudson and the Delaware and the capes of Virginia, to break up the sense of class in the forests while the struggle for property went on.

He wrote too much. He should have let the Americans alone, for he could understand only the English aspect of them, and his fastidious ear made a jargon of their speech. He should have lived in a world where there were no magazines, with their constant urging of the established writer to write more than he wills, and their subtle molding of his work to the stock emotions of vast audiences. He should have seen his Saga early in its length and breadth—and gone to some Walden Pond to write it—and stopped when he had finished. I do not know whether he was a great artist, although there are passages in *The Indian Summer of a Forsyte* and in *The Apple Tree,* and *In Chancery* and elsewhere, which only a consummate artist could write. Yet certainly he had that insight which is given to someone in every generation, and which, if used, explains us to ourselves. He had a message. I use that word with reluctance, for a message means usually a dogmatism, a moral, and designates that part of a book or a lecture which sticks in the memory like a lump of undigested dough. None of this in Galsworthy. Rather he is the moving finger that writes. You see in him, often through clouds of words, what the Greeks saw in Sophocles, the moral meaning of a generation. Sophocles dealt in heroes and in a superb style of heaven-sent rhetoric. Galsworthy treats of stiff old men, hiding beneath Anglo-Saxon phlegm or a dry humor inappropriate to tragedy, the powerful prejudices, the passions, of a people heart-wrecked by their devotion to property, but become great because they identified property with the welfare of a state. Yet both Sophocles and Galsworthy are concerned with fundamental morality. And this is what gives dramatists and novelists magnitude, precisely as the power to realize, to make their problems live as a Soames, as an Irene, as a Hamlet, is what makes them novelists and dramatists.

I have said little of Galsworthy's plays because this essay is not concerned primarily with literary criticism, and for Galsworthy the stage (so I think) was only an escape for the emotions aroused by those unavoidable contradictions in a society supposedly founded on justice which stirred his humanitarian spirit to a pitch that only drama would assuage. The theater never gave him room. It exaggerated the lesson at the expense of the background in which the true moral lay. He saw best pageant-wise, not drama-wise. His strength, like so much English strength, was in the slow tenacity of descriptive narrative, not in quick symbols or isolated event.

Galsworthy is just dead, and America, in which he was as much honored as at home, and perhaps more widely read, may well take stock of what his insight may mean for us. For ours is a country bred in the English tradition, though intensely changed by circumstance, a country not devoid of character as the English and as Galsworthy understood character, not unaware of the code of duty, for of the Puritans who gave fiber to that code the best came here, not without the desire for order which was so strong in all the Forsytes, nor the sense of fairness, nor the instinct to be humane.

Our problem has been different. We have had to contend with less rigidity of ownership, we have been able to escape many responsibilities in the easy recourse of our oppressed and our turbulent to the spaces of the West, we have been far more fertile in experiment. But to suppose that the karma which pursues all greed for Things, all obsessions with property, is to be spared us, would be unrealistic. Our karma is different. We threw out our Soames Forsytes a generation ago—the selfish individuals, the so-called builders of American prosperity, men not too scrupulous, who believed that in making themselves they were making America, and attained a certain bad eminence of character from their loyalties so energetically if so selfishly pursued. Yet those pirate captains of the last generation of American industrialism in their way were patriots, as Soames Forsyte was a patriot.

Are there any patriots left? In our sectional blocs? Among our tariff mongers? In our local interests? Among the veterans? In Congress? Undoubtedly, but it has been months since we have heard from them. One grows skeptical. Is there any character in our new society to take the place of the old character of individualism? Is the humanitarianism which the last generation suppressed in business and exuded upon foundations and universities, more vital now that the strong men who took with the right hand and gave with the left are gone? Is the beauty which they, like Soames, forced out of their lives, and then sought, like fugitives, in pictures, and bronzes, and opera, and Tudor Gothic, where it took the form of property—is it dealt with more intelligently today? Is religion? Is love? This is what an American thinks, what he must ask, as he reads Galsworthy, seeing in the special English problem a reflection of his own. And we understand the grim sadness of Soames Forsyte at his life's end, self-critical, skeptical of the future; and we realize, as Galsworthy the idealist was forced by his own imagination to realize, that life is a series of defeats and compensations, of values frustrated to the peril of the race, of character that may emerge as a result of frustration—or may not.

The nineteenth century, liberal, progressive, hopeful, intensely possessive, was a laboratory of human nature. The books of John Galsworthy are a report of what happened in the English section, which was so much then the center of the modern world. If the reader reflects upon the story of how Soames Forsyte bought, and how he lost, Irene, who was the symbol of the "life that is wild and young" which belongs to the Cyprian alone, he may sum up the whole matter by saying that love and Irene fell victims to property, yet from their loss stoicism shaped that character which gives to society a backbone if not a heart. Where are our own minds at this end of the age of possessiveness? Have we the self-knowledge of Soames Forsyte in his Thames-side gallery? Can we hope like

thé couple in Noel Coward's *Cavalcade* for a future for our
country of dignity, and greatness, and peace again? Or must
we live our own Forsyte Saga to its end, and wait for a John
Galsworthy to tell us what it meant?

Lytton Strachey

By EDMUND WILSON

*Mr. Wilson has published a novel (*I Thought of Daisy, *1929) and some poems, but his reputation is firmly built upon his critical writing.* Axel's Castle *(1931) is one of the most significant books of literary criticism which has appeared in America since the Great War. For Mr. Wilson's social judgment one should turn to* The American Jitters, *a series of social criticisms, written with biting satire.*

IT IS often the case with first-rate people that their lives seem to come to an end just when they have finished performing their functions: they put all their energy and passion into accomplishing their particular work and then when the work is done they—sometimes very suddenly—take leave.

In nothing else, it seems to me, did Lytton Strachey prove his first-rate quality more clearly than in departing when he had said what he had to say. Strachey's chief rôle was of course to blast once for all the pretensions to moral superiority of the Victorian Age. His declaration in the preface to *Eminent Victorians*—"*Je n'impose rien; je ne propose rien: j' expose*"—was certainly not justified by his book. His irony here was so acid that it partly dehumanized his subjects. The essays on Manning and Dr. Arnold, though the technic gives an effect of detachment, have a force of suppressed invective. And the essays on Florence Nightingale and Gordon, written with the same biting metallic accent, make the subjects less sympathetic than we feel they deserve to be. In attempting to destroy, for example, the sentimental reputation which had been created for Florence Nightingale, he emphasized her hardness to such

From *The New Republic*, September 21, 1932. Used by permission of the author and *The New Republic*.

a degree as to slight her moral seriousness and the deep feeling behind the force that drove her. Only occasionally does he let these appear: "O Father," he quotes her as writing, "Thou knowest that through all these horrible twenty years, I have been supported by the belief that I was working with Thee who wast bringing everyone, even our poor nurses, to perfection"; and "How inefficient I was in the Crimea, yet He has raised up from it trained nursing." Such a woman must have been more than the mere demon of energy which Strachey made her.

But from *Eminent Victorians* on, Strachey's ferocity steadily abates. *Queen Victoria* is already a different matter. Both Victoria and Albert in Strachey become human and sympathetic figures. He is said to have approached them originally in the mood of *Eminent Victorians* and then found himself relenting. Victoria is not caricatured like Florence Nightingale: she is presented simply as a woman living, for all her great position and her public responsibility, a woman's limited life. To Strachey's Victoria, being Queen is a woman's personal experience, a matter of likes and dislikes, of living up to social obligations. This is the force of the famous deathbed scene, perhaps the highest achievement of Strachey's irony, though so often stupidly imitated since by people who have appropriated the cadences without appreciating the point:

Perhaps her fading mind called up once more the shadows of the past to float before it, and retraced, for the last time, the vanished visions of that long history— passing back and back, through the cloud of years, to older and even older memories—to the spring woods at Osborne, so full of primroses for Lord Beaconsfield—to Lord Palmerston's queer clothes and high demeanor, and Albert's face under the green lamp, Albert's first stay at Balmoral, and Albert in his blue and silver uniform, and the Baron coming in through a doorway, and Lord M. dreaming at Windsor with the rooks cawing in the elm trees, and the Archbishop of Canterbury on his knees in the dawn, and the old King's turkey-cock ejaculations, and Uncle Leopold's soft voice at Claremont, and Lehzen with the globes, and her mother's feathers sweeping down towards her, and a great old repeater-watch of her father's in its tortoise-shell case, and a yellow rug, and some friendly flounces of sprigged muslin, and the trees and the grass at Kensington.

Victoria has lived through the Victorian Age, has stood at the center of its forces, without knowing what it was all about.

But in his next biography, *Elizabeth and Essex,* Strachey produces a somewhat similar effect without the same ironic intention. *Elizabeth and Essex* seems to me the least satisfactory of Strachey's books. His art, tight, calculated, French, was ill suited to the Elizabethan Age. His Elizabeth, though a fine piece of workmanship like everything he did, is worse than metallic, it is wooden. It concentrates so narrowly on the personal relation between Elizabeth and her favorite that we wonder, glancing back to *Queen Victoria,* whether it was really altogether Victoria who lacked interest in the politics and thought of her time, whether it was not perhaps Strachey himself. Certainly Elizabeth lived in a larger intellectual world than Victoria, yet we get almost none of it in Strachey: in general we do not feel that the fates of the characters are involved with the larger affairs of history. The personal story is told with insight, but then, after all, Michelet tells a thousand such stories, taking them in his stride. And we are aware for the first time disagreeably of the high-voiced old Bloomsbury gossip gloating over the scandals of the past as he has ferreted them out in his library. Strachey's curious catty malice, his enjoyment of the discomfiture of his characters, is most unpleasantly in evidence in *Elizabeth and Essex*. His attitude toward women—Florence Nightingale, Mme. Duffand, Queen Victoria, or Queen Elizabeth—was peculiar in this, that he was fascinated by their psychology without feeling any of their attraction and rather took pleasure in seeing them humiliated. He almost invariably picked unappetizing feminine subjects and seemed to make them more unappetizing still. His study of Elizabeth in the light of modern psychology brings her character into clearer focus, but the effect of it is slightly disgusting: it marks so definitely the final surrender of Elizabethan to Bloomsbury England.

Lytton Strachey was changing with the tendency of his time. The fury of *Eminent Victorians* evaporates: there is hardly an accent of protest left in him. The revolt against Victorian pretensions ends in emptiness and faintly scabrous psychology. Strachey now recapitulates his view of history, and this view is simply that which I have already mentioned in connection with Anatole France—that view which has played so important a part in bourgeois thought in its later phases, in Anatole France and in Flaubert, in Henry Adams and T. S. Eliot—the idea that modern society represents some sort of absolute degradation in relation to the past.

In *Portraits in Miniature,* which seems to me one of the most remarkably executed of Strachey's books, he traces, through a series of thumb-nail sketches of for the most part minor historical and literary personages, the evolution of modern society from the Elizabethan to the Victorian Age. These personages, by very reason of their special interest or small capacity, supply cultures particularly clear of the social and intellectual bacteria at work during the periods in which they lived. Strachey begins with Sir John Harington, who in Elizabeth's reign invented the water-closet, and goes on through seventeenth-century types: an amateur scientist, a truculent classical scholar, an ambitious university don, the leader of an uncouth Protestant sect; eighteenth-century types: a French abbé who consorted with the philosophers, a French magistrate and country gentleman who insisted on his rights, a lady of sensibility—and ends with Mme. de Lieven, whose surrender to the middle-class Guizot marks for Strachey the final capitulation of the magnificent aristocratic qualities which he had admired in Queen Elizabeth. And a second series of miniatures, which reviews the British historians from the eighteenth-century Hume to the Victorian Bishop Creighton, the historian of the Papacy, points a similar moral.

The industrial, democratic, Protestant, middle-class world is a come-down, says Strachey, from Queen Elizabeth, from Racine, even from Voltaire (both these last great favorites of Strachey's, to whom he devoted admirable essays). When one considers the great souls of the past, the present seems dreary and vulgar—the Victorian Age in particular, for all its extraordinary energy, was an insult to the human spirit. This is the whole of Strachey; and when he had said it as pointedly as possible in the fewest possible words, he died.

But not only did Strachey in his writings point a historical moral: he illustrated one himself. In his gallery of English historians, he himself should come last. Certainly one of the best English writers of his time—one of the best English writers in English—he makes us feel sharply the contrast between the England of Shakespeare and the England of after the War. Shakespeare is English and expansive and close to the spoken language. Lytton Strachey, whose first published book was a history of French literature, is so far from being any of these things that his merit actually consists in having written like the French in English. His biographical method, though novel in English literature, was already an old story in French: Sainte-Beuve was the great master of it, and Strachey's tone resembles his. And the weaknesses as well as the virtues of Strachey's style are the result of his imitation of French models. He is pointed, economical and precise, but he is terribly given to clichés. The penalty of trying to reproduce in English the chaste and abstract vocabulary of French is finding one's language become pale and banal. No wonder the age of Shakespeare turned wooden and dry in Strachey's hand. And by the time he had reached *Portraits in Miniature,* he was merely repeating belatedly in England a kind of thing which Frenchmen like Anatole France had been doing for fifty years. He was not only imitating the French, he was imitating their bourgeois culture in its decadent stage.

Strachey's real originality and force are seen best at the beginning of his career—in *Eminent Victorians*. There, just at the end of the War, he stripped forever of their solemn upholstery the religion, the education, the statesmanship and the philanthropy of the society which had brought it about. The effect on the English-speaking countries was immediate and drastic. Biographers set themselves to seeing through and ironically exposing celebrities until they became a nuisance and a bore. The harshness of *Eminent Victorians* without Strachey's learning and bitter feeling, the intimate method of *Queen Victoria* without his insight into character, had the effect of cheapening history, something which Strachey never did: for though he was venomous about the Victorians, he did not make them any the less formidable. He had none of the modern vice of cockiness, but maintained a rare attitude of humility and admiration and awe before the spectacle of life. But the Americans and the English have never been able to feel the same again about the legends which had dominated their past. Something had been punctured for good.

Those Eminent Victorians

By HOWARD MUMFORD JONES

Howard Mumford Jones is Professor of English at the University of Michigan. Besides being a brilliant scholar in English and American literature, Professor Jones is also a poet and playwright. He is now in England (on a Guggenheim Memorial Fellowship) where he is writing a life of the Irish poet, Tom Moore.

OUR present economic chaos has been given its full measure of discussion, but I have been moved to wonder, in following such of it as I could, why we write and talk about unemployment and the problems of the machine age as if these particular questions were entirely novel and strange, and why, in view of the ineffectual way we handle them, we continue to patronize the nineteenth century, the central problems of which were similar. Indeed, I go even farther. I think it high time to re-examine that whole maligned period, not only for what it may teach us in new adjustments, but for what it offers in tolerance and wit as well.

We are all too familiar with the attacks on the Victorians. They conjure up the hair-cloth sofa, the Sunday-school tract, the antimacassar, the what-not, the bustle, and the unhygienic skirt. Victorianism is the elder generation. Victorianism is the pretense that if you do not name a thing, it isn't there. Those who dislike to discuss sex merely in terms of biology are apt to be classified with the lady who noted sadly the difference between the home life of Cleopatra and that of our dear Queen. Those who admire Gladstone (if anybody does) are Victorians, albeit those who admire Disraeli (and the Victorians admired him enough to make him premier) are not. To talk of duty, honor, the obligations of being a gentleman, the responsibilities of matrimony, or the sacredness of religious belief is to be Victorian. The Victorians were so bent on being moral that they ignored the unpleasant aspects of life. They had no use for art which was not ethical; they displayed, it is alleged, an embarrassing familiarity with the purposes of the Almighty. Did not one of them proclaim that God's in his heaven and all's right with the world, though the world was palpably maladjusted; did not another sing aloud that he was going to be Queen of the May? Victorian stuffiness, Victorian decorum, Victorian prudery, Victorian solemnity!

Well, in one sense they had a right to be solemn. The first half of the century, like our own, was a period of recurrent crises, but whereas we confine our discussions to "serious weeklies" and long-faced conferences and ineffectual newspaper editorials, the Victorians were of the opinion that the national conscience was concerned, and sought in their writings to arouse thinking on the subject. Our own fiction is monotonously compounded of sex and psychology; we pooh-pooh the purpose novel; and (except for Upton Sinclair) almost no contemporary author of importance is concerned in fiction to arouse public interest in public questions. The Victorians thought otherwise. From the day when Bulwer Lytton in his first novel converted Pelham to utilitarian thought, to the day when George Gissing laid down his pen, a consciousness of the importance of man to society and of society to man is a constant theme in nineteenth-century fiction. Mrs. Gaskell and Charles Kingsley cry out against social injustice. Thackeray studies the adjustment of the parvenus and the upper classes. Disraeli outlines a political philosophy in the Young England novels, a genre in which Trollope followed him. George Eliot bases her books on a social philosophy, and to George Meredith a reading of life is a reading of earth. Similarly the poets— Tennyson, Mrs. Browning, Swinburne, Meredith—are aware of political issues and turn them into beautiful and enduring verse.

Now I am far from thinking that literature is any better

for being sociological, but most of us will agree that literature tends to be better when it is written with a "large discourse," and I confess that the relative thinness of American fiction since our own Victorian age ended seems to me to arise from the fact that it is based on a very narrow reading of life—the reading which sees the be-all and the end-all of the novelist's business as sex and psychology. And I wonder, in view of the relative brittleness of most contemporary fiction, whether we are quite entitled to patronize the Victorian novelist? Have we mastered the art of the novel so completely that we can afford to dismiss as naïve a Dickens who, more than any other single figure, in the opinion of his contemporaries, made readers aware of social chaos in England? Our solitary exhibit in the way of broad canvases and social satire is Sinclair Lewis (perhaps some would add Dreiser), a humorist of great power, but is it not odd that whereas we produce only one of this kind, the Victorians produced a score?

I have said that the problems of that period and our own were similar. On the one hand, there was, for example, the inherited system of the universe. There was God, whose wondrous hand the nightly stars hymned as of old. There was an intricate and reasonably formed universe which He had invented, and everywhere traces of His handiwork could be found. There was the Anglican Church as by law established. There was man, who certainly had a body, and who was presumed, as even Shelley admitted, to have a spirit and probably a soul. There were the Queen, God bless her, and England's wooden walls, and the Duke of Wellington. In fact, there was a noble world inhabited by noble beings. And then there came crashing down on the Victorians a bewildering variety of changes, discoveries, and revolutions.

Startling theories of geology ruined the comfortable chronology of the King James Bible and reduced the life of man to an inconsiderable second in infinite time. Astronomical investigations extended the regions of heaven until earth was lost in infinite space. More and more it appeared that man was a great deal lower than the angels, and about the middle of the century he appeared to be a good deal closer to the animals. A succession of brilliant investigations in science smashed the good old comfortable mathematical universe of the eighteenth century into bits. In the heavens there was only anarchy, and on earth nature was red in tooth and claw. The Anglican faith was split by a schism which sent some of its most brilliant minds into the Roman Catholic fold, and Arnold later pleaded in vain with the Puritans to return to the Established Church. Could it be that the old system was wrong? The system that seemed as certain as the Duke of Wellington and as invincible as the Life Guards at Waterloo? Amidst the wreck of matter and the crash of worlds the Victorians clung to one essential belief—they were not under any circumstances going to admit that human life was any less interesting or important or dignified or noble, even though the heavens fell and hell blew up—in fact, one of them, Frederick Denison Maurice, helped in the explosion. They did their best to reconcile the smashing impact of the new science, which threatened to reduce everything to anarchic materialism, with their inherited belief in the dignity of human life. If we are today anything more than certain worms writhing in midnight, we owe our sanity to the Victorians. They conserved the human tradition, and without the human tradition, we should be stark, raving mad.

While the physical universe was crashing around them, the political and social world, too, seemed to be going to pieces, as Carlyle and others gloomily observed. The fixed and immutable laws of political economy, traced logically to their tragic conclusion by Ricardo, McCulloch, and the Manchester School, seemed to indicate that modern life would have to be one of increasing misery. They saw poverty in the streets and heard revolutions across the water. From 1820 to 1870 the Victorians struggled with depressions at home and counted a succession of crashes abroad; yet the streets of London, unlike the streets of Paris, Berlin, Vienna, or Richmond, never ran red with blood or echoed to the tread of a conquering army. The Victorians went into the nineteenth century with an England that was in many ways the little old England of

Walpole's time, and they emerged with an empire that, with all its defects, was the most remarkable the world had seen since Rome. Theirs is one of the most extraordinary examples of national continuity and astonishing readjustments in the history of mankind.

How did they manage it? I suspect we have overstressed Victorian prejudice; for they managed it by a tolerance for unexpected developments which far surpasses ours. They were capable of absorbing strange food. They made a Jewish novelist prime minister of England, despite his curls and his waistcoats; and I need not comment on the chances of either a Jew or a novelist, much less both, being elected President of this enlightened republic. They elected an atheist to parliament, and when parliament threw him out, they continued to elect him until not atheism, but parliament, gave way; and I hardly need mention the possibility of electing a Charles Bradlaugh to the Senate of the United States. They suffered a group of aliens to tie up the business of the House of Commons night after night under the leadership of O'Connell and his followers; and I cannot imagine delegates from the Philippine Islands and Porto Rico enjoying the same liberty in the House of Representatives. Huxley told a bishop to his face in a public meeting that in his opinion the bishop was a fool and hinted that he was a liar; yet Huxley served on more public commissions (or so his biographer states) than any other British scientist. Would an American professor in a state university be similarly honored? I think we have talked too much about Victorian moral conformity.

You cannot, said Burke, indict a whole people; and it is difficult to indict a whole century. That the Victorians (to confine ourselves to them) had their characteristic weaknesses is evident; but one grows weary by and by of so monotonous and one-sided an argument and longs for a little more attention to a few obvious facts.

For example, one is confronted by the charge of moral prudery. It is evident one can retort that the Victorians were often refreshingly immoral, and if this form of argument is hilariously absurd, it will at least awake the jaded attention of modern critics. Against the charge that the Victorians insisted upon the standards of middle-class respectability for all forms of conduct, let us set some bits of biography. The period opens in 1837, with the arrest of Thomas Griffiths Wainewright, artist and designer (the friend of Charles Lamb), who poisoned various harmless persons, partly for cash and partly for pleasure, and closes with Oscar Wilde, who wrote charmingly of Wainewright, and whose particular form of vice even our advanced generation has not brought itself to condone. The philosophical thought of the age was largely shaped by John Stuart Mill, who ran off with another man's wife, and its most characteristic novelist is George Eliot, who lived for over twenty years quite openly with a man she was not married to, for the sufficient reason that he was another woman's husband. The most amusing essay of Thomas De Quincey, who did not die until 1859, is a whimsical defense of murder considered as one of the fine arts, and his best-known work is an esthetic description of the dreams of an opium-eater. Rossetti took chloral; James Thompson drank himself to death; and from Ford Madox Hueffer's absorbing *Memories and Impressions* I cull the following pleasing anecdote concerning a visit paid by William Sharp to the house of Philip Marston, the blind poet:

"He found the poor blind man in the clutches of the poet I have just omitted to name, crushed beneath him and, I think, severely bitten. The poet had had an attack of delirium tremens and imagined himself a Bengal tiger. Leaving Marston, he sprang on all fours toward Sharp, but he burst a blood-vessel and collapsed on the floor. Sharp lifted him onto the sofa, took Marston into another room, and then rushed hatless through the streets to the hospital that was around the corner. The surgeon in charge, himself drunk, seeing Sharp covered with blood, insisted on giving him in charge for murder; Sharp, always a delicate man, fainted. The poet was dead of hemorrhage before assistance reached him."

And in the same book I am reminded that Madox Brown, "whose laudable desire it was at many stages of his career to redeem poets and others from dipsomania, was in the habit of providing several of them with labels upon which were inscribed his own name and address." The poets, when too drunk to get about, were then brought by cabmen or others to Fitzroy Square, where the maid and the cabman promptly put them into a bath and made them drink strong coffee, the bath being selected because the poet would "not be able to roll out and injure himself." But let us continue.

Charles Dickens, in the minds of many the chief purveyor of Victorian sentimentality, separated from his wife and quarrelled incessantly with his publishers. George Meredith left his first wife, the daughter of Thomas Love Peacock, and celebrated in *Modern Love,* published in 1862, not a triangle situation, but a quadrilateral one. M. Lafourcade, the French student of Swinburne, points out that Richard Monckton Milnes owned a library of erotica, introduced the poet to the works of the Marquis de Sade, and encouraged him to write poems celebrating various sexual perversities, that are unpublished and unpublishable. Among Swinburne's friends was Sir Richard Burton, whose chief masterpiece cannot for obvious reasons go through the mails. Swinburne himself got drunk ("and how drunk he used to get!" writes Julian Field, an Oxford student who knew him); indulged in the most outrageous language; and was frequently referred to by the erudite Furnivall, the Shakespeare editor, as "Pigsbrook." As for the literary groups with which the Victorian period closes, their "morality," as any reader of Holbrook Jackson's *The Eighteen Nineties* knows, was a little to seek—Francis Thompson took opium, John Davidson killed himself, Aubrey Beardsley is remembered for decadent drawings, and Ernest Dowson's brief career was scarcely memorable for ethical balance.

Now of course these tergiversations do not prove anything except as they raise doubts about careless judgments on the Victorians. As it is sometimes argued, however, that facts like these are exceptional and that the true tone of Victorianism is to be sought in the work of Tennyson, Browning, Thackeray, and Dickens, let us look at some of it. There is no doubt that Dickens invented Little Nell and Paul Dombey; that George Eliot wrote a Sunday-school story in *The Mill on the Floss;* that Tennyson was often sentimental; and that Browning was an irritating optimist. But is this all the story? Is there anywhere a more vigorous denunciation of cant and hypocrisy than in the novels of Dickens, the creator of Mr. Pecksniff and Mr. Chadband and Mr. Podsnap? Thackeray certainly complained that he could not write with the openness of Fielding, but if the author of Becky Sharp and Major Pendennis was really hampered in depicting them, the fact is not patent; if there is a more appalling picture in brief compass of human greed and depravity than in the story (too little read) of the Honorable Mr. Deuceace as set forth by Mr. Yellowplush, his footman; if there is anywhere a more succinct statement of the lack of connection between worldly success and the official principles of that success than *Pendennis,* I do not know where it is. George Eliot undoubtedly wrote *Silas Marner;* but exactly what moral lesson is to be drawn from the loss of Mr. Tulliver's fortune, and what is the precise application of the seventh commandment to the life of Dorothea Brooke? Has anybody surpassed the sharpness with which Trollope pictured worldly clergymen in the Barchester series, or worldly aristocrats and parvenus in the parliamentary novels? Is any reader of Disraeli still of the opinion that cynicism was unknown in the nineteenth century? Did or did not the Victorians produce those great eccentrics, George Borrow and Edward Fitzgerald, the author of *Hajji Babba,* and the author of *The Way of All Flesh?* The Victorian novel begins, if you please, with Peacock the satirist and closes with Meredith volleying arrows of silvery laughter; it includes the great apology for the natural man to be found in *Lavengro* and *The Romany Rye;* and it numbers among its principal exhibits (a fact frequently forgotten) the serried titles of one Thomas Hardy, who was emphatically of the opinion that God is not in his heaven and that all is not right with the world.

As for poetry, let us look at Tennyson, that arch example of all the Victorian qualities. Arthur, it must be admitted, is not much of a man, but what about Ulysses? *Enoch Arden* is rather bad, but what about the poem which reads:

> Raving politics, never at rest—as this poor earth's pale
> history runs,—
> What is it all but a trouble of ants in the gleam of a million
> million suns?

I cheerfully surrender Galahad to anybody who wants him, but this same Tennyson wrote *The Revenge;* and if the true test of poetical worth is pessimism (for so our modern argument seems to run) I submit in evidence this product of Tennyson's last years:

> Act first, this Earth, a stage so gloom'd with woe
> You all but sicken at the shifting scenes.
> And yet be patient. Our Playwright may show
> In some fifth Act what this wild Drama means.

And then there is Browning. On the literary exchange Browning stock has at present sunk to its lowest level since the organization of Browning clubs, and there are almost no takers. I do not count myself among the Browning enthusiasts, but even the author of *Pippa Passes* is entitled to fair play; and I would merely observe that the famous phrase about the exact whereabouts of God with respect to the rightness of earth is not spoken by Browning *in propria persona,* but by Pippa herself as part of the dramatic action of the story, which has for its end to show the unconscious effect that the words of one human being may have in the lives of others—a theme not unknown to our stream-of-consciousness novelists. And this same Browning, so cheery, so irritatingly glad, had a fine eye for a scoundrel, as witness *Mr. Sludge the Medium* and *Prince Hohenstiel-Schwangau* and *The Bishop Orders His Tomb at St. Praxed's Church;* argued on occasion that it was better to be vitally immoral than passively moral; stole an invalid woman from her father; and (unless I am much mistaken) set a fashion for writing dramatic monologues which the admirable E. A. Robinson and other modern poets are still following without surpassing.

The truth is that, instead of inventing "Victorianism," the Victorians engaged in incessant warfare against the cant and hypocrisy they inherited from the maudlin sentimentality of the eighteenth century. At the opening of that epoch Shaftesbury taught that there was inherent in the human heart a something which his disciple, Hutcheson, was to label the "moral Sense." In the innumerable volumes of Daniel Defoe England read that nothing succeeds like success; that when you have money you ought to invest it prudently; that a bad woman can be made good by putting her funds out at six per cent; and that a wicked pirate becomes respectable when he retires to trade and to overreaching his fellow-man in a bargain. The fashionable pens of Steele and Addison were presently at work refining female manners in the direction of modesty, good sense, and prudery; admonishing noblemen not to duel, drink, or gamble, but to follow the example of Sir Roger de Coverley and look after their tenants benevolently and morally. Soon on the stage you learned that female delicacy is always to be protected—read the *Conscious Lovers* for an example; and if you attend the *London Merchant,* which moved the acid Mr. Pope to tears, you learned a good sound moral lesson as to the fate of the idle boys—for the apprentice takes up with a prostitute, embezzles money, shoots his good old uncle, is caught, repents, and is hanged, to the accompaniment of such a salvo of moral platitudes as no Victorian novelist ever dreamed of.

And the doctrine was continually preached throughout the eighteenth century. What are the novels of Richardson but involved Sunday-school lessons in a low and prudential order of morality? What is Fielding's *Amelia* but an object lesson in the domestic virtues? What are the poems of Edward Young except lessons in religiosity? What is *The Vicar of Wakefield* (in this connection at least) but a lesson in impossible goodness, and what is Samuel Johnson, among other things, but a dispenser of ethical commonplaces? No, it is not in the Victorian age that heroines begin to faint on the slightest provocation; it is in the novels and plays that preceded the nineteenth century. Nineteenth-century writers, with all their faults, never preached so ostentatious a morality as did Richardson, nor taught, like Defoe, that money is the test of virtue. No religious poetry of the Victorian era is as lugubrious as Young's *Night Thoughts* or Hervey's prose *Meditations Among the Tombs*. The moral story for young was really founded by the heavily virtuous female writers of the eighteenth century, and the moral tale flowed from the pens of Samuel Johnson, Mrs. Barbauld, Hannah More, and John Gay long before Little Nell died and Colonel Newcomb was called away and Tito ruined Romola's life.

Of course this is not the whole truth about the eighteenth century, but it is a truth critics of Victorianism ignore when they declare that the Victorians, forgetting the glorious freedom of Byron and Shelley, invented a pall of morality and snuffily turned from art to the sermon. Their leaders did nothing of the kind. They took what had been given them and made the best of it. They were a race of rebels. They had little use for the ethical codes which had cramped average human conduct for a hundred years and which, reinforced by the eighteenth-century reasoning of the utilitarians and the laissez-faire economists, threatened to cramp human conduct still. Indeed, we read them ill if we continue to forget that they were struggling with the great burden of "morality" which they inherited from the century before them.

There still remain, however, the undeniable Victorian Sunday, the black clothing, and the sober faces in the faded daguerreotypes; the solemn discourses of John Ruskin and Matthew Arnold; Herbert Spencer and Bishop Wilberforce, Mrs. Hemans and Mrs. Humphry Ward. But even granting them, there is yet another aspect of the Victorians which we all too often neglect. We fail to remember that this gloomy age is likewise the age of British humor and that the nineteenth century has actually given more first-rate humorists to English literature than any other century in the long roll of English letters.

The wit of the century which invented *Punch* is perhaps its most enviable possession. The Victorians did not take themselves half so seriously as we take them now. Anecdote after anecdote exists to prove that the period was a time of exuberance and gaiety. William Morris, for example, stepped to the head of the stairs in that amazing household which contained the pre-Raphaelites (when they were not joyously quarreling) and called down to the cook: "Mary, those six eggs you served me for breakfast were bad. I ate them, but don't let it happen again." There is Edmund Yates's biting comment on Thackeray's first lecture, when, asked his opinion of the performance, he meditated solemnly and remarked with becoming laconicism: "Very good. Wants a piano." Swinburne on one celebrated occasion met Tennyson at the house of a friend and said, "We understand, of course, that Arthur is Prince Albert and Guinevere is Queen Victoria, but, Tennyson, who is Launcelot?" There is W. S. Gilbert's famous comment on Beerbohm Tree in *Hamlet*: "Funny, without being vulgar." There is, in short, an endless stream of anecdote and persiflage which makes Victorian letters and memoirs an infinite delight.

In fact, when drollery is almost a major theme in the Victorian period, it is wonderful to see how critics forget to account for it. The age begins with Sydney Smith, who once dryly remarked: "Benevolence is a natural instinct of the human mind; when A sees B in grievous distress, his conscience always urges him to entreat C to help him"—and from that witty punster goes its scintillating way to Oscar Wilde, the epigrammatist. Was there ever such a feast of humor as Victorian fiction alone presents—the brilliant pages of Disraeli, the inimitable Dickens; Thackeray, over whose "Victorian" novels there plays a constant stream of satire and fun; George Eliot with her great comic peasant creations; George Borrow with his joy in life and humor; Trollope and the vagaries of cathedral life; the wit and wisdom of George Meredith? And as if this were not enough, there are the great eccentric novelists from Peacock, the irresistible, to Mallock's *The New Republic* and John Davidson's half-mad concoctions. There is Browning, a master of grotesque satire; Tom Hood—and when next it is argued that the Victorians could not call a woman's "limb" by its right name, let the cynic read *Miss Kilmansegg and Her Precious Leg;* there is the long succession of verse humorists from Father Prout to Charles Stuart Calverley. How in the name of common sense can a period be writ down as unmitigatedly solemn which produced Edward Lear and the *Ingoldsby Legends,* Lewis Carroll, and W. S. Gilbert? Has any one arisen in this earnest age to create another Pooh-Bah or a new *Pirates of Penzance?* Had anybody until *Of Thee I Sing* was written laughed at the Senate as Gilbert laughed at the House of Lords, and do we dare treat our bishops as airily as that great man depicted the Bishop of Rum-Ti-Foo? It would appear from all this that the Victorians were not all such grave deacons as the world imagines. In fact, I believe that the absurd seriousness with which we read novels based on the fairy-tales of Freud, and ponderous works of fiction based upon the insubstantial fabric of disordered syntax and stream-of-consciousness anarchy must awaken mirth among the Victorians. And I think we might profit from the Gargantuan gales of laughter which come to us across the what-nots and set the patent rocking-chairs a-rocking, and which, blowing more softly, sigh through the woods where Alice and the White Knight walk forever to the delectation of mankind.

O'Neill and Æschylus

By JOHN CORBIN

Besides having been dramatic critic and editorial writer for THE NEW YORK TIMES *and* THE NEW YORK SUN, Mr. *Corbin has served as critic of* HARPER'S WEEKLY, *as literary manager of the* NEW THEATRE *(New York), and on the editorial staff of the* ENCYCLOPÆDIA BRITANNICA. *Among his books are the following titles:* AN AMERICAN AT OXFORD *(1902)*, A NEW PORTRAIT OF SHAKESPEARE *(1903), and* THE UNKNOWN WASHINGTON *(1930)*.

IN THE subject-matter and title of *Mourning Becomes Electra*, Eugene O'Neill claims comparison with the most revered of Greek dramatists, and both critics and public have so far honored the claim as to make his play the outstanding success of the current season on Broadway. This popularity, moreover, is only the climax of a steady ascent through plays no less somber and harrowing—*The Emperor Jones, The Hairy Ape, The Great God Brown, Anna Christie, Strange Interlude*. Here is a phenomenon which, to use a fine old locution, may well give us pause. Nothing one half so arresting has occurred in the world of the theater since Bernard Shaw proclaimed his intelligently farcical comedies as "better than Shakespeare."

Now Shaw, as the world well knows, is not only a humorist but a professional egotist, endowed with all the grimaces and the exultations of the circus-tent barker, and there is abundant precedent for a success of ballyhoo. At one time, to be sure, there seemed to be danger that he was overplaying his part, alienating the public that had most need of, and could best re-

From *The Saturday Review of Literature*, April 30, 1932. Used by permission of the author and *The Saturday Review of Literature*.

spond to, the provocative tonic of his gibes. I remember discussing this danger with one of his oldest friends and warmest admirers. William Archer not only admitted it but added a fear lest what had begun as an outward flourish, an attitude studiously costumed, might presently strike inward corrosively, like a poison garment. Fortunately such fears proved unfounded. Bouncing humor carried the day. But Eugene O'Neill, God knows, is no humorist. And, so far as his attitude toward the great public is concerned, no dramatist was ever more modest, more finely and courageously self-respecting. Yet this very austerity has had a reward beyond Shaw's self-exploitation, even with the tired business man and his rubber-tired wife.

Something has happened in the world of Broadway, a thing of which O'Neill, if not prime mover, is certainly the worthiest and most impressive exponent. Time was when prophets of progress raged against the tyranny of the "happy ending." Pollyanna sat enthroned, lisping the gospel that all living is a glad, sweet song, that human pain and frustration must be banished from our thoughts—and, *a fortiori,* from the theater. Of this gospel, William Winter was the most impressive exponent. When reminded that Shakespeare made adulterous love a theme of his greatest tragedies, that the Greeks did likewise not only with adultery but with incest, he quoted Browning: "The less Shakespeare he." So Hamlet and Mark Anthony go to't, Clytemnestra, Phædra, and Œdipus! The managerial mind judged likewise, though in terms of its own. After Richard Mansfield had scored successes in *Arms and the Man* and *The Devil's Disciple,* Shaw's agent urged *You Never Can Tell* upon the great chief of the so-called Syndicate. He refused the play on the ground that the public wouldn't spend good money for the painful privilege of an evening with a dentist and a dentist's chair. Another enthusiast suggested to the most intelligent and public-spirited of the Syndicate managers that the *Agamemnon* was upstanding drama and might be eked out in the Athenian manner with a comedy after-piece—*The Cyclops* or *Alcestis.* Daniel Frohman replied, not without a twinkle, that in New York, there weren't enough Greeks. A decade later he would doubtless have said, "Yes, we have no Athenians!"

In brief, playwrights found themselves forced to think of the drama not primarily as an art but as an entertainment, and entertainment was conceived in the terms of laughter and blissful tears. Clyde Fitch alone had courage to deal honestly with the darker realities of character and conduct—feminine jealousy in *The Girl with the Green Eyes* and feminine mendacity in *The Truth*. These were comedies, but his last play, *The City,* produced after his untimely death, applied the same method to more masculine and dramatic vices, incidentally anticipating *What Price Glory* in the exploitation of cuss-words. To-day the public that once doted on Pollyanna, and still doesn't know Æschylus from an escalator, sit staring through five mortal hours of lust and murder, adultery, and incest, until their bums ache and the edge of the seat cuts their knees, swayed only by a rapturous conviction that one simply must be intellectual in order to register socially.

Incidentally, of course, there has been a vast improvement in both the artistic quality of the drama and the intelligence of the playgoing public—or perhaps we should reverse this statement, rating as incident or by-product the fact that Broadway has gone highbrow. Of either phenomenon there was scant promise a brief dozen years ago when O'Neill became known to us through his one-act sea plays. Those who praise the decade just past are curiously blind to the advance in the theater, which has been as great as the advance over the novels of Henry James and Howells and Stephen Crane has been negligible. The author of *Bound East for Cardiff, In the Zone,* and *The Long Way Home* taught us that sheer character is of prime value in the theater, though it evokes no derisive laughter and gives us no trace of that "sympathy" with human frailty which is essentially self-approbation. Of character as O'Neill portrayed it the touchstone is the stark reality of human suffering, faintly illumined at best by an aspiration that is groping and dumb. In the true sense of the word it is passion, and that is a thing that was as lamentably absent from American drama before O'Neill as it is lamentably absent from the modern novel of the sexual libido.

To develop such passion in the theater requires a dramatic instinct and a dramatic technic as simple as they are strong. For the "situations" and the "great scenes" of his predecessors, O'Neill had as little use as for their comedic laughs and their saccharine tears. No contrivance was visible in his plays, no effort of any sort; yet the human heart somehow revealed itself, caught in the meshes of that most tragic fate which is character—what one essentially is and must remain. In progressing to plays of a full evening's length, O'Neill remained true to his loyalties. He even added to them. Few things dismay a commercial manager so deeply as a multiplicity of scenic "sets," involving initial outlay and constant expense of stage hands. In this respect Ibsen himself became a strict economist. O'Neill put down what was on his mind in the form in which it came to him, piling up scenes with the result that very few of his plays are commercially viable. But his development as an artist was untrammeled. His power of evoking atmosphere was that of a poet; his imagination ranged from the mystic inspiration of the high seas to the soul-destroying penury of New England hills, from the opulent splendors of great cities to the peace of Caribbean islands in moonlight. The vivid truth of his characterizations expanded in proportion—the starved poet and mystic of *Beyond the Horizon;* the love-crazed stoker of *The Hairy Ape;* the black Napoleon, terror-stricken, of *The Emperor Jones;* the faithful prostitute Anna Christie. You will have to range the civilized world to find such a gallery of dramatic portraits, of dramatic passions so deep and widely varied.

Then came a change the imprint of which may be easily grasped today by reading the plays. The artist who scorned the trumped-up "situations" and "great scenes" of the "well-made play" fell for the newer fashions in technical *tour de force;* indeed he lavishly added to them. It began with *The Hairy Ape,* which echoed the Continental fads of stylisation and expressionism. So long as the burly and upstanding Yank remained in his normal mood and in his stoke-hole, the world he envisaged was shown in its normal guise; but under the impact of the scorn of him voiced by a beautiful young deck passenger, and of his perverse love for her, her up-town world took on attitudes absurdly toploftical and visages of a simpering superiority that could only be rendered by putting the actors into masks. Startling as the effect was, it was sound enough psychologically and perhaps added to the impression of Yank's impassioned delirium. But the fact remained that this partial expressionism rendered impossible any complete and truthful representation of one party to the dramatic struggle. It is perhaps irrelevant to point out that the great masters have resorted to no such obvious methods in depicting the tortured soul, though the calm citation of Æschylus gives us a text. But it is not without significance that the device forced O'Neill to depart from the detached impartiality and sturdy truthfulness of his previous plays. Especially significant is the fact that he has not repeated it. To black-lead one half the world is as futile a device as to whitewash the other.

The interest in startling technical devices remained, however, and it continued to be fused with a tendency to subordinate character to psychology. In *The Great God Brown* the mask appeared again; but this time it was used to make obvious to the audience the difference between native impulse and the more-or-less artificial self which one presents to the world. Each actor carried a rubber false-face expressive of his assumed attitude and, as often as O'Neill judged that the audience required to be told that he was socially tarrididdling, he clapped it over his visage. Practically, the effect was far less successful than that of the masks in *The Hairy Ape*. While the actor was speaking, his chin worked up and down against the rubber, with the result that the lips of the mask moved with precisely the expression of a goldfish gaping against its bowl of glass. But that was the least of the damage. No actor needs to be told that the two great instruments of his art are his voice and his facial expression. Those masks reduced the voices behind them to an inarticulate monotony, void of tone color and vibrant force, and all facial expression to a single idiotic grimace.

In *Strange Interlude* the obsession with inward or subconscious mentality reached its climax, and with it audacity in the matter of technical stunts. In order to reveal unmistakably the wellsprings of impulse O'Neill resorted to a curious combination of soliloquy and aside. With incessant iteration, all the people on the stage become deaf-mutes, lay figures, except the one of them who, for the time being, is permitted to expound wordily the dark secrets of his libido. I shall not attempt a defense of the rigid realism of the well-made play championed by the once new school of Pinero and Henry Arthur Jones. At the time Bronson Howard, who took himself with some seriousness as Dean of the American Drama, protested against it and registered his protest by putting at least one soliloquy and one aside into each if his plays. Doubtless it is true, as the Victorian realists contended, that character is most convincingly revealed in action and in the give-and-take of dramatic dialogue; but it is also true that, in addition to Bronson Howard, William Shakespeare occasionally made his characters address themselves or the audience. In our modern drama not the least of improvements is an abandonment of the dull, material realism of the eighteen-nineties in favor of a plastic freedom and imaginative intensity comparable to that of the great Elizabethans. All that I question is the extent to which O'Neill has used the old devices—a matter of mere technical efficiency.

In justice to O'Neill's craftsmanship, it should perhaps be added that the reason for so much self-communion on the part of his characters was less technical than psychologic. His interest in the subliminal mind is now so great that he takes it as his hero. As clearly as in Freud's great work, *The Interpretation of Dreams,* the protagonist is an impulse to wish-fulfillment primarily colored by the Œdipus complex. The people of the play themselves speak the familiar patter. One of them is strongly attached to the young heroine but is prevented from making love to her by an affectional preference first for his mother and then for his sister. He defers his declaration until both are dead and the young object of what normally would have been love has passed through half a dozen sexual relationships to her change of life. O'Neill's attitude toward this fellow is obvious in the fact that he makes him a writer of jejune conventional novels void of passional reality. Also, with an irony more self-willed than intrinsic, he makes him a declaimer against the Freudians, who yet welcomes "with a strange passionate eagerness" the idea that the Supreme Being is no male but our universal Mother. In brief, *Strange Interlude* is primarily not life in the living but a tract on the new psychology.

As to the originality of Freud's method and the effect of his teaching upon his profession there is scarcely room for two opinions. He has revolutionized psychotherapy. Very seldom does it happen that an achievement so richly deserves the epithet of epoch-making. As to his specific results in detail the case is far otherwise. As yet psychology has merely touched the surface of the subliminal mind. Whole regions of power remain to be explored, from amazing mental feats like those of the "lightning calculator" and the "spirit" control who improvises "Martian" languages to the feats of faith-healing which are at once spiritual and physical. Freud himself stresses the narrowness of the field he has conquered. Nor are he and his disciples agreed within the compass of their field. In this very matter of the nature and power of the Œdipus complex, which so fascinates O'Neill, Freud's foremost disciple Jung is radically opposed to his master. Only the amateur psychoanalyst seems able to escape doubt as to the finality of his knowledge. But, like another crudely multitudinous phenomenon of the libidinous complex, his name is Legion; and too often he deserves the same Gadarene fate. The new psychology is mainly founded on the antics of ailing and shaky minds and has too often been exploited by such.

In itself, O'Neill's interest in technical exploits and in the Book of Freud is perhaps no subject for regret. Few things are as stimulating, in any art, as the free quest of new methods and new subjects. The ultimate test, however, is not their novelty but their viability. O'Neill has had no followers in the use of mask, soliloquy and aside, and has himself apparently abandoned them all. What remains in his technic is its primal quality, a simplicity, solidity, and sincerity that rise to a certain massive beauty.

As to qualities of characterization and emotional conviction one can only record personal impressions, with all possible modesty and candor. I was among the first to acclaim the masculine vigor and emotional intensity of the earlier *dramatis personæ,* the rich color and variety of atmospheric evocation. In the later plays I find nothing at all comparable to the hairy stoker Yank, to the mystic dreamer of *Beyond the Horizon,* to the rawly feminine Anna Christie, to the savagely dominant and savagely superstitious Emperor Jones. In abandoning the objective for the subliminal world, or so it seems, O'Neill has plunged us into the drab and tenuous regions of late twilight. Freud himself is on record against this preoccupation with the mental underworld. "Action and the conscious expression of thought mainly suffice the practical need of judging a man's character. Action above all deserves to be placed in the first rank." It is a rule as sound in the drama as in psychology.

Undoubtedly the psychological plays have power to hold the attention. The multitudinous public does not sit five hours at a performance that bores it, swayed only by eagerness for the uplift. Much must be granted to O'Neill's power of dramatic speech and to his skill in unfolding a dramatic narrative. Nor is it for nothing that the stuff he deals with is lust and murder, adultery and incest. The tabloid mind has stuff in plenty to feed on, even as it assumes the attitude intellectual. And has not O'Neill the authority of Freud when he assures us that we, personally, each and all of us, are swayed by passion hitherto unheard of in the theater? One is so deeply and so pardonably interested in anything that tells one, tells one intimately and amazingly, about oneself. What Molière's bourgeois gentleman felt upon learning that all his life he had been speaking prose was a joy faint and dim compared with the joy of discovering that our most seeming-virtuous thoughts are in reality incestuous. Even more than these solemn new subjects, this solemn psychoanalytic predicate has served the purpose of jocular Shavian ballyhoo.

It is high time to inquire into the provenience of this master complex. In reality it is quite different from what Freud, and with him O'Neill, have made many or most of us believe. Of all people Œdipus was least guilty of it. When he learned from the oracle of Apollo that he was fated to marry his mother, he fled in horror from home and kingdom, to the uttermost corner of the earth. There, as a reward for routing the Sphinx in a contest of wit, he was acclaimed as King and given the Queen as consort. She was in fact his mother, her face having doubtless been lifted; but the union was so far from being passional, or in any sense Freudian, as to be a marriage of convenience. When the horrible truth was borne in upon the court of Thebes, Jocasta hung herself and Œdipus, having scratched out his eyes, fled to the wilderness to die in wretched poverty. There was no libido, no complex, in either; quite the reverse. The idea would have been as impossible to an Athenian as to a Victorian. Even the impulse to adultery was made the theme of only one Greek play, the *Hippolytus* of Euripides, and that during what was regarded as the decadence of the drama. In O'Neill the incestuous impulse is represented as, in point of fact, frustrated; one thing we are spared. But as a determinant of character and fate it is everywhere given the Freudian prominence.

And so, by steps ascending as easily as those of an escalator, we arrive at Æschylus. Whether mourning becomes him we do not know, for he never dons it. No spirit ever lived more courageous and triumphant. It is not merely that he fought through the Persian war and was wounded at Marathon. In confronting the problems of life and fate also, his head became bloody but remained unbowed. Steeped as he was in his native polytheism, in a religion as barbaric in its origin and its basic ideas as it became superficially beautiful, his soul strove always toward a monotheism quite comparable to that of the Christian Trinity. There was no question whether Zeus was She. He was "the great master-worker," "subordinate to no other power," a deity as stern and just and all-pervading as the Hebrew Jehovah.

> The air is Zeus, Zeus earth and Zeus the heaven,
> Zeus all that is, and what transcends them all.

Nor did Æschylus subscribe to the barbarous conception of fate so often attributed to him as to the other Greek dramatists. Sophocles could write,

> Once a House has suffered the shock of a great god's
> wrath
> The curse pursues its children even to the very last.

And this is precisely the fate O'Neill visits upon his House of Mannon. The whole point of the Agamemnon trilogy is that Orestes and Electra are rescued from such blind fury. To Æschylus as to Shakespeare fate is conceived in the terms of character as expressed in deliberate action and speech—the thing we have been and are. Citing the "ancient saw" which attributed to the gods an insensate zeal in punishment, he adds his own individual and rebellious creed: "For I, apart from all, hold this my creed alone, that only impious deeds breed cursèd offspring, sons like the parent stock. In every house that loves and does the right, fate evermore brings issue good and fair." The Agamemnon trilogy is founded on this enlightened, this almost Darwinian, idea. It is only in obedience to the oracle at Delphi that Orestes kills his mother, murderess and adulteress though she is. When the ancient barbaric fates, the Erynnies, pursue him to punish this blood-guilt, he takes the manly and forthright course—performs every rite of purification and appeals for justice against his grisly pursuers to the oracle at whose bidding he had acted. The case is brought to the bar of judgment—Æschylus against the old theology. Apollo appears as witness for Orestes, and Athena decides the case in his favor. Nor is that all. The horrible Erynnies are themselves converted, becoming the Eumenides or "friendly ones"; and they gratefully take up their abode as such at Athens, having become

> Well-doing, well-entreated and well-honored,
> Sharing the land best loved of all the gods.

There is no better example of the katharsis of Aristotle, though the Œdipus trilogy of Sophocles and all the great plays of Shakespeare might be cited to the same effect. Those who are attuned to tragedy are no less consoled and strengthened by it than that other public is consoled and strengthened by the comedy of vapid optimism.

With the problem of the origin of evil, of its divine purpose, Æschylus struggles on no better terms than other mortals. But his conclusion is at least no worse than ours. Suffering and self-sacrifice may be made a sacrament. "Pain is gain"; the "wisdom that profiteth" is "achieved through sorrow"; "woe-recording care makes the unwilling yield to wiser thoughts." It is thus by a privilege of pain that "Zeus leadeth men in wisdom's way." Whatever may be said of this philosophically, it is devoutly spiritual, conducive to "self-reverence, self-knowledge, self-control." And at least the pragmatic philosopher will commend it as a faith for those who go forth to Marathon.

In *Mourning Becomes Electra* very little is to be found of either Æschylus or Sophocles, except indeed the great length of their trilogies. The normal human horror at incest becomes an agreeably interesting Freudian libido. The upstanding manhood of Orestes, his hard-fought battle for spiritual release, becomes a weak-kneed and neurotic pessimism ending in suicide. O'Neill's Electra herself is so tainted in mind that she willfully renounces escape to the brighter world and closes all doors and shutters, the more deeply to enjoy the gloom of the House of Mannon. It is the curse, the primal curse, of Erynnies who refuse to become Eumenides. That is clear.

Not so the answer to a very natural question as to the monstrous sin from which O'Neill's curse sprang. Old General

Agamemnon, back from our Civil War, is much the same heavy patriot he was on his return from the fall of Troy. No curse in him. The Orestes, far from murdering his mother, is warmly yet innocently Freudian toward her. So far as the record goes, the blight on the House of Mannon sprang from a rivalry in love between two long-deceased ancestors, and it was so far from being incestuous as to be centered on a domestic servant—which is to say that this alleged Æschylean curse sprang from the French nursery maid.

Is it possible that O'Neill's interest in technical stunts and morbid psychology registers a decline in his creative powers as great as the concomitant increase in popularity? That is a question of taste which may not be disputed, of the ultimate judgment of critics and public which it would doubtless be rash to forestall. One thing, however, is already subject to approximate demonstration. The earlier plays, somber and painful as they were in subject, had no trace of morbidity and pessimism. In the hour of his death, the hero of *Beyond the Horizon* has a sense of the privilege of pain as valiant as that of Æschylus. "Only through contact with suffering," he says to his dull but well-loved brother, "will you—awaken." His staunchness in enduring fate is as marked throughout as that of blind Œdipus; and as night closes in from his earthly horizon he has Hamlet's courage to see in death the ultimate felicity.

Shavings from Shaw

By ROBERT BENCHLEY

Bob Benchley is now known to all cinema enthusiasts for his movietone "shorts." He writes "The Theatre" regularly for THE NEW YORKER *and is known to all who ever saw a Model T, for his essay "Lesson Number One"* (OF ALL THINGS).

R EVIEWING a play by Shaw is an ungrateful task at best, for, no matter what the reviewer may say, he must necessarily make himself out something of a whippersnapper. It is agreed, I suppose, that Shaw is a really Great Man, otherwise he could not, wearing a full beard, have his picture taken in a bathing suit (a test of greatness which even Napoleon could hardly have come through with complete success). It is also agreed, I hope, that anything that Shaw writes has distinction, not so much because it is always good, but because it is so much better than anything else of its kind. So either to praise or to pan Shaw must seem equally presumptuous on the part of a man who, even in his most luxuriant season, can raise only a fragment of a mustache.

Let us say then, in all humility, that *Too True to Be Good* is not Shaw at his best. It is not Shaw at his worst, for he has toyed with the movies like an elderly kitten with a ball of string, but it is rather as if the Great Irishman had forsaken his abstemiousness for one night and, under the mellowing influence of several rum punches, had indulged in that prerogative of all good stews, reminiscent and repetitious philosophizing. *Too True to Be Good* seems to be the work of someone who has been reading too much Shaw and has nothing to add to it—except, as the bun wears off, a despairing "Whatever is to become of us all?" Following the late lamented "A Night of

From *The New Yorker*, April 16, 1932. Used by permission of the author and *The New Yorker*

Barrie" at the Playhouse, we have "A Night of Shaw" at the Guild. But don't think that you couldn't spend worse nights.

The slightly drunken and phantasmagorical nature of the proceedings is heightened by the structure, or lack of structure, of the piece and the heterogeneous makeup of the cast which has been assembled, with rare abandon on the part of the Guild, to act in it. It is like one of those dreams that one has in which Ludwig Lewisohn wins a sack race and a visit to the Aquarium at the Battery ends one up in the Taj Mahal. "Then it seemed as if Bea Lillie came on, dressed in a sort of bathing suit, and talked with a British colonel, only it was on more of a mountain, and Hope Williams was there, having just got out of a great big bed somewhere near London and put on a Greek peasant's costume to chase her mother around a big rock labeled 'St. Paul's.' Then I woke up." This nightmare feeling of not knowing what in hell is going to happen next, together with the bright colors of Jonel Jorgulesco's settings, helps considerably to keep those heavy eyelids open and to lend a certain excitement which Mr. Shaw's reiterated views on vegetables, war, inoculation, and the British army could not possibly have furnished had the scene been laid in a drawing-room.

During the first, and very bad, act you think that maybe it was a mistake to put Miss Lillie in the part of the nurse, for her own (unfortunately not inimitable) comedy tricks threaten to eliminate Shaw entirely from the proceedings. But as the show wears on, it is Miss Lillie's personal comedy which makes the whole thing bearable, and the more she eliminates Shaw, the better you like it. It may be presumptuous to look askance at Shaw's philosophizing, but when he essays gags he lays himself open to comparison with the lowliest gagster, for a gag is a gag, whether it be pulled by George Bernard Shaw or Lou Holtz, and most of Mr. Shaw's gags are perfectly terrible. If Miss Lillie were not there to lend grace to them by a slight and regal inclination of the head or a convulsive dip into a candy box, matters in *Too True to Be Good* would be in a parlous state on many occasions. It may not be good Shaw, but neither is Shaw in this instance.

The rest of the cast, with the possible exception of Miss Williams, who needs a good scene by Philip Barry or Donald Ogden Stewart to fit her particularly immobile type of acting, do wonders with the old material at hand. Ernest Cossart as the Colonel, Leo G. Carroll as Private Meek, Frank Shannon as the evangelical sergeant, and Claude Rains as a strange man with an umbrella, all place Mr. Shaw greatly in their debt. But it is Hugh Sinclair, a young Englishman who has been doing some excellent acting in a very quiet way for some time (ever since he stopped playing Miss Lillie's accompaniments in vaudeville), who takes the one important thing that Shaw has to say and makes it seem ten times more important by his inspired reading of it as the final curtain comes down. I have never seen an audience stopped short in the midst of its hat-reaching as Mr. Sinclair stopped that opening-night audience at the Guild Theatre. Standing at the front of the stage, after dismissing the rest of the cast one by one in the manner of a finale to a Charlot revue, this young man, representing, it is to be supposed, Shaw himself, confesses the bankruptcy of the world in general and of himself in particular. "I am by nature and destiny a preacher. . . . But I have no Bible, no creed; the war has shot both out of my hands. . . . I stand midway between youth and age, like a man who has missed his train; too late for the last and too early for the next. What am I to do? What am I?" Here, for the first time, we see what Shaw has been saying in all this vaudeville. He has been throwing everything he has said before into a melting pot and the residue is dross, because, with the world's spiritual market as it stands today, it is unnegotiable. Whether it is what Shaw has written or the way in which Mr. Sinclair reads it, the fact remains that the final speech of *Too True to Be Good* is a thrilling, and rather terrifying, thing to hear. No more convincing proof of Shaw's real stature in the world today could be had than the panicky feeling which comes over you as you hear this despairing cry coming out from the gathering fog as the curtain falls. If this brave general admits defeat, then the army is indeed lost.

Loin du Bal

A Letter to Mr. Shaw

By STARK YOUNG

Mr. Young is one of the editors of THE NEW REPUBLIC, *to which he contributes weekly articles of dramatic criticism. From his long list of published material the following titles show his wide range of literary interests:* GUENEVERE *(play in verse), 1906;* THREE PLAYS, *1919;* THE FLOWERS IN DRAMA *(essays on the theater), 1923;* HEAVEN TREES *(a novel), 1926;* THE STREET OF THE ISLANDS *(short stories), 1930.*

Note—THE SHEWING-UP OF BLANCO POSNET *(1909) was conceived by George Bernard Shaw after reading Tolstoy's* POWER OF DARKNESS. *The Shaw-Tolstoy correspondence is partly reprinted in Archibald Henderson's* GEORGE BERNARD SHAW, HIS LIFE AND WORKS. *For still further information upon this point see Archibald Henderson's* GEORGE BERNARD SHAW, PLAYBOY AND PROPHET. THE NOTORIOUS MRS. EBBSMITH *(1895) is a play by Arthur Wing Pinero.*

WHEN I was young, dear Mr. Shaw, in a very negligible small place in the South, a village, of course, with its shakedown of ancient wrong conventions, bardolatry and meat-eating, there was a cousin who used to play on her square piano an old piece, "Invitation to the Dance," and with it another, "Loin du Bal." You are announced to arrive in America not very long hence, for a day only, it seems. By one of those foolish things of the mind, associations and what-not, ever since I heard this news and every time I think of it I am reminded of my cousin's music. You are the guest, I suppose, and America the dance at which

From *The New Republic*, February 22, 1933. Used by permission of the author and *The New Republic*.

you are expected; or, perhaps, we are the beings still far from *le bal,* which is you; for your whole career has been in the nature of a dance. The small squeak I want to make at you I have asked various persons whose taste I value to give me their judgments on, whether it is bad taste or not to say it. They say not. I console myself with two thoughts, or rather three. First: space in print—vulgarly known as publicity—of almost any sort so long as it is devoted to you, has always been your heaven. Second: you yourself have always reserved the right to say things, as you did when you were invited to Irving's funeral or when you sent to *The New York World* upon the death of poor Arnold Daly—who had been among the first with your plays in America—your celebrated cable about the rarity of spontaneous combustion: I mean to say that you have not always studied certain such dainty matters of politeness as might concern me now in addressing you, a famous man, no longer young and about to pay us a call. Third: one of your many virtues is that you have recognized sincerity when you saw it, though for the sake of your debate you have sometimes chosen to shut your eyes.

I read not long since of your landing in an Indian port and, apropos of the situation there, your saying that they need not mind too much; England, also, had its untouchables: let, for example, a duchess marry a butcher and see what an outcry would arise. I was ashamed of you. In the midst of that blood and the long suffering in India—about which you have at home said brave, sound things—for you to think only of a jibe with one of its eyes on a British audience, hoping, by the old tricks, to hit them and make them smile at the same moment—a safe moment thus guaranteed—was pitiful. What must the Indians have thought; how quietly in their own midst must some of them have been disgusted with the Dominion seer, pretty much as Tolstoy sat on you when you sent him *The Shewing-up of Blanco Posnet* and wrote effectively of God and God's development! No matter how quietly some among them may have stood in their meditations while you trotted the globe, they must have known that in the very first place, even, it was not true. Any child knows that England is filled with pill-makers, bitters-makers, and what-not in trade who win titles, or chorus girls married to great lords, and that the only obstacle between the butcher and the duchess is that he should kill enough beeves to contribute to the party campaign or the royal charities. Could you not, even in those rich and now tragic lands and seas, go without the little news lines in the newspapers of America and England? We might let it go as senile were it not in line with your old tricks. The sum of all this is only to beg you not to land in America at all. You will be sure to say silly things.

I am mindful of your long, valiant life, that vitality in you, that standing up—trusting to your wits to make it safe, which it always turned out to be even after your *Common Sense About the War*—for what you saw was right, that high partisanship undertaken with enthusiasm and doubly so if it offended the Athenaeum Club, William Archer, and the sober islanders. I hate to see you come to America and be silly. I know, too, the labor by which you perfected the instrument you use until you came to be among the marvels of English prose. I know the dedication, battle, and circus you have kept up in order to place your thoughts, and the thoughts of such Europeans as you chose to lean on, with the English-speaking public. I know how soon in your career you were working among the books of the British Museum, acquainting yourself with movements and theories yet strange to Britain, where, as the French say, all good little philosophies go when they die. You indeed supplied a combination of knowledge, wit, courage, and exhibitionism that put over matters which the brains of others had quietly given birth to. You, as you yourself have said, had a talent for elucidating and tidying up, an intellectual dustman—the phrase is your own—who taught people not only to take on new ideas, which they are ready enough to do for the sake of mere newness, but to get rid of the old stock of dead matter. Sometimes I have thought that your two chief blessings, in the way of gifts, were, first, a passion for getting into new forms, for those whom they might serve, deeply social ideas; and second, an enjoyment of shocking not only people who might thus be roused into life or brought in line with what you preached—anyone might enjoy such successful shocking—but also of shocking people who would never understand those ideas at all. The moral purpose of the first led you to being an artist. In the second, the satisfaction it gave the imps and vanity in you kept you going; it helped, too, keep Pan alive in you.

The gods, masquerading as the Life-Force, out of which you have got no few conceptions and more copy, put on each of us his particular curse, I suppose; your curse has been that you are so made that you cause people to think first of you, not of your subject—how often have you marred a crusade of yours by throwing yourself suddenly in, Shaw the wit, as if one could sacrifice everything but one's vanity, could never leave off tinkering at the fiction of oneself! Your pranking as reformer and tight-rope walker, social thinker and wit, Fabian and faun, at the same time, hamstrings many an honest answer from honest men whom you know to have solidity and intelligence, but who cannot play your half-guerilla, half-unfair game. You have waxed impassioned over unfair advantages one man may enjoy above another and you have hymned the fairness of Socialism, while using somewhat unconscionably for the fight your own advantages in brains, your unscrupulous jestings and thrust, as if this sort of strength and strategy had nothing parallel to the capitalists' ways. Even about sex, look at you. Play after play skipping about over marriage beds and the heats of clerks, women, poets, and life in general, railing over excess, preaching the sexual regulation of people who cannot be, like you, busily engaged, energetic and entertained, and all this, mind you, with scarcely a chance taken as to broad words, good, bawdy, plain talk and hit the nail on the head. That touchy matter of word frankness—theorize and be gasped at, but such is only a dangerous game of sorts. And yet to be taken as a virgin, an acolyte, that would not do, it would be insincere and it would be harmful to the reception of your ideas popularly as not deriving from a real man. How you took care of that: "I liked sexual intercourse because of its amazing power of producing a celestial flood of emotion and exaltation of experience, which, however momentary, gave me a sample of what may be the normal state for mankind in intellectual ecstasy." The momentariness we will not take up, since we do not know whether it is measured in the light of the private or of the eternal. A way of getting to heaven. Nobody could too confidently debate that. It is, of course, only a redusted Renaissance theme, but which of our Coition Sects puts it so well? My little point, also, then, you will have taken care of: "Some people are born with a terrible desire to be laughed at; this has prevented me becoming a great author."

I remember when, as a student from the country, I first encountered your works, at an age younger than you were when you struck Ibsen. Even then, I remember, I was not taken in. I saw the verve and the delight, the smashing of fronts and top hats, the knowledge, the courage, the whizz and great talk of it all. But I saw also the shock method you used, saying things almost obvious in a way that made what might be modest preaching, gentle science, or debatable sociology sound as if those who readily accepted it were essentially outraged at it. Behind this was your theory of irritation; that nobody will trouble about anything that does not trouble them. Even then I saw by the pleasant glow under my skin that the whole business was flattering me; to the charm of the rhythmic and delicious speech was added the enchantment of secret blarney. I saw, also, alas, and just as clearly, that the ego or the imp was omnipresent. This was a man who would babble in Zion. There was no tremor, no pulse, no power of beauty or the shadowy world or strength or joy that would shut up that self. It was a great deal, of course, this self; but was no great shakes to displace the stars, the long silence of night, the clouds one over another, from people's regard; and the same is true of great thoughts, profound ideas, passionate beliefs—the author's shadow replaced them all too often. Long before then when Ibsen dawned on the London few, your friend, Graham Wallas, after reading *The Wild Duck,* said that when he "came to the end of the play, the bottom fell out of the universe." One can only ask what sort of a universe was this that you and your friends dwelt in that an Ibsen play could knock the bottom out of it, or any play for that matter? However, this was one way of fighting for Ibsen and the new theater from Europe.

Your Shakespeare scandal—imagine it in America unless Mr. Ford or Edison had said that Shakespeare was less great than himself!—came under the head of this Ibsen crusade. You can thank your very wise biographer, Mr. Archibald Henderson, for making clear your real devotion to Shakespeare. What you objected to was Shakespeare's thought, his social comment and so you went on and actually got a rise by claiming to be greater than the bard. That, of course, is one way of conducting the battle; you might have added almost that Phidias put no electric switchboard in the Parthenon, and what a blight on the Psalms wine is. All through Mr. Henderson's book there are points you could have sanely followed, if only he could have written your biography before you were born—now there's a theory of biography with meat to it that you have missed!

Lately I have run through your two volumes of dramatic criticism, belonging to the '90's. They are still engaging, persuasive; they still play tricks with one's natural processes in argument; they are often basic, free of an epoch. They had their influence. Pinero, for example, who after some years of apt theater writing got himself off into problem piddle-paddle which he could fabricate but not digest. In fact what rash, brash thousands of dramas in English since then, full of reality, problems, situations and social comment! I have read over your *Cymbeline* criticism: "Stagey trash of the lowest melodramatic order," and so on. Very well, dear Mr. Shaw, knock off the particles of this Shakespeare play. What remains? A basis of living substance, poetic glow, breathing pulse, free vitality. And now with time what remains of *The Notorious Mrs. Ebbsmith* and of a good deal of your own drama already, with the matter grown stale? Very little of anything. But what is the basis of drama, as it passes from epoch to epoch, style to style, thought movement to thought movement? Why, the same thing that remains in all life: living substance, et cetera. But I shall not like a village school-teacher or a British vicar bite at that Shaw-Shakespeare bait. The Duse-Bernhardt criticisms, long famous, are better cases in point. Bernhardt, heavily plastered with make-up, "her lips red as a newly painted pillar-box, she is beautiful with the beauty of her school, and entirely inhuman and incredible." Duse on the contrary is everything opposite, one is at liberty to look at her gray shadows, her wrinkles, what life has written, et cetera. It all makes a fair distinction in a sort of general way, it is very persuasive, it carried on the fight for the new theater. Duse wrote you a letter of appreciation, as well she might. For that matter, dear Mr. Shaw, Duse when she had been in America two days sent me a telegram asking me to see her, she wanted to tell me that what I had written of her had changed her state of mind in coming to America. She repeated this remark to others and asked me to come to Asolo that next summer. That ought to be for a writer of theater criticism a sort of *nunc dimittis;* it was to me, though I bring it in only to bolster my right to an opinion at the moment. For all the charm of your article, much of it could as readily be turned upside down; Ellen Terry knew better, for she saw how easily Bernhardt took the elevated rôles, her mask was perfect for it. The myth of Duse's not making-up is nonsense—you do not quite say it but the public got it some-where—I have never seen make-ups so subtly contrived as hers were to the mask. Duse's realism was in large part that of the Italy of Dante in poetry, Mina da Fiesole and Donatello in sculpture, and the mingling of the realistic and the exotic in D'Annunzio; and she told me herself that she detested doing *Ghosts* with its parochialism and its lying heroine.

It may be that all this worry of mine comes only from an old devotion, though I must confess such works as *Too True to Be Good* with the old tried tricks, the insistences and that appalling bourgeois sermon at the end, have almost finished me. It may be that your championships, your quips, causes, assaults, refusals, some of your scenes, your revival of real dialectic in the English drama, lead me to be jealous of the impression you make here in America. And I am indeed your debtor. And yet even as I say this I cannot help remembering, two years ago in Florence, a phonograph record of yours, something about English diction, which laid us all low with embarrassment for you; and another time in a huge moving-picture place in New York. You were talking from the screen, the old Shaw-ego-joke, turning your head, praising your profile, the crowd looking dumbly on, most of them not knowing who you were.

This could lead to my last point. You are one of the great showmen in literary history. No man is popped more into print than you and very few ever with such lasting reiteration. I think you should be reminded how apt you are to give the sense not of ideas but of a vaudeville of thought. You have spoken of your need to discipline your wit; another version would be to discipline your exhibitionism; that is if you will come to America and will say silly things. Do not be misled by the headlines of our New York newspapers; Peaches Browning and Al Capone got just as many. Remember that that specialty of yours, which has so circulated and so maimed your gifts, is the one thing America shines in and is skeptical about: advertising. It is too bad that one of our major sins you are not in a position to attack. If the reporters make you sound sillier than should be, well, they have done so with you before and for years; somebody said that if a man's wife calls him prince charming in public the second time it is his own fault. What a pity that on this visit you could not for once speak straight out, forgetting the fear of dullness. We need you badly; but we do not need your fiction of yourself.

The Maverick Turned Bell Mare

By CAMERON ROGERS

After his graduation from Harvard in 1923, Mr. Rogers joined the editorial staff of WORLD'S WORK *magazine and later became its book review editor. Since 1929 he has been editorial manager of W. R. Grace and Co., New York. Among Mr. Rogers's books,* THE MAGNIFICENT IDLER—THE STORY OF WALT WHITMAN *(1926), and* OH SPLENDID APPETITE! *(1932), a book of essays, are particularly significant.*

Note—A maverick is a wild, unbranded animal. A bell mare is the leader of a herd, so-named because of the bell she wears. See the essay by H. L. Mencken on page 335.

HENRY LOUIS MENCKEN, editor of *The American Mercury,* has been, for a period of roughly twenty-five years, a force in American Letters. For the fifteen years just past he has been more than that. He has, in himself, composed, almost indisputably, the most powerful critical influence at work in this country, and certainly the one most constantly discussed, combated or applauded. He has been variously estimated. To the late Stuart P. Sherman, for example, he was a critic for flappers. To Frank Harris he was one of the best critics in English. To Edmund Wilson he is a genuine artist; to Carl Van Doren, a writer resembling in some fashion Poe, Whitman, and Mark Twain; to Burton Rascoe, a natural product of American traditions, training, and character; to the Irishman, Vincent O'Sullivan, a product as American as pumpkin pie or a Riker drug store; and to L. M. Hussey, a writer who is primarily emotional and creative, and so, therefore, primarily an artist.

He has, in other words, possessed and administered in his critical writing so individual and vital a personality that contemporaries have been unable to pigeon-hole him or gauge to their satisfaction the precise sphere of his influence and the validity of his opinions. During the last decade Mencken has constantly defied those who would explain him, catalogue him, and so spike his guns. His strength has been his nonconformity, his brawling disagreement with accepted canons of American life, customs and behavior, and until recently this strength had remained undiminished. Now, however, it is definitely impaired and for two reasons. One is that he has been accepted and his protestant clamor no longer attracts an attention either startled or reverent. The other, that he has done his work, and having written with an admirable emphasis of things about which he knows a great deal, he now either chooses or is forced, or both, to write of things about which he knows very little.

In his time Mencken has constituted, for many intelligent people, a sovereign formative influence. But his time is very nearly past because the premises of his prosecutions have become too familiar, and a rising generation will persist in regarding him, not as an enlightened Ishmael bawling wisdom in the waste places of American boobery, but as a quite orthodox, though still forceful, editor with a failing for repetition. For a prophet to be with honor in his own country means the end of that prophet qua prophet. Mencken is just such a one. The Shermans, the Munsons, and the Calvertons, the Pattees and the Boyntons have ceased to strive with him and so have ceased to impel him to a greater, more raucous, and more inspiring diapason of ridicule. He will continue to uncover in American life those preposterous beliefs, shibboleths, and manners at which he has been mocking for years, but in so doing he will no longer occasion amazement. For he has taught too many pupils to observe these things for themselves, and he has taught them so thoroughly that they no longer require his schooling.

However, it is not yet to be inferred that Mencken is, quite hopelessly, a spent man. If there is ever in the United States a national prohibition of tobacco, for instance, or a Constitutional instrument forbidding the further glorification of the American girl as directed by revue producers, his voice may again be raised in all its ancient plenitude and with all its ancient epithets of scorn. But, unfortunately, it seems quite likely that in that time there will be voices younger and stronger, voices compact with an invective perhaps even more rigorous than his own, so that, in the main, his usefulness is at an end.

But let us, in the light of all this, a light which would seem to reveal an epitaph, examine the substance of his career.

He was born in Baltimore in 1880, educated at Knapp's Institute and the Baltimore Polytechnic, and was inducted into professional journalism at the age of nineteen. He served as a cub reporter on the *Baltimore Herald* and his first printed piece of reporting was the following terse statement of fact:

"At Otterheim Memorial, United Brethren Church, Roland and Fifth Avenues, Hampden, Charles H. Stanley and J. Albert Loose entertained a large audience last night with an exhibition of war scenes by a cineograph."

An item which, taken in relation to his now notable phobias, seems filled with a gentle irony. This was in 1899. In 1900 he contributed a few short stories to such magazines as *Leslie's,* and Ellery Sedgwick, then conducting that periodical, was so favorably impressed by one story that he offered Mencken the post of associate editor. Mencken, refusing this, became Sunday editor of the *Baltimore Herald* in 1901, city editor in 1903, managing editor in 1904, and editor-in-chief in the following year at the age of five and twenty. His abilities were so manifest that when in 1906 the *Baltimore Herald,* to employ a graphic idiom, "folded up," he was appointed news editor of the *Baltimore Evening News,* then Sunday editor of the *Baltimore Sun,* during which latter employment he emerged definitely from comparative obscurity in the rôle of the militant and always audible critic. It was during this period that he commenced to fall upon what he considered to be the frauds of the day. He laughed at the New Theater idea then sprouting in New York, gibed at Richard Mansfield, and engaged to cry up the dramatic talents of George Bernard Shaw.

Almost at once people began to read his work, a few with applause, a great many with frequently expressed distaste. In 1908, at the suggestion of Theodore Dreiser, an author in whose behalf he has long battled with adverse opinion, he became literary critic of the *Smart Set* and for the next six years applied himself with his peculiar gusto, here to criticism of books, there, to that of personalities, and everywhere to that of the orthodox texture of American life. He conducted a column in the *Baltimore Sun* entitled "The Free Lance," and instantly aroused an opposition that would have appalled a less resolute character. Mencken fed on opposition, probed, flayed, laughed coarsely, and wooed enemies. He made no effort to enlist a following, and, of course, secured one, but one which, fortunately, remained small as compared to the foe.

In 1914, with George Jean Nathan, whom he had met and with whom he had formed a friendship four years earlier, he became joint editor of the *Smart Set* and as such, during the next ten years, achieved his fullest significance as a critical influence not only in American letters but in an increasing degree in American life. In 1924 he was instrumental in founding *The American Mercury* and became its editor, and since 1924 he has become less and less the spokesman of an intelligently caustic minority, but more and more the accepted and almost supreme arbiter of men and women whose mental processes he has now ceased to astonish any more.

Here, briefly and in rough chronology, is the substance of Mencken's career. He is not an old man but he raised his voice when he was, comparatively speaking, so very young, and he has used it so consistently, that he has already given us his all, told us all he knows, taught us all that he has to teach. For there can and should be no such thing in the world as a sound critic of life in its every aspect, and to function as just such an agent of the Omniscient Intelligence is palpably his present ambition. Indeed, it is the only sign that he gives of having passed fifty. While his writing, as his biographer, Isaac Goldberg, points out, remains that of a young man, the subjects upon which he employs it balk at conclusive treatment. His mind's eye, trained once upon specific evils, frauds, and follies, seeks now to encompass the whole hodge-podge of universal errors, and these are too diffuse, too complex, too vague in his own understanding, to permit success. One may concisely trace the progress of this abandonment of an impregnable position for one which does not exist at all, in the six volumes entitled *Prejudices,* and which contain, the first of them the best work of his *Smart Set* days, and the last of them his still rigorous but increasingly meaningless disquisitions on "The Nature of Man," "Government," "The Nature of Love" and the like. These, written, it is true, as only he can write, are not meaningless save for one cardinal reason. They are not incoherent or unintelligent or dull. They are meaningless simply because Mencken knows very little more about any of them than do his readers, and about some of them, it is quite possible, rather less.

When he took a specific man or book and built around such a subject an edifice of shrewd comment, sometimes devastating but frequently excellent criticism, and always revealing statement, he was as nearly infallible as any critic can be, and more inspiring, infinitely more influential and effective. If you will look into the first volume of these *Prejudices* you will find estimates of H. G. Wells, Arnold Bennett, George Ade, and others which judged by any but a purely academic standard of criticism, surpass any kindred work of our times. They shocked many critics, even surprised the late Stuart P. Sherman, himself, before he came to New York, an excellent commentator upon letters, into a pallid satire of rebuke, but they will outlive far more pretentious critiques, even, perhaps, far more scholarly ones, because of a validity and fierce perception elsewhere unequaled in this generation.

It has been authoritatively stated that Mencken is not a literary critic at all but a critic of his times in all their manifestations. This, to precisely this extent, is true. He is not, *sui generis,* a literary critic such as, let us say, was Hazlitt. Nor is he, however, *sui generis* of his times. In him the functions of both are so nicely combined as to achieve a double result. An author, a book, or even a public figure such as the late William Jennings Bryan, is the glass through which Mencken looks at his times, examines their magnified defects and forms his conclusions. Remove that author, or that book, or that personage, and he stares at a landscape too vast to be comprehended by any human critical retina, too sprawling, too general for any instructive scrutiny. Through his glass he has been able to particularize, to concentrate upon one social malady, expose its symptoms, prescribe for them and pass on to another. But without his glass he is lost. He sees everything and at the same time nothing, and so is able to diagnose with no more authority than might the authors of those very evils which he would cauterize with the hot-iron of his mockery. Mencken, writing objectively and with a specific target for his criticism, has been an important influence upon the development of the contemporary American mind. Writing subjectively upon general human problems, he has been and will remain ineffective.

It is significant, here, to observe that it was when he ceased to be Mencken the Maverick and became the bell mare of the herd, that he translated himself from one critical see to the other. When, ten or fifteen years ago, he pointed out to an outraged majority that H. G. Wells, who had once been "the most brilliant, if not always the most profound, of contemporary English novelists," had yielded to a "process of gradual and obscure decay," he awoke hard feelings but also many intelligent readers to the realization that Wells of late had, in fact, been producing novels which were not only dull but pitifully commonplace. It is true that he did not at once materially damage Wells's American sales, but he had bred a severe disaffection in the ranks, incited a rebellion in many minds, against the touted clap-trap of once talented but now empty English authors. Ten or fifteen years ago the attitude of American criticism toward Wells or Bennett was an attitude not critical in the least. Men acutely perceptive to the faults of American authors reviewed *Mr. Britling Sees It Through* and abased themselves before its very ordinary qualities as though the hand of God had wrought them. Mencken, though his work in this respect has been far from completely successful, changed all this. In a word, he was honest. Instead of writing testimonials he wrote criticisms, and that he should dare to do so caused such men as Stuart P. Sherman to look upon him as an intolerable boor, and that class of readers of which Sherman was the spokesman, then by far the largest in the country, to do likewise. But, in the minds of a few, Mencken had sown the seed. While Sherman did all the thinking for his flock, Mencken taught his to think for themselves. And since Sherman was not a critic of contemporary letters at all, but a man of sound scholarship merely in the tradition of letters, he actually impeded the development of individual critical thought while Mencken cried it on.

But at that time Mencken was the Maverick and he continued to be so with every clay icon that he smashed and every false standard of excellence that he attacked. Also, he continued, and more and more perceptibly, to mold the minds of a group of men and women which grew larger year by year. His ultimate reception by the herd was the inevitable result, and almost coincidentally he renounced objective criticism, threw away his glass, and assumed the conduct of the Omniscient. It is not, of course, inconceivable that such an action was forced upon him by the fact that of late years he has had very little at which to aim. When the occasion arises, when, as happened in 1925, he has a Bryan at which to shoot, he will be again Mencken the Maverick. But with this distinction. Ten or fifteen years ago he was a maverick to Stuart P. Sherman's army of bottle-fed intelligences. Today he is a maverick only to an army which is bereft of any intelligences at all. Yesterday he at least had intelligences with which to work. The trouble is that he worked with them too well and showed too many of them the light. Today he can be of no more use because there remain too few.

Mencken's writing, the prose style which has been his weapon, has remained, it is gratifying to observe, comparatively unaffected by his critical apothcosis. This style, like its possessor, made enemies, awoke at one time a considerable academic uproar and a strange disquiet even in the breasts of his warmest admirers. At its best it is clear, forceful and witty. At its worst it is boisterous, affected, and sometimes in bad taste judged by any standards of writing. Stuart P. Sherman, whose opinions touching style were always sound, esteemed it as being hard, pointed, forcible and cocksure. It is, certainly, all of that. Its faults, in point of fact, are few and candid.

Like his friend and one-time co-editor, George Jean Nathan, Mencken has a weakness, more, a vice, for needlessly interpolating into his prose a variety of German expressions which add nothing to emphasis of content and which constitute so naïve an effect of sophomoric cleverness as to astound readers who revere his abilities. If these expressions were French instead of German how palpable would seem the absurdity of their usage by an otherwise first-rate author writing in the English language. The fact that they are in a tongue, for some reason considered less precious by the herd, somewhat diminishes the mischief, but only in the case of his unilingual admirers who, if they possess any feeling for good writing, will still object. Mencken, it would seem, cannot write police when he means police. He must write *Polizei*. If he refers to scholars a mysterious compulsion directs that he write *Gelehrten*. Does he wish to speak of the Home for the Aged? Then he puts hand to dictionary and plucks out *Greisenheim*. Or if he wishes to make use of the word employment or simply to mention the day's work, the same obscure inhibition forbids him to put on paper the English word and he inscribes *Geschäft* instead. He has actually disfigured an otherwise delightful essay on Huneker by hammering into the opening paragraph the word *Doppelschraubenschnellpostdampfer*. And why? Merely to avoid the necessity of writing twin-screw mail packet. Such a procedure makes, of course, for an effect at once ridiculous and uncouth and is, if you like, the worst flaw in his style. But save for an occasional abuse of such expressions as pish-posh, and a sometimes tedious reiteration of such nomenclature as Homo Boobiens, Boobus Americanus, and the rest of that familiar terminology, it would be hard to find its equal.

Indeed, as a medium of satire, invective, or praise, Mencken's style has no equal, even today when he has nothing more about which to write and has fallen back upon subjects to the expositions of which no style might lend a reasonable coherence or a tolerable validity. His style is not polished. It is frequently ungraceful. It is as bare of ornament as is an elm of leaves in January. But it remains as memorable as the date of one's birthday, and most especially does it so remain to those men across whose backs it has been laid. In this connection I quote briefly from *Prejudices*. Mencken gives a paragraph from the works of a well-known man of letters, then appends the most succinct, expressive, and completely short-winded piece of unfavorable criticism that I have ever read.

"Whenever in a world-historic war the side of righteousness has triumphed, a great overflowing of art has followed soon upon the fact of victory. The noblest instincts of mankind—aroused in perilous moments fraught with intimations of mortality—have surged and soared, beneath the sunshine of a subsequent and dear-bought peace, into an immeasurable empyrean of heroic eloquence. Whenever right has circumvented might, Art has sprung alive into the world, with the music of a million Easter-lilies leaping from the grave and laughing with a silver singing."

Upon which Mr. Mencken:

"With the highest respect for a Magister Artium, a pedagogue of Columbia University, a lecturer in Miss

Spence's School and the Classical School for Girls, and a vice-president of the National Institute of Arts and Letters—Booh!"

How that one single brutal monosyllable pricks the balloon of intolerable rhetoric! It is precisely symbolic of what has been Mencken's rôle in contemporary letters, and as seen through them, in contemporary life. No one has been able to cry "booh" with such authority or effect and the pity of it is that he should persist in continuing to do so at something which is too big for him and which he does not comprehend.

What Is a Poet?

By MARK VAN DOREN

Brother of Carl (editor-in-chief of The Literary Guild of America) and husband of Dorothy (associate editor of THE NATION), Mark Van Doren is poet, critic, and lecturer (Columbia University) in his own right. Besides writing critical studies of John Dryden and Henry David Thoreau, he has published six volumes of his own poems, one, JONATHAN GENTRY, a long narrative poem.

———

POETRY speaks for itself. But poets, curiously enough, do not; and so it is time that someone speak for them and say what they would say if they spoke in prose. It is time that they be defended against the silent charge—all the more damning because it is so silent—that they are a special race of men and women, different from all other creatures of their kind and possessed of faculties which would make them, if we knew them, only too wonderful to live with, not to say too embarrassing. I should like to relieve them from the burden of being queer. Poets are supposed to be a suffering race, but the only thing they suffer from is the misapprehension that they are endowed with a peculiar set of thoughts and feelings—particularly feelings—and that these endowments are of the romantic sort. It consists, to speak for the moment historically, in the notion that the poet has always and must always cut the same figure he has cut during the past hundred years or so. It consists in expecting him to be a Shelley, a Keats, a Byron, a Poe, a Verlaine, a Swinburne, a Dowson. He may be another one of those, to be sure; but he also may be any kind of person under the sun. My only conception of the poet is that he is a person who writes poetry.

From *The Nation*, June 1, 1932. Used by permission of *The Nation*.

WHAT IS A POET?

That may sound absurdly simple, but it is arrived at after reflection upon the innumerable kinds of poetry which poets have written, and upon the baffling variety of temperaments which these poets have revealed.

Here is the figure we have set up. A pale, lost man with long, soft hair. Tapering fingers at the ends of furtively fluttering arms. An air of abstraction in the delicate face, but more often a look of shy pain as some aspect of reality—a real man or woman, a grocer's bill, a train, a load of bricks, a newspaper, a noise from the street—makes itself manifest. He is generally incompetent. He cannot find his way in a city, he forgets where he is going, he has no aptitude for business, he is childishly gullible and so the prey of human sharks, he cares nothing for money, he is probably poor, he will sacrifice his welfare for a whim, he stops to pet homeless cats, he is especially knowing where children are concerned (being a child himself), he sighs, he sleeps, he wakes to sigh again. The one great assumption from which the foregoing portrait is drawn is an assumption which thousands of otherwise intelligent citizens go on. It is the assumption that the poet is more sensitive than any other kind of man, that he feels more than the rest of us and is more definitely the victim of his feeling.

I am tempted to assert that the poet is as a matter of fact less sensitive than other men. I shall make no such assertion for the simple reason that to do so would be to imply that I knew what kind of man the poet necessarily was. My whole point is that the poet is not anything necessarily. He may be sensitive, and he may not; the question has nothing directly to do with his being a poet. Certainly there have been poets with very thick hides. We have to account for the fact that Browning looked more like a business man than he did like a poet—whatever a poet is supposed to look like; that Horace was plump, phlegmatic, easy-going, shrewd, and sensible; that Dryden was an excellent trader in literary affairs; that Pope was so insensitive, at least to the sufferings of others, that he poured an emetic into the tea of a publisher with whom he had quarreled; that Li Po and most of the other great Chinese poets

193

were government officials; that Robert Frost is to all outward appearances—and what other appearances are there?—a New England farmer.

There is reason for supposing that no artist is as sensitive in one respect as the man who is not an artist. He is not so likely, that is, to be overwhelmed by his own feelings. Consider what he does with his feelings. He uses them, deliberately, for the purposes of his art. The ordinary man—meaning for the moment the man who is not an artist—may be so affected by the death of a parent, for instance, that he becomes dumb. There was Daudet, however, who at the funeral of his mother could not help composing the room where he stood into a room that would be the setting of a new story. He was using his feelings, together with the scene which called them forth, for an ulterior purpose. The artist is callous, and must be so in order to keep his mind clear for the work he has before him. So also the poet must be sensitive to words, rhythms, ideas, and moods; but in the very act of perceiving them clearly, in realizing them for what they are worth, he distinguishes himself from the race of men who feel and only feel. When we read the poetry of a man like Pope who was extraordinarily, almost abnormally, susceptible to the charms of verbal music we can have no doubt that he was, in that one department of his existence, all sense. We are not justified, however, in going on, as a recent biographer of the little man has done, to attribute to him a sensitive heart. As a matter of fact he had another kind, and in the ordinary man it would be denounced as an ugly one.

From the notion that the poet is deeply affected by life we often proceed to the notion that he cannot stand a great deal of it; we say he dies young. To be sure there are the English romantic poets—Shelley, Keats, and Byron—to support our error, and to be sure they are always conspicuously present in spirit when poetry is under discussion, since it was their generation that gave us our conception of poetry and the poet; we still are in the romantic period. But even as we talk this way we seem to forget their contemporary Wordsworth, who lived in perfect peace till he was eighty. We forget that Dryden lived to seventy, Shakespeare to fifty-two, Browning to seventy-seven, Tennyson to eighty-three, Milton to sixty-six, Herrick to eighty-three, Spenser to almost fifty, and Chaucer to an even sixty. We disregard the great age of Homer when he died, at least if the traditions be true. And anyway the ancient traditions about poets have their significance. For one of them was that poets die old; hence the bust of Homer, wrinkled, composed, resigned, with sunken eyes. The three great tragic poets of Greece died old indeed; Æschylus at sixty-nine, Sophocles at ninety, and Euripides at seventy-five. Vergil and Horace gave up the struggle in their fifties, Lucretius committed suicide, it is said, at forty-three or forty-four, and Catullus, like Shelley, was extinguished at thirty; but Ovid, for all his banishment to a cold, uncomfortable part of the world, and his probable suffering there, lived into his sixtieth year; and Ennius, first of all the known Roman poets, saw seventy. Dante had a hard life, but it lasted fifty-six years. Racine went on to sixty; Goethe expired peacefully, calling for more light, at eighty-three. And what of the greatest English poet in recent times? Thomas Hardy, who did not even begin to be a professional poet until he was more than fifty-five, wrote ten volumes of verse after that, and when he died at eighty-eight was busy with the preparation of a new volume, which appeared posthumously!

Another burden of which I should like to relieve poets is the burden of being strangely wise. They have been called prophets, I believe, and seers; clairvoyants, informers, transformers, and what not. All this, too, in spite of the impracticality attributed to them. Indeed, there seems to be a connection between the two attributes. The poets know nothing of the world, but they may tell us a good deal about life; not life as we live it, but life—shall we say?—as we ought to live it. Simply by virtue of their stupidity in ordinary affairs they somehow become conversant with extraordinary affairs which we ourselves shall never experience but which it might be rather nice to hear about. So runs another legend, and one as romantic as the rest. For it has no foundation whatever if the whole history of poetry be taken into account. In a primitive tribe the poet is also the medicine man, the priest, and the foreteller of future events, since it is in verse that these functionaries speak. Among savages, then, the poet is a prophet. But nowhere else. The division of labor has gone on; the prophet is the prophet, in verse or in prose as the occasion may be; the poet is the poet, and always in verse. The poet is a sayer, not a seer. Wordsworth brought on a considerable confusion by insisting that the poet is one who goes to Nature for her secrets, which are substantially the secrets of existence, and then comes back with the dew of knowledge on his lips. The poet, in other words, is equipped with a peculiar mind which enables him to plumb—or fathom, or penetrate, or see through, or pierce; the phrase matters not—the world's appearances. For us the mere appearances, for him the reality behind. Thus he not only cursed his successors with the responsibility of being prophets; he cursed them also with the duty of being acquainted with Nature, and of pretending to some sort of mastery over her. The truth, I suspect, is that the poet is no more of a magician in this respect than the scientist is. And think of the poets, long ago and since, who have never been the least bit interested in the out-of-doors. Dr. Johnson said that he was unable to tell the difference between one green field and another. Milton got his flowers and mountains out of old books; Spenser got his landscapes out of sixteenth-century woodcuts; Dante read Nature as a work in theology; Horace was comfortable in the presence of his hills only when a few friends from Rome were with him to drink wine and make remarks about life; Vergil in the country was concerned with husbandry and the diseases of sheep; Ovid would not look at a tree unless it had once contained a nymph.

The poet may think anything, feel anything, do anything; he may or may not be a wanderer; he may or may not love his home better than any other plot of ground; he may love children; he may hate them; he may be restless under the pressure of a domestic establishment; he may get his chief joy out of a wife and kitchen; he may inhabit a palace; he may shiver in a garret; he may be noble; he may be mean. He is not limited, in other words, more than other men. Yet we go on limiting him. And to what? To a simpering, humorless, pious, nervous existence which for all the world we should be unwilling to share with him. No wonder we don't like him, and no wonder we don't really enjoy reading poetry.

Civilization and the Poet

By JOSEPH WOOD KRUTCH

Joseph Wood Krutch, who is now one of the editors of
THE NATION, *began his editorial work when he joined the
staff of that weekly as dramatic critic in 1924. In 1926 Mr.
Krutch helped to establish The Literary Guild of America.
Among his books of literary criticism,* EDGAR ALLAN POE: A
STUDY IN GENIUS *(1926) is especially noteworthy.* THE MODERN
TEMPER *(1929) is his best-known work.*

"THE world," said Emerson, "seems to be always await-
ing its poet," and though the saying is a true one we
are, perhaps, not wrong in supposing that the need of
our particular world for "its poet" is more than usually acute.
Emerson certainly intended the term to be taken in its widest
significance to mean the possessor of one of those articulate
imaginations which can communicate a sense that the world
of our experience has a unity and meaning, and it is certainly
just from the absence of any such sense that we suffer. Our
best writers of verse themselves define rather than triumph
over the prevailing mood produced by the feeling that we are
lost in a meaningless chaos. But the phenomenon is not merely
literary and we lack a satisfactory life for the same reasons
that we lack our comprehensive poet. Poems and civilization
are alike the result of affirmations sweeping enough to make
form out of what seems confusion.

Nor is this analogy between the kind of affirmation which
makes poems and the kind which makes civilizations merely
an analogy. The poem and the civilization are parallel phenomena—one occurring in the realm of thought and the other

in the realm of action, but each the result of some passionate faith inclusive enough to give form either to living or to contemplation. Each implies an imagination powerful enough to interpret in humanly usable terms the data present in the consciousness, but each implies also that these data shall be capable of such interpretation; and the first question which inevitably arises in connection with contemporary conditions is the question whether or not the data of the contemporary consciousness is susceptible of such a humanly usable interpretation.

It has long been suspected—justly or not—that an *Iliad* was easier to write in the year 1000 B.C. than it would be today. The anthropomorphic religion and the naïve patriotism of the primitive Greeks were in themselves so simply human, so in harmony with instinctive human thought and behavior, that they made easily possible the attempt to see human life as ample, significant, and harmonious. But this religion and this patriotism were themselves possible only because these primitive Greeks knew so little of nature that they could construct a universe made almost exclusively from the materials which they found in themselves and could people it with gods made in their own image. Since their time, knowledge has been constantly busy with the criticism of every structure erected by the human mind. It has been posing ever more difficult problems to the imagination which would arrange that knowledge into a humanly satisfactory pattern, until men have begun at last to wonder whether or not any imagination is equal to the task, whether we have not been overwhelmed by knowledge (or what seems like knowledge) and compelled to witness a triumph of Nature over Art.

Many of the data which the imagination has found it so difficult to find a place for in any humanly useful conception of the universe as a whole are, of course, scientific. The pattern into which we have arranged what we know of nature is obviously incompatible with those conceptions of man's place in it which underlie some of the noblest poems as well as some of the noblest civilizations. Science has also encouraged certain tendencies of thought which increase the difficulty since it has promoted, for example, a general distrust of the validity of spontaneous conviction and a tendency to seek out the prejudice behind what seems to us at first sight our most inevitable affirmations. But it would be a mistake to suppose that all knowledge of the sort which makes epic poetry or epic culture difficult has been the result of scientific thought.

The artist himself, hardly less than the scientist, has peered into many dark and unlovely corners. He too has the passion, perhaps ultimately fatal, for knowing; and that passion has led him on, horribly fascinated, from discovery to discovery. Hence the satirist and the realist, no less than the astronomer and the biologist, stand between us and any Homeric conception of the world amidst which we live. Zola, Baudelaire, and Ibsen; Gissing, Hardy, and Dostoevski—these men, hardly less than Darwin and Freud, have disillusioned mankind with the universe and with itself. Though perhaps none of them actually discovered anything, all called our attention to much and made it an inescapable part of our consciousness. Doubtless there are, in all their works, few ugly facts which Shakespeare did not in some sense know. But there was a meanness in human nature and a sordidness in human fate which he could somehow disregard, which he could blithely ignore in a fashion no longer so easy. This meanness and this sordidness have been examined with a care and described with a force which rendered them no longer negligible. Art has acknowledged them; and for that reason they have become, not merely facts, but facts which have taken their place solidly in the human consciousness.

For this reason, also, they must be dealt with, and any imagination which proposes itself as competent to make art out of the modern world must find a place for them, whether the work which it is endeavoring to create be literary or social. There is no golden age of faith, of simplicity, or of ignorance to which we can return—unless, indeed, society as we know it should suffer some overwhelming catastrophe which would break the whole continuity of its development and return the few straggling survivors to savagery. Those eccentric converts to fifth-century paganism, thirteenth-century Catholicism, and seventeenth-century Anglicanism, who propose to live and write as though they were in the heyday of the culture which they have chosen, are mere refugees whom few will follow.

Few would seek to deny that modern life has its compensations, or that many of the experiences peculiar to it are delightful. The very sense of freedom associated with it, even the sense of having escaped the restrictions and the burdens which convictions impose, seem sometimes more than enough to compensate for any losses entailed. But few would refuse also to admit the curiously disjointed or fragmentary character of this life. Whole sections of our experience, both pleasurable and the reverse, seem not only unconnected with one another, but positively incompatible. Some—like those which arise out of the cultivation of romantic love, of honor, and of our personal integrity—are apparently survivals from a world already dying; others—like those connected with power and speed and freedom, with our plunge into the material richness of the modern world—seem to give us hints of a way of life still imperfectly organized and imperfectly understood; but these two classes of goods are mingled without being combined.

The very cynics whose documented relativism mocks any attempt to spell Duty or Justice or Right with a capital letter find themselves passionately devoted to defending Communist victims of police clubs or denouncing the Society for Suppression of Vice with bursts of oratory whose appeal is wholly moral. Lovers who rediscover the value of those illusions which are very old nevertheless change mistresses or wives with a facility which is very new and seem determined to live several lives for the very reason that they are incapable of leading one. Even humanitarianism, perhaps the most characteristic of our attempts to live nobly, does not dare to examine the foundations upon which it rests for it is devoted to the task of saving human lives without being really sure that human lives are worth saving.

What appears to be lacking is any logical or even any emotional connection between our various motives, various beliefs, and various impulses; any sense that they are a part of one whole or that they could be put together in any fashion which we enable them to reinforce one another. We are overwhelmed, not only by the diversity of knowledge, but also by the diversity of possible deeds, of possible values, and of possible judgments. Such artists as we have offer us constructions whose essential deficiencies arise out of the fact, not that they are artificial or partial, but that this artificiality or this partiality is so glaringly, so unforgettably evident. And if we babble of the necessity of seeing life steadily and seeing it whole we babble without conviction because we are struck by the fear that the more steadily we see it the less will it appear to be any whole which we can comprehend.

We may realize that the wholeness which seemed to characterize certain previous philosophies or civilizations was illusory, and that the connections between the parts of any previous peoples' experience were purely imaginary connections whose existence was merely assumed. But that realization does not help us very much because it is the inability to imagine or assume any such connections for ourselves which constitutes the difficulty and we do not know even where or how we ought to begin.

But let us grant that art, in the broad sense in which it has here been defined, is still possible; that the apparent triumph of diverse and alien nature is only temporary. Let us assume, that is to say, that a modern world, complete and unified, will emerge. Is that world close enough for us to imagine, even vaguely, what it would be like?

Certainly the prophets who proclaim its coming differ widely enough among themselves, but probably the most polite and respectable among them are those who assure us that civilization is not to be remade but only salvaged and that the new world will be more like the world of the past than the world of this present. Some of them, like Mr. Chesterton, are sure that if only beer flowed as freely as it once did in Merrie England we should all very happily put our trust in the Pope and all would be well again. Others, like Professor Millikan, have faith in telescopes and confidently expect that we shall some day construct one which will discover the ten commandments written in letters of fire a hundred thousand light years away. But they agree in the essential, which is that we need only to recover a few principles which we have lost in order to get along very nicely in the world we now know. But polite and reasonable as these prophets seem, there is, nevertheless, something singularly tame about their gospels, something plaintive and elegiac about their pleading, something which seems hardly adequate to influence very effectively a world which may not know where it is going but which is certainly going somewhere under the force of impulsions not to be controlled by the pious suggestions of frightened respectability. The men who speak most earnestly of the claims of authority are the very ones whose voices most conspicuously lack its ring and it is, paradoxically, those who tell everyone to do as he likes who have achieved the largest following. If leadership is to be recognized by the confidence with which it asserts itself, if art is to be known by the power and the persuasiveness we feel before we can analyze, then the beginnings of the new world which may be forming are to be sought among those who are concerned with nothing less than with mere conversation.

Wherever this world of ours competes directly with the past, it loses. Its religions are anæmic and foolish; its poems and its pictures often seem to be trivial and feeble; just in so far as their aims and methods are identical with those of the past. But in certain other activities it exhibits a competence which seems, in comparison with previous efforts in the same field, as nearly superhuman as the competence of Shakespeare seems superhuman in comparison with the efforts of our contemporaries to write tragedy in blank verse. Its instruments for measuring the stars, its machines for hurtling through space, are successful beyond the wildest dreams of previous ages; and the most significant thing about them is not that badly articulated or rationalized faith in their importance which is sometimes expressed by philosophers or humanitarians, but that passionate and implicit faith in the immediate, unassailable value in the thing itself which made them possible.

Whatever else we may say of it, we know that the ecstasy of the pilot is authentic and that it is communicated unreasonably to society. Crowds carry transatlantic fliers in triumph from the field just as crowds are said to have carried Cimabue's Virgin in triumph through the streets of Florence; and each crowd acts for the same reason—because it has recognized a kind of achievement which it can understand. The world is not interested in machines because they save labor or because they increase production. These are the excuses it makes to itself. It is interested because it is interested, because its heart is there. Concerning them it has made one of those affirmations which really count because the affirmation was made spontaneously and does not need to be defended. In that case the will to believe did not explain its rights; it believed.

Even those of us who are, by temperament and education, most attached to values of another sort and, for that reason, least capable of feeling what many of our contemporaries feel, catch at moments some hint of it. We drive in their cars, fly in their airplanes, and live in their cities. We are caught up by this world, gasp with its excitements, and, by moments, we too, forget the other world to which in quieter moments we feel that we belong. But we cannot completely identify ourselves with the representatives of the present. The very inarticulateness of their philosophy, of their poetry, if you will, baffles us. The world of speed and power and exactitude in which they live is a world which still exists only upon the periphery of the consciousness. It is known chiefly through instincts and reflexes, not through ideas. It is, in other words, a world not yet given form by art, a world which has been directly experienced but never successfully thought out. Since no symbols have been found for its aims or its joys it cannot be substituted for—it cannot even take its place beside—those worlds which have a different kind of existence in the consciousness because they have been symbolized and interpreted in terms appropriate to that consciousness. Yet the materials may possibly be there. Art has, in the past, many times revealed to mankind perceptions, emotions, and valuations of which it had not known itself capable.

No one can say beforehand whether or not the new interests and the new ecstasies are capable of being thus humanized. Certainly it is difficult to conceive any connection between them and those which a Shakespeare celebrated. Certainly they seem less outgrowths of previous interests than something radically different, and it may be that they are entirely inexpressible in terms similar to those which literature uses. Perhaps the tendency of the plastic arts to abandon the imitation of nature for pure geometry is merely one relatively comprehensible sign of a break with tradition which is destined to be more complete than even the most extravagent of the "post-," "neo-," or "sur-" schools can imagine. Perhaps the wildest eccentricities of the "modern" poets may be taken as evidence either that poetry is beginning to grapple with the problem or that it is disintegrating under the realization that the problem is not capable of being grappled with.

But in any event there is no escaping the fact that much of the old world has grown dim. The academicians who plead for standards in art, the versifiers who talk of taste in poetry, the moralists who plead that we still *can* believe what our fathers did—there is not one of them whose voice has more than a spectral quality. Even those who believe them righter than their opponents must confess that the conservators are, at least, no match for those who do not bother even to answer. Vitality is all on the other side and those of us who confess our inability to accept the modern world without reservation or to say what can ultimately be made of it, do feel sure, nevertheless, that vitality of some sort is as indispensable to art as it is to life; and we shall take courage again when we find somewhere some evidence that the values which are dearest to us can be affirmed with a passion equal to that with which scientists, technicians, and mere sportsmen daily make the affirmations by which they live.

It is only in the sense which has been here implied that there can be any meaning to the statement that life is art and that esthetics can take the place left vacant by religion and morality. To say that is to say only that one work of art may be replaced by another; but the other must still be found. Some unified aim, some hierarchy of values, some sense that something is supremely worth-while, must impose itself upon us with a self-justifying inevitability.

What we seem to have is an embarrassing profusion of almost equally unsatisfactory possibilities. What we lack among the advocates of each is an imagination strong enough to make that possibility seem inevitable. Nor is it, so long as this is true, worth-while to affirm any abstract faith in art. If love and honor and duty can be salvaged then someone must write about them in a fashion which carries conviction. If we are to get along without them, then someone must describe a world from which they are absent in a fashion which makes that world seem still worth the having. And it is just its failure to do either of these things quite adequately which reveals the weakness of contemporary literature.

This latter has enjoyed, at moments, its triumphs of honesty and accuracy. It has even, at moments also, transcended these virtues in order to achieve beauty—that quality which we attribute to anything when it makes reality seem identical with desire and convinces us that what ought to be is the same as what is. But contemporary literature is too fragmentary and too varied to rank among the supremely great literatures, much less to assume unaided a task which the literatures of other times could perform only with the help of philosophy and religion. It is—like ourselves—doubtful, divided, eclectic, and experimental. It has never succeeded in making us believe anything wholeheartedly or for long. It has given us no self-justifying image because its creators have achieved no self-justifying vision.

We know that this world of ours is interesting. The very vividness of its never-failing stimuli and the very richness of the possibilities which it is continually suggesting, make us unwilling to sacrifice any of them. Even its distresses are so exciting that we are not convinced by those who long for a return to the good old days and none of the unities which have been proposed seem to include enough. What we long for is the ability to function in this complicated world as easily and as freely as others seem to have functioned in a simpler one; to find life, not merely exciting, but satisfactory and meaningful as well. We want to see it whole but we want also to see it all; to find a name for every one of its sensations, an explanation for every one of its phenomena, and a justification for every one of its values. We want a philosophy which is more than merely cold and reasonable, a philosophy whose ultimate expression is one of those works of art which seem not only to sum up but also to justify a civilization.

Perhaps some of these desires are incompatible with others. Perhaps all satisfactory affirmations are partial, and perhaps they seem satisfactory only because they make us forget what they are not able to include. But if this is so, the very fact that we are not able to forget anything about the world in which we live is proof that such an affirmation has not been made. And, at least until it has, we shall continue to long for some attitude which would unify the modern consciousness without depriving us of any of those fragmentary goods which it affords. Only one thing is certain. We shall know what artist we ought to accept when we find ourselves accepting him and we shall know what authority ought to be obeyed when we find ourselves obeying it. Life may be an art—but only when it is characterized by art's spontaneous inevitability.

Does Music Have to Be European?

By ROY HARRIS

Roy Harris is a young American composer from Oklahoma. In 1926, after hitch-hiking across the continent, he arrived unannounced in New York. His ANDANTE FOR ORCHESTRA *was performed in the Lewisohn Stadium. Because of the merit of that work, Mr. Harris won a Guggenheim Fellowship which provided the opportunity for study in Paris.*

A MERICA is vast and elemental; America is desperately struggling to wrest social balance from her omnivorous industrialism. America is rolling plains, wind-swept prairies, gaunt deserts, rugged mountains, lonely rockbound shores, seas of wheat and corn stretching on to the elastic horizon, cotton and tobacco fields, fruit orchards, little bare mining towns huddled on the sides of mountains, lumber camps, oil fields, and New England mill towns; America is smoking, jostling, clamorous cities of steel and glass and electricity dominating human destinies. America waits calmly between the Pacific and the Atlantic while the tide of the Mississippi rises and falls with the seasons.

Americans are more than the civilization which they have thus far built. This civilization is only some temporary prerequisite which we are too near to evaluate. Americans will live through today's institutions and inevitably create new institutions. We are the plastic stuff of nature; we mold ourselves to meet the exigencies of survival. Our climate and our social, political, and economic customs are producing characteristic Americans by the same biological process by which characteristic Frenchmen, Germans, and Englishmen were molded, from the same Aryan race stream.

Our dignity is not pompous, nor our profoundest feelings suppliant; our gaiety is not graceful nor our humor whimsical. Our dignity lies in direct driving force, our deeper feelings are stark and reticent; our gaiety is ribald and our humor ironic. These are moods in which American composers are born and which surround them, and these moods produce unique values of beauty, a different feeling for rhythm, melody, and form. It is precisely this spontaneous native feeling for distinctly different musical values which makes the problem of the serious American composer so especially difficult. His moods are not warmed-over moods of eighteenth and nineteenth century European society, nor is his musical material rearranged and retinted formulæ of the standard classics. Consequently, our audiences, teachers, and critics and our imported conductors and performers are confronted with musical values with which they are unfamiliar.

Our rhythmic impulses are fundamentally different from the rhythmic impulses of Europeans; and from this characteristic rhythmic sense are generated different values in melody and form. Our sense of rhythm is less symmetrical than the European rhythmic sense. European musicians are trained to think of rhythm in broad, symmetrical meters, while we are born with a feeling for its smallest specific units and their possible juxtapositions.

For instance: given a 4-4 meter, the European will generally think $(1+2+3+4)$ in quarters, or in eighths $(\overline{1,2}+\overline{3,4}+\overline{5,6}+\overline{7,8})$ or in sixteenths $(\overline{1,2,3,4}+\overline{5,6,7,8}+\overline{9,10,11,12}+\overline{13,14,15,16})$; but the American is very apt to feel spontaneously $(1+\overline{2,3}+4)$ in quarters, or in eighths $(\overline{1,2,3}+\overline{4,5}+\overline{6,7,8})$ or in sixteenths $(\overline{1,2,3,}+\overline{4,5,6}+\overline{7,8,9,10}+\overline{11,12,13}+\overline{14,15,16})$

The American does not think these rhythms out first as mathematical problems; he feels them in terms of spontaneous musical ideas; to cut them out of our music would be to gainsay the source of our musical impulses. Our struggle is not to invent new rhythms and melodies and forms; it is to formulate them into such clear notation that their character will be preserved in performance. Time and again I have heard my American associates play rhythmic-melodic phrases which sounded natural and spontaneous but which were very difficult to define on paper. In lecturing to groups I have repeatedly played rhythmic melodies before showing their notation on the blackboard. Invariably some musician in the audience will venture the comment: "They don't look like they sound." They look complicated; they sound simple and natural. The new type of form which is evolving from these rhythmically freer melodies also looks difficult and sounds natural. There is nothing strange about this American rhythmic talent. Children skip and walk that way, our conversation would be strained and monotonous without such rhythmic nuances. What is strange is that repetition could have been so insidious as to accustom our ears to the symmetrical rhythms which predominate in eighteenth and nineteenth century European music.

Contemporary European composers also employ freer rhythms in their music, but the rhythms are written into the music. They do not fall naturally into spontaneous melodic lines. They sound like they look on paper—difficult. Stravinsky's *Les Noces,* for example, sounds like an imbroglio of rhythmic patterns. When Ravel attempted to incorporate our rhythmic sense in his violin sonata it sounded studied because he had not felt the rhythm in terms of musical phraseology. Even Bela Bartok, who has been deeply influenced by Hungarian folk song, often writes superimposed rhythms which are intellectual conceptions rather than spontaneous musical impulses.

The problem of American composers is not one of authentic creative impulses; it is rather the lack of an indigenous musical culture which would provide adequate performances, receptive audiences, and intelligent appraisals.

The growth of musical culture is manifested in three ways:

the understanding and discriminating appreciation of audiences, the development of interpretative musicians, and the production of characteristic native composition. Audiences are the roots of musical culture; interpretative musicians form the professional body of music; and original composition is the final fruit. And musical culture, that strange plant of civilization, develops in much the same way as a tree develops; roots, body, and fruit are interdependent. Obviously, there can be no body of interpretative musicians until there is already an audience to feed it, nor can there be a growth in musical composition until composers have the necessary experience of hearing their works performed and appraised by capable and sympathetic interpretative musicians.

Thus far American audiences have developed upon imported music and imported interpreters. This does not mean that we are unmusical. It simply means that our people have been preoccupied with the building of economic empire; that cultural pursuits were not pressing issues and so we had to procure their products from nations who had already passed through the initial stages of civilization. As late as the time of Bach, German courts procured their music and their musicians from France and Italy. German church organists, choristers, and composers grew on German soil, and it was not until they produced the choral-variation forms which grew out of the Lutheran church service that Germany really began to develop musically. It is natural for a young society to import musical culture. Every European society has done so except France, and her troubadours accepted their notation from the Roman Catholic Church.

It was natural and necessary that we import interpretative musicians and with them their native music; and because America was conceived as a democratic and capitalistic society, there was no court life and music had to be sold as a competitive commodity. We were culturally green and budding, we were gullible and easily browbeaten. It was good business to import a musical personality and watch the eager, excited, socially exploited, and curious American dollars roll in. Barnum was the first big Showman. He imported Jenny Lind, Ole Bull, and others. He plastered his artists with a thick coating of "hokum." He prospered and set a precedent. The practice of this precedent has been considerably toned down, but with the aid of subtle advertising technic and newspaper circulation it is even more widespread and far-reaching.

But it is also natural that a society should outgrow the pre-digested musical culture which it needed to import from a more mature society. Each society needs to experiment with its own wings until it is self-sufficient. American society has gladly accepted music from Europe and paid for it with a stream of gold. We accepted European notation, scales, and instruments.

Reproducing machines, records, and radios have cost us heavily. They have led us to form habits at the very turning point when we would naturally have been throwing off European influences. Each invention has carried such an interest in sheer ingenious mechanical achievement that it has been possible and economically profitable to go through the same stages of musical development again. First in the concert halls, then with the reproducing records, and now with radio, the American public has been and is still being led through the same imported musical literature and the same "personality hokum" about European "Maestro" interpreters. The business men of music have learned a lucrative formula.

The "great American public" has been very efficiently trained to know that it prefers an endless reiteration of the "standard classics"—meaning the best works of eighteenth and nineteenth century Europe, especially German instrumental music and Italian opera. It has been trained to believe that the moods, melodic styles, harmonic idioms, sequential forms and rhythms of that music are the final undivided cream of human experience, and that anything else is distinctly *not* music. And, finally, because there is a saturation point beyond which human attention cannot focus, American audiences are learning to demand and pay for the mechanical perfection and personal idiosyncrasies of *prima donna* performers. The social significance of music is being smothered in commercial dickering.

Toscanini knew that he would not dare to appear in any European country without presenting works of native composers, proof of which is his performance of native works in every European capital. Toscanini also knew perfectly well that he would not antagonize American audiences or critics by touring Europe with the New York Philharmonic Orchestra, without presenting one single American work. European critics commented on the irregularity of the proceeding, but our own critics accepted it as a matter of course.

Until American audiences refuse to be browbeaten by foreign conductors, performers, and commercial critics, until we can accept adequate performances and performers as the natural prerequisites of musical culture and become absorbed in the content and meaning of the music itself, American composers cannot hope for much support.

The professional body of interpretative musicians divides naturally into *participating* interpreters (conductors, orchestral men, and soloists) and *appraising* interpreters (teachers and critics). Of the participating interpreters, conductors and their orchestras are by far the most important resource of native composers. In the first place, conductors and their orchestras have a closer and more stable relationship to the community which supports them. Touring virtuosi must master a few programmes to mechanical perfection. They then tour all over the world simply repeating the same programmes and employing the same publicity leads in each place.

Naturally, such a touring virtuoso is very chary about including any modern works on his programmes. His livelihood depends upon steering the safest course from one musical port to the next and he trims his sails accordingly.

On the other hand, conductors and their orchestras cannot afford to be too limited in their repertories. They play to the same public each week for the whole season and their repertories must be representative. Unfortunately, the relationship of the American composer to American orchestras and their conductors is so far not a very fruitful one. In the first place, most of our conductors and orchestral men were born with European temperaments and were surrounded during their most receptive and plastic years with European musical traditions and idioms. They do not readily respond to our serious music. As a general rule they understand and prefer the commercial jazz idiom because it has a very steady rhythmic pulse, because its harmonic texture is obvious, its form elementary, its moods light, and its orchestration effective. Or, if a professional gesture of social courtesy is unavoidable, the conductors generally programme some American composer whose idiom and moods are frankly post-Wagnerian or post-Strauss or post-Debussy, and who has learned to capture some of the orchestral effectiveness of these composers. But conductors do not relish the emotional content of our stronger native music; and, above all, they resent the technical difficulties of its rhythmic patterns and forms.

Such music requires a new receptive approach, a concentration and plasticity in which neither the conductor nor his orchestra can rest on their experience. But most of our orchestras are lacking in plasticity because of over-drilling on the most esoteric nuances of the standard literature. They have learned this literature and can go on giving it ad infinitum without much effort. Such repetition tends toward technical and spiritual sterility. And this sterility not only deadens the orchestral men; it makes listless, sated audiences. It becomes a vicious circle—concerts become dry-as-dust institutions, audiences become undemonstrative masses. Leopold Stokowski has felt this so strongly that he has initiated as part of his daily routine the sight reading of new scores. Consequently, the Philadelphia Orchestra has an amazing sight-reading facility and a plastic receptivity to new musical idioms which certainly justifies this forward-looking policy. We can only hope that such a plasticity is an early symptom of what is to follow.

But so far characteristic American works are side-stepped if possible. If too much pressure is brought to bear, they are very often given what is professionally known as a "scratch" performance. American audiences have been trained to mechanically perfect performances of Tschaikovsky, Brahms, César Franck, Wagner, Rimsky Korsakoff, and contemporary Europeans, and they know that Bach and Beethoven are good regardless of performance; when they hear an American work poorly performed they conclude that the work was not good. Unacquainted as they are with the composition, they do not realize that the musicians are so uncertain of their entrances that they are afraid to give forth clear, clean-cut phrases and that consequently their tones are dull and muddy. Under such conditions an American work sounds forlorn, faltering, and uncertain and suffers by comparison when placed next to a standard work which the men can play with their eyes shut. This is a typical experience of the American composer, and with it comes the lukewarm applause of audiences and friends, who were disappointed, and the damning with faint praise by the critics who have not yet learned how to make the necessary allowances in their appraisals. The same problem is even more acute during the popular summer seasons where only one rehearsal is given for each performance.

Albert Coates, English conductor and composer, stated recently in a newspaper interview, "Had I been born an American, I doubt if I'd have had a chance—in this country at least."

It is doubtful whether this condition will be radically changed before we have a new crop of young American conductors and orchestral men who were born with the American moods and American rhythmic sense in their blood. Unfortunately, the young Americans who thus far are being admitted into our major orchestras are so apt to be impressed with the honor of their opportunity and with the desirability of absorbing the traditions of the seasoned Europeans around them that they often become more rabidly prejudiced than the routine men are.

If American music is alien in our concerts, it suffocates in the atmosphere of our pedagogy. Naturally, the objective of teachers and schools is the public success of their pupils, and their pupils are predominantly students preparing for public careers either as performers or as teachers. Prospective teachers must learn definite harmonic systems, definite contrapuntal methods, definite crystallized forms to sell again to pupils.

I recall a conversation with a very intelligent teacher who had frankly admitted that authentic composition must create and solve its own problems, that consistency of procedure could be the only rule to vital creative work; but when I criticized the teaching of definite crystallized rules I was answered somewhat as follows: "What can I do? These people come to me to learn something definite which they can teach to others for a living." This teaching of definite rules about harmony, counterpoint, and form, this academic emphasis on rules that have been culled from the most obvious formulæ of obsolete styles is of course so much deadwood which experience must burn out of young students' minds before they can have any intelligent understanding of the nature of American music. As one of our prominent composers once said to his former teacher, "Your theories prepare American students to meet our own problems about as much as drilling prepared the Hessian soldiers to fight the American colonists." Prospective performers must prepare to meet the professional requirements of managers—*i. e.,* to present the musical literature of eighteenth and nineteenth century Europe. They must build a salable repertory; they must learn the classics first.

This procedure is no malicious boycotting of American music; it is a natural and, for the most part, unconscious acceptance of the concert world as it exists today. But the result is that during their most receptive and plastic years young embryonic teachers, performers, conductors and orchestral men have been obliged to neglect the melodies, rhythms, and moods which are in their blood.

One of the sorest problems which the American composers must face is the prevalent incompetence of commercial critics in appraising new works which they have never before heard. There are, of course, a few exceptions to the rule, but a first-rate critical faculty is as rare as a first-rate creative talent and requires as much training. Most commercial critics accepted their positions as an escape from the wear and tear of the profession for which they prepared themselves. Some critics use their responsibility as an opportunity to work off their literary ambitions and naturally concentrate on literary phraseology rather than critical acumen. Few critics were especially prepared in ear training, musical analysis, and breadth of musical culture. Many of them probably admitted it frankly in the beginning, but their position demands the gesture of authority and they are so coddled by managers and professional artists that they soon lose that first perspective. It is much easier to learn to juggle words in the simulation of authority than it is to develop the musical authority itself. And even if they were especially gifted and trained to be competent critics the commercial routine of having to write long articles on virtuosic interpretations of the same *genre* of music day after day, month after month, season after season would dull their sensibilities. In fairness, it must be added that even if they had the conscientious initiative to grow and keep abreast of contemporaneous output, their routine leaves no time or energy for growth. The power of these critics, through their influence on box-office receipts, is far out of proportion to their merit.

Finally, can American composers become socially and economically adjusted? It is my personal conviction that talented American composers will find an economic support more readily than they will find a social adjustment. There are many fellowships of recognition being offered for distinguished work—the John Simon Guggenheim Memorial giving a stipend of $2500 annually for two years, the Pulitzer prize of $1500, the Prix de Rome giving three years of economic leisure in Rome are some of the outstanding honorariums. (Unfortunately, all three of the above-mentioned honorariums require the recipient to go abroad for his creative period.) But there is an increasing concern for the economic stability of composers. The Eastman School of Music, the Juilliard Foundation are both publishing serious American works. Then, there is the publication *New Music,* edited by Henry Cowell. Probably the most significant policy is that of the Cos Cob Press. This publishing house contracts with American composers for the rights to all works written in a stipulated time, advancing a generous sum of money. This policy immediately raises the composer to economic citizenship and the degree of social well-being that goes with it.

But the problem of social adjustment is a very difficult and many-sided one for the serious American composer. I have already shown that American compositions are not presented often enough or well enough to acquaint American audiences with American composers. This one condition alone makes the American composer remote. The first problem of all composers in all times is that of achieving a subjective calm sufficiently continuous and focused to enable spiritual and mental co-ordination. The solution of this problem depends on his finding and adjusting himself to an environment in which he may develop slowly and naturally, and this applies to a physical as well as a social environment. Man is so constituted that before he can profit from an intimate contact with nature he must first be at peace with himself, and this peace requires social adjustment.

How to serve society as a composer, how to become economically and socially recognized as a worthy contributing citizen, how to establish durable human contacts with individuals or groups is a harassing problem. The shifting scenes of our social and economic environments are so fluctuating, so crowded with heterogeneous influences, such a helter-skelter race of commercial jockeying, that it is very difficult to strike any bedrock economic or human relationships. Our economic system has fostered the productive psychology within such narrow limitations that no allowance is made for the leisure which is necessary for productivity in the arts. Immediate utility has become such a raucous slogan of our civilization that it is difficult for a composer to avoid the devastating position of being elbowed aside by unschooled and thoughtless acquaintances into an apologetic attitude. King Ballyhoo and his thick-hided henchmen rule the roost. The problem of social and economic adjustment is doing more to destroy talented American composers than any other problem.

But not only the destiny of individual American composers is at stake. The issue involves the musical expression of over a hundred million people today and on into the waiting tomorrows. It is healthy to formulate creative impulses; their repression is unhealthy and dangerous to society. We are entitled to free musical speech. And music cannot speak to people until it is embodied in living tones. When foreign conductors and soloists refuse to perform our works they are denying American creative musicians the right to speak to American people. When they surround us with the idioms of eighteenth and nineteenth century European masters, and thus indirectly insist that these idioms must be our ultimate musical values, they are very subtly and circumspectly curtailing our musical liberty and our pursuit of musical happiness. They are arresting the development of the unique intimate musical values which only can express the immediate environments of the millions of human beings who happen to constitute American society. We will not be able to withstand this foreign influence in our musical life until enough American individuals realize that we cannot *buy* musical culture any more than we could buy a home environment. It must be believed in, cultivated, and used.

America is developing a distinctly different civilization from Europe, Asia or the Orient, and our percentage of musical creativeness is high. But there is the possibility of stifling the ultimate musical expression of America. The musical creativeness of a society *can* be stifled, as history so emphatically illustrates in the case of post-Reformation England.

If we as a people attain the intelligence and strength to prefer our own subjective values, we will develop an indigenous music. The innate creative power is patently insistent. Our musical destiny awaits action.

I'm Signing Off

ANONYMOUS

SOME time ago, under the usual pressure, through the good offices of an influential friend, and with no previous experience in the business, I entered radio station XXX as announcer and utility man. I am, I suppose, of average intelligence and sensibilities, of a typical American background and adequate education. Additionally I own to a decent general knowledge of music and a proficiency at the piano and in singing. I am — I confess it reluctantly — the average young man. Station XXX (not a thousand miles from Fifth Avenue) is correspondingly average, representing the typical large American broadcasting station.

I arrived, much flustered and slightly apprehensive. The business manager, Mr. A., told me to "look around for a day or so and get the hang of it." And for three days I did nothing more than that, observing what Milton Cross, one of the better-known announcers, termed in a New York *Herald Tribune* article "the very highly specialized activity" of the "art" (his word) of radio announcing.

I observed how the microphones, condenser, and carbon were placed in their varying relations to instruments, singers, speakers, and announcers; observed the effects of certain wall surfaces upon microphone reception; listened to voices that "blasted" and produced "peaks," and to voices that did not. I learned something of the mechanism and management of the mixing panel. I learned the necessity of programs that ran smoothly and on time, and of average quick thinking on the part of the studio staff. I learned that an "artist" was anyone who entered the studio in a professional capacity.

Then abruptly I added to my stock of knowledge. The

From *The Forum*, February, 1932. Reprinted by permission of *The Forum*.

business manager informed me that I was to go on the air this evening, I was to get in there and show 'em how it was done, I was to put that smile into my voice, give 'em that winning personality. And so he came finally to his peroration: "Now, B., I know you're a college man . . ."—I was, along with five million others—". . . well, don't show it! I'm educated myself, but I don't even let the fellows here know it. They don't like it. Public don't like it. Give 'em what they want when you announce. Way to make good!"

I should have been prepared for this information, but I wasn't. And it staggered me. I had assumed that my business, since it had to do with English speech, with a wide range of knowledge, and with the entire library of music, would make unlimited demands on my mental furnishings. I was to learn later that the only virtue proper to the great announcer is showmanship.

First of all there was the run of the day's work. Did it suggest art in content or arrangement? Was it well-balanced, varied, amusing? Did it rise occasionally to the plane of normal intelligence, taste, and cultivation; did it at seemingly intervals bear the blazon of the vaunted educational institution which the majority hold the radio to be?

Well, from seven to eight in the morning was the children's hour, and as such quite legitimate and laudable, filled with much ringing and clattering of bells, buzzing of clockworks, mechanical hoots, and the other effects which, all program directors are convinced, children love. Included also was an adventure yarn by "Captain Bert," which was advertised as having been drawn from his actual experience. Captain Bert, though well-qualified for his post, hard-working, and absolutely dependable save when overtaken by *la crise juponnière,* was pressed for time. So I undertook the writing of true adventures for him to sponsor. I remember with a little mortification and with great pleasure his exploits in Borneo, for example. Borneo, by the time I had done with it, was as savage and thrilling as a circus poster, and Captain Bert was a hero cased in triple brass. One morning he engaged in a hand-to-hand struggle with two full-grown orangutans — and did them in, what's more.

Following the Captain's epic doings came jazz and allied popular music from eight o'clock to ten. From ten to ten-thirty, home economics. The purpose behind this program was commendable: in theory, the women of the city profited, as did the station and the sponsoring grocer. But unfortunately the "Kitchen Kourse" was as new as my presence in Station XXX. And the woman in charge, while she had the requisite elocution teacher's "vocality," was otherwise inexperienced and furthermore busy. So I stepped into the breach. My first paper—on pies—was interesting if not sound. It was in fact definitely lyric; by hewing closer to Shelley than to Fanny Farmer I managed to avoid flare-backs from knowledgeable housewives and at the same time to win the omnipotent business manager's approval.

From half-past ten to eleven I played the piano and I sang ... and I began to learn many things about music from my audience of a million as well as from Mr. A. Such as: that the "C-Sharp Minor Prelude" is good for a down any time; that the march from Prokofieff's *L'Amour des Trois Oranges*— as fine a piece of musical humor as ever was written—is "terrible"; that Shutt's *A La Bien Aimée* is "a good deal highbrow"; that the public wanted *good* music and that I'd better sing "Somewhere in Old Wyoming." Thereafter I sang "Somewhere in Old Wyoming" and told comic stories, cherishing one invaluable truth that by process of trial and error I had discovered. Which was, that my public liked the better music only when a recognizable and famous man executed it, or when by dint of weary repetition the music itself had become familiar and therefore acceptable. Exceptions may be taken, I know; but the rule holds.

For the next half-hour, a program devoted to the selling of a fraudulent electro-therapeutic machine. And then thirty minutes of old-fashioned church services, to the material profit of both the organizer and the station.

By that time it was noon at XXX and we settled into our

paying stride. To be sure, stray wedges of the clock were given over to bridge forums, historical reminiscences (whatever they were), travel talks, epi-Guestric poets and critics. But the stock commodity for the afternoon was this: ten minutes of market reports, five minutes of police alarms . . . and sponsored dance music.

Somewhere between six and midnight an hour's tribute was paid to the sober-sided muse. An orchestra played, or, more likely, a string trio for cheapness' sake. This is a typical offering.

Twilight	Friml
The Garden of My Heart	Ball
In Elizabethan Days	Kramer
Serenade (The)	Schubert
Scarf Dance	Chaminade
Kamennoi Ostrow	Rubenstein

The final number here, Rubenstein's bell-ringing exercise, shared honors with *À La Bien Aimée* as the peak of "high-brow stuff."

A tenor sang—usually this sort of cup-shotten program:

Somewhere in Old Wyoming
Promises
Forgive Me
Until We Meet Again, Sweetheart
So Beats My Heart For You

It is possible, of course, that since the radio has rendered musicianship unnecessary the "artists" were themselves deceived. They may have thought that they were recreating a profusion of masterpieces. Yet I credit most of them with the knowledge that their repertories were depraved and dull. In the dark outside lay some monstrous primitive carnivore, Our Public, slightly confused with the official who signed the checks, ready to crunch the bones of their reputations if they made a single false step. I say they knew better. But had they done better they would have fared worse.

With trio and with vocal soloist gravity was ushered in and

out. The city's merchants would have none of it, and therefore neither would Station XXX. For the rest of the evening there was usually a "drama," in which the villain and the English language were struck down simultaneously. And there was dance music, some of it good, some bad, all of it jazz.

The programs of the contributing orchestras were wonderfully simple in plan: they were practically identical. To assure myself of this fact, I drew up a sort of frequency chart a few months ago. During one week the following musical numbers were played not less than five times a day, not more than eight, at our station:

> The King's Horses
> You're Driving Me Crazy
> Three Little Words
> Fine and Dandy
> Walkin' My Baby Back Home

And they continued to sound as frequently for weeks after. It seems like months.

This is not quite all of the day's labor. We at Station XXX make one truly remarkable effort that is worthy of special notice. On Sunday "Uncle Tim" holds his Kiddie Karnival. Under the yellow shimmer of Uncle's teeth the usual theatrical minors perform for an hour and a half; the usual piercing and uncertain notes are struck, blown, and wrenched from instruments. Through some kind of magic, music which would be atrocious if played by a visible adult becomes charming when played by an invisible child. Verses are recited or audibly forgotten to an accompaniment of toys drawn across the floor of the studio, because confusion and inadequacy are dear to the nursery heart. Uncle Tim reads the comic strips in a suitable treble. He makes kind, avuncular fun of his Kiddies. Merry childish laughter bubbles up continually to the microphone, under the watchful and expert baton of the uncle.

The next day I saw the resulting letters from the adults for whom this infantile circus was operated; not so many letters, of course, as we would have taken in a few years ago, but

still baskets of them. They criticize, suggest, condemn. And
for all their mistakes and their pencil smudges, we give them
consideration, because through them speaks the voice of God—
disguised, naturally, as the potential customer. We listen too
when the divine utterance employs the telephone. Once during
my apprenticeship I informed the microphone that to my way
of thinking a certain notorious mammy-singer was a foul
comedian and small potatoes compared with Groucho Marx.
Within three minutes we had seven telephone calls beginning
thus: "Say! Who does that announcer think he is, anyway!
Callin'——no good! Are you goin' to let him get away with
that sort of stuff?"

So much for the events of the day at our temple of the
muses. I need only say of it that I found room for
thought, those first few weeks at XXX. Undoubtedly we
made money here and were a thriving business. But were we
also good entertainment, high art, higher education? I could
find no justification here for Mr. Cross's lofty attitude. Indeed,
the moments came more frequently when I looked upon the
microphone as a malefic talisman capable of extreme perver-
sion, capable of transforming princesses into scullery maids,
full of pernicious charms and brazen in the use of them.

I examined further into my profession. I went from our
programs to our managers and announcers. Surely, I thought,
if radio is an instrument of enlightenment and the humanities,
I should be able to reveal very special qualifications in its high
priests, altar ministrants, and acolytes.

The president is a shrewd business man whose reading list
is headed by *V. V.'s Eyes,* and who once when I was practicing
Bach—for very private reasons—informed me that he *liked*
Chopin.

Our vice-president is likewise a shrewd man of affairs; and
in addition he has a tact which is lacking in his superior, for
he is content to deal with the finances of the station. Though
he does not acknowledge his ignorance of simple radio technic, of music, and the art of English speech, he at least does not
attempt to interfere with our operations.

Not so the production manager. Shortly after I came here he told me that he too was a "college man"! He toils through the difficulties of our mother tongue like a disabled oyster barge through a heavy sea, and he once referred to that famous English poet, Coolidge. His ignorance of music is exaggerated in its scope; he fails to distinguish between a Strauss waltz and a military march, between a "major" and "minor," a duet and a quartet. But he superintends production, because he has "a good business head" and "knows how to handle men."

In Mr. A., the business manager, we have what is generally called a dynamo: that is to say, his voice is sharp, his movements brisk, his personal appeal to merchants potent, his capacity for error theoretically *nil*. I found that he is the most significant figure in our station, because he is its most adept salesman and because he believes in and enforces his personal tastes. It is admitted that his selling ability is an excellent thing. But his preferences in speech and music, while wonderful, are not excellent. When he corrects good orchestration into bad, good balance into bad, good continuity, voice manner, and pronunciation into bad, I occasionally protest. His answer is, "You're right, but the public don't know what you mean. Maybe 'lingerie' is what *you* call it, but 'lawn-ju-ray' is what the women buy on the counters. So give 'em lawnjuray!"

Through Mr. A., D & T Maiers, Clothing Merchants, buy half an hour on the air and thereafter feel privileged to dictate every detail of their entertainment. If they say that the word is "en-sem-bul," or that such-and-such is too slow or too soft or too dull, then it is all of those things. If they want the six current numbers played—and they always do—then the six are played. If they say that an announcer with a barytone voice must coo in a tenor fashion like the great Joe Blank at Station YYY, then the announcer takes a gargle and coos. Unquestionably the brothers Maiers have sound mercantile instincts, and thanks to them Station XXX is a thriving concern. But I do not find it in the Gospels that a business man is necessarily a compendium of all taste and knowledge.

Next to the Maiers in authority comes the gallery of our

production staff and announcers—men who have been courteous and generous to me, for whose sake I and my station must remain anonymous in this article. We have had various backgrounds: one of us was formerly a real estate agent and longshoreman, another was in the Coast Guard, another a professional baseball player, another an engineer, and so on. That none of them has had a formal education is irrelevant. But that they have not acquired knowledge informally, that they have never undergone the severe testing which develops a sure taste, that they have no reading, no musical appreciation, that they lack the equipment which should figure most importantly in our profession—this is strictly relevant and a little tragic. These men, whether they will it or not, are powerful agents in formulating the taste, speech, and habits of mind among a million people. Mr. Cross wrote that "announcers must be ever alert about their diction, enunciation, inflection of syllables, and, may we say, voice humor." He even added that "there are scholars among us." Therefore I thought it fair to expect an inoffensive use of English and a well-groomed manner, if nothing else, from my fellow barkers. I rarely heard it.

On the other hand, I frequently did hear Uncle Tim, whose type is common in the radio world. Like so many of us announcers, he was once an actor, having spent fifteen years elaborating minor rôles in a Tom-show. The results are astonishing, though not unique. There is a great deal of the zoo in Uncle Tim, a trait which is shared by almost all radio "uncles" and "captains." Before his microphone he is full of a soft, childish laughter, and of charming conceits and fantasies; he plays a great deal, so to speak, with his verbal tail, cracks nuts, eats straw, chatters excitedly, and so on. The tempo of his speaking is afflicted with an extraordinary *rubato,* which may be represented thus in musical terms: *sforzando accelerando—sostenuto—accelerando subito—largo largo.* "Down . . . in the . . . well there was . . . (*very quickly*) the cutest little mou-ou-ou . . . (*pause, then a gasp*) . . . sie and when he was at . . . home he . . . was . . . in-a-we-e-ell."

To a layman this may not immediately suggest the human

voice, but Uncle Tim's manner is popular and leads many merchants to Mr. A's office. The rest of us do not hesitate to imitate him, since we too must sell. We are radio's high-pressure salesmen, and must poke the rabbits down the gullet of that reluctant anaconda, our public. The trouble is that radio's only staple product is amusement, which is not the result of violence.

Last of all I came to those masters of the lean and racy or the fat and colorful prose—the writers of continuity. By the terms under which I drew my very respectable salary I was also of their number. Continuity, I learned, falls into two divisions—"commercial" and "sustaining." The former is high-pressure ad-writing, and the latter is that vivid matter which introduces and interrupts all programs, whose function is gracefully to cushion the radio mind against too abrupt an impact with music, ideas, and oral sounds.

I learned what everyone these days is aware of, that the advertising announcements are viciously long and in consequence are a contributing cause of radio's ill health. For a number of our half-hour sponsored programs I have written scripts eight or ten minutes in length. A certain featured "entertainment" at our studio regularly alternates two minutes of paid speech with two minutes of music.

I further learned that "air-ading" has to be written, not untruthfully of course, but . . . well, forcefully. I can honestly say that in Station XXX I have not invented a single concrete textual lie, having found such technic to be childishly inefficient. In place of the lie we put misrepresentation; with due regard to the penal code we state a low-grade truth, a safe generality. So far, so good. There is something too lamblike, however, in a simple truth. And the dominant flavor of advertising is wolf rather than lamb. So by heaping up illogical inferences, implications, slippery suggestions, and repetition we raise the low-grade truth to a proper selling plane—as necessarily we must if we are to inflate our patrons' desires up to and beyond the size of their pocketbooks before delivering them over to our clients. But unfortunately for me, I have the sort of mind that is unable to see the difference between a trap set for a creature's leg and a trap set for his subconscious self.

Sustaining continuity is another thing again, quite removed from the market place. Here the *littérateur,* the gifted Englisher of thoughts, the maker of dreams and creator of atmosphere—here the verbal genius of the radio hits his stride. And here, I thought, is a line which Messrs. the talented business men will not overstep.

They didn't. But another force did, a special tradition of taste which rules in all broadcasting studios and which in my opinion is on a level with the idealism of the tabloids. Under its tutelage I am forced daily to write English prose that is indescribable. The trick is easy, and I hereby place the secret at the disposal of any continuity writer who may wish to win the backslaps of his manager and the hearty approval of his "radio family." Overstate all emotion, violate all laws of restraint, use the tritest phrases, the most extravagant similes, the most drenching sentimentality. Strain for cheap verbal effects, employ commonplaces once the property of Chautauqua lecturers and politicians. Walk heavily and use a big stick. In short, write as wretchedly as you can. I quote an example:

"When you look into the heart of a great diamond, unearthly glory flickers up into your eyes. But when you read its story, you can see the broad ribbons of blood that flow through its lovely current. When you pronounce the names of the great stones, the air throbs with harmony, and you seem to hear the waves of poetry breaking with a crystal sound over the far shores of romance. But, reading of their adventurous lives, you shudder as you hear the laughter of the demons that watch over these blazing beauties."

One important use of continuity is to interrupt. Never allow your announcer to say: "Next you shall hear . . ." or, "The song that follows now is called . . ." Exaggerate! Force! Be puerile! Give the script a horse-drench of virile showmanship. Like this: "The *baton* of our *chef-d'orchestre* (pronounced in various ways) presents now for your musical consideration. . . ." Or, "With bows for brushes and notes for pigment our instrumentalists paint a picture for you of that old sweetheart of yours, 'Somewhere in Old Wyoming.'"

My proud stomach does not revolt too fiercely when as announcer I salt down the jazz programs with excrescences such as these, for the words and music are mated to each other and to the audience. But I am sickened when I am obliged to ballyhoo Schubert and cheer him on as if he were a famous quarterback doing a broken-field run. I should rather like to hear honest music honestly presented, listen to the play of honest minds, away from this sticky, hypocritical fug of emotion, fellowship, and uplift, barren intellects and conceited ignorance.

I should enjoy telling the people that the six current jazz tunes they are about to hear are poisonous after a week of repetition; that this political speaker has called his audience gullible idiots just five minutes before going on the air; that this continuity which I pronounce should be hissed off as stuff of ill effect; that the prize jars of mayonnaise will *not* go to the writers of the first one hundred letters received at the station but will be scattered about where they will do the most good; that this critic and book reviewer has the literary tastes of an hyena and the critical equipment of a beachcomber and that a chain bookshop is "obliged to him" for puffing its particular list; that the air is full of miasma and dullness and they'd best come out of it.

I imagine that after saying these things I should be short on job but very long on self-respect.

Perhaps conditions at another station would be more tolerable, but I doubt it. I have visited many of them, have met, talked with, and listened to many announcers, attempted to speak with directors of programs and music; I know as dinner companions one or two heads of the business not utterly unimportant. And I venture to say this: that where there is but small flint, tinder, and fuel, one does not look for a bright fire.

Concerning radio at large, my experience and observation has furnished me with three propositions that to me seem almost axiomatic. First, that broadcasting is by its nature inevitably an educational and a cultural agent. Second, that as long as the present staff of men is in and above the studios any educational or cultural shift must be a downward one. Third, that, given the weakness of public protest, radio will not be forced to mend its ways or alter its current methods of milking the public cow.

The very widest possible view of national broadcasting has not led me to abate the edge of these contentions. It is a macrocosm of which Station XXX is an elemental and model part. The analysis which I have tried to make of my own studio may be applied with identical results to the largest one. The national chain announcers share the defects of their lesser-known brothers: instead of displaying whatever small enlightenment is theirs, they exploit their illiteracy over the air. They are quite at home, for instance, with the pronunciation of tongue-twisters and the hard ones out of McGuffey. Dictionary in hand, they can deal with "disestablishmentarianism"; they know their etiquette when faced with peacock brains and beccaficos. But serve beans, and they eat with their knives. Within the past two days I have heard a noted altar ministrant in one of our metropolitan fanes deliver himself of "im*p*otent," "pictewer," "of*t*en"—and, in imitation of an aspiring provincial dowager, "lond," "ond," and "monner." That is not the lack of higher education; it is the complete lack of any education whatsoever.

Happily for their peace of mind, the great announcers are preserved from the thought that they are imperfect. Most of them are too busy aping a crowd of gentlemen talking at ease to speak at all naturally—from Lower-Oxford-on-Upper-Ohio they bring an Oxonian accent that would make Buddha blink. And they are so absorbed in the blossom of their own perfection that they touch things which they should not dare to handle: one of the hearty-bluster school, for example, presumes to broadcast events at a boat race when he cannot rightly distinguish a rowing slide from third base.

As for the continuity that these men read, it would be an unpleasant and useless task to set down examples here. The national chain programs they announce are no better. To be sure, we may hear a few good programs, some of them extraordinarily so, and they hang like rich jewels in an Ethiop's ear. The fact is, I suppose, that while an hour of excellent entertainment justifies itself, it cannot justify a whole week or month of tripe. Pleasure in music is not, like truffles, to be taken at the long end of a pig's nose; nor is an oasis of any real benefit to a man if he dies in the desert trying to reach it.

Conscious that isolated periods of decency do not make amends for insufferably long stretches of maladroit advertising and pseudo-entertainment, the two national chains have during the last six months made strenuous efforts, in the news columns, to improve conditions. Famous concert names and bureaus have been merged with them, and the air was full of promise. But the results have been negligible so far. The genuine artists have disappeared, overwhelmed by the mass of "artistes," or their programs have been shorn of interest by the advertiser. Perhaps something will arise later from this official union of talent with commerce. Meanwhile, in our great depression, the many questionable hours return handsome profits to the stations.

The station managers, of course, defend themselves by saying that they must give each class what it wants. If so, then their position is indeed an unhappy one, for the air policy of Something for Everyone threatens to result in Nothing for Anyone. And so arises an amusing paradox. They are able neither to understand and accomplish the function of leadership nor to dismiss it. Like a man with a live wire in his hand, they can neither use it nor drop it.

Let us be fair. The blame does not rest entirely with the radio executives. Above them are the advertisers, grimly determined that the people *shall* desire, *shall* buy. In order to impose their will they threaten the air men with no physical violence; they merely flourish a check—and the air with its public attached is sold to them. The advertiser has bought an hour on the air as he would buy a pound of cabbage. He owns it. And what he says goes! Add public apathy, and the list of evils is complete. The abuses are almost traditional by now, and under their influence radio, like Disraeli's statesman, having been for seven years a bore, is now become an institution. It may be that, in spite of the honest effort being made in certain quarters, its further course must remain unaltered.

Yet I have imagined an ideal broadcasting station. Its owner (myself) will be a man who does not have to make money every hour of the day. Its announcing and production staff will be men of education who will have undergone special training in the arts of speech, music, and restraint. Its continuity writers will be few, their output limited, and the quality of it inconspicuously good. Its advertisers will have the power of suggestion but must leave the command to those who know more about the business in hand than they do. There will be no hypocritical pretense to public service; the programs will make no attempt to present something for everyone—they will be aimed frankly at and above a presumptive upper-middle class; they will accept Broadway standards only in comedy and dance music.

If the quality of these programs cannot be maintained eighteen hours a day, then the station will be on the air for half that period. If under these conditions the station cannot be successfully operated, it will be closed. The public and the advertiser will find the tabloids and the billboards sufficient to their cultural and commercial needs.

Football Myths

By HERBERT REED

Herbert Reed used to write under the pseudonym, Right Wing, for THE NEW YORK EVENING POST. *His book,* FOOTBALL FOR PUBLIC AND PLAYER *(1913), shows his remarkable grasp and understanding of the game.*

D OWN on the floor of the Yale Bowl one of these crisp November Saturday afternoons; on the clipped surface of the beautiful field enfolded by the Palmer Stadium at Princeton; in the Harvard Stadium just outside Cambridge; and elsewhere in unnumbered enclosures, twenty-two young men will fight out a mimic warfare the most enthralling to be produced in any nation.

High up behind where we are sitting with rugs about our knees as the sun sinks and the shadows fall from bleak West Rock, or perhaps across the plain at Champaign, the chirping instruments of the telegraphers, the "bugs" as the operators call them, will carry the news of victory or defeat to a thousand newspapers. And the chances are that the summarized story as it travels over the wires or through the air from the microphone will begin somewhat in this fashion: "Yale's high-powered machine swept roughshod over So-and-So this afternoon, swinging into action the famous Rockne system as transplanted from South Bend by Adam Walsh, one of the famous coach's ablest pupils."

There will be new heroes to write about, to be sure, but the high-salaried coach, and above all the "Machine" will be the burden of this song of Big Business in football, this ballyhoo of the "miracle coach." However, it so happens that without a

From *Scribner's Magazine,* November, 1932; copyright 1932, by Charles Scribner's Sons. Reprinted by permission of the author and *Scribner's Magazine.*

flock of football players the miracle coaching is not forthcoming, the best system in the world does not function. There are no Robots in modern football. Indeed, there seldom were. In the rare cases where they still persist their records are not impressive. When the "miracle coach" wins, it is the System that does it—when he loses, individual players are to blame. However, systems have their merits if sufficiently elastic, while machines have none.

At the present time there are two great systems spread over the face of the land, the Rockne and the Warner. At first glance they are machine systems, simply because they show the effects of patient and persistent drill, and the institution that has not the time for that drill had better let them alone. But away down at the bottom they rest on the possibilities of individual brilliance of a higher order than anything even the Golden Nineties had to offer.

Just the other day I stood on the field at practice with a couple of the best coaches in the country, who have not, however, combined journalism or recommending hair-slickers or spats with their coaching.

"What I need right now," said the football chief in question, "is a good dog-house runner and a couple of tackles. With as many replacements as possible. You know, outside the passing, this game is played down in the dirt. That's where we've got to go if we want to win. And on top of that, I'm still looking for the divine spark." Not a word about the system.

Such a thing as a football machine appears only on paper and never on the field. In every planned play, even the much-vaunted "perfect play" staged now and then for a touchdown by the products of the late Knute K. Rockne's coaching system, there are developments that appear only as the play gains momentum, which affect its apparent precision, the precision that gives birth to the machine idea, and eventually results in its success or failure. An excellent example of this, the maneuver that gave rise to the expression "the perfect play" in the first place, was the 65-yard run for a touchdown by Chris Flanagan of Notre Dame against the Army at the Yankee Stadium four years ago. The element that made this play successful was the fact that the Army left tackle was two feet out of his prescribed position. Had he been on correct post the play perhaps would not have been called, or at least would not have resulted in a touchdown, and therefore would not have achieved perfection. Plenty of kudos goes to the quarterback who called the play instantly, having seen the flaw in the opposing defense. Thus, not any machine but that rugged individualist, the quarterback, really was responsible for the touchdown and consequent victory.

In seeking to destroy this machine myth I go farther and state that there *never was* a football machine in the whole history of the game. Not even Fielding Yost's famous "point-a-minute" machine of the Nineties, which in the end was totally dependent upon the fact that a young man named Heston was the fastest man for fifteen yards in football clothes who ever stood upon a gridiron; not even the great Haughton Harvard teams in which precision was so beautifully developed after the famous coach had attended a Plattsburg training camp where he was initiated into the mysteries of squads right (the peculiar path of No. 3 in the rear rank being the path of a Harvard halfback today in one of the Crimson's best ground-gainers). It was under Haughton, too, that both signals and plays moved to a perfect rhythm, set in practice by the tick-tock of the metronome. Yet not even in the earliest days of Haughton were his great winning teams machines.

It is probable that most Harvard and Yale men, and a large section of the football public in general, remember the return of Haughton to coaching at Harvard, when his machine beat Yale by a field goal kicked by a slender chap named Victor Kennard. On occasional Saturdays it is my pleasure to sit at a certain field very close to the famous Vic Kennard, renowned spare part of the Haughton machine. Victor's job these days is scouting. Like Jimmy Knox, the daddy of all football scouts, he watches annually just one team for the Crimson, duly charting everything that team has shown in public for the benefit of Eddie Casey, present Crimson head coach, and his aides.

Referring to the incident that made him famous, Kennard says, "There certainly were things going on that season that Percy knew nothing about." Kennard had been told that he was expected to win the Yale game by a dropkick, which would be his only function, and that he would be called in cold to do it. To the icy-mannered Haughton Victor was just exactly a spare part in his football machine, which he had geared to go deep into Yale territory but feared could not cross the goal line. First the worry over the proposed task began to cost Kennard weight, and pretty soon not a little sleep. As the game drew near he endured the agony of nightmares in which he saw himself called in and failing dismally at his appointed stunt. Of all this acute suffering Haughton knew nothing until long afterward. But Nourse, the Harvard center, who was to pass the ball for the crucial kick, began to study the slender kicker, and at last Kennard unburdened himself. So between them they hatched a plot. Nourse told the other players that when Kennard was called in they were to be near their places, but not set, some of them standing upright, but all making sure to be on side. Nourse would crouch at once and shoot back the ball. And so it happened. The Yale players were caught flat-footed, not one of them set for the charge, and so hopeless was the chance of blocking the kick, that both teams stood upright and watched the ball sail over the bar and between the posts. In the course of the play only two men on the field were in action. So victory went to Haughton's machine through the individualism of two men.

It is true that the great backfield of Logan, Bradlee, Brickley, and Mahan, with Tack Hardwick blocking out tackles and backs on a system of his own invention which no coach ever taught him, followed as closely as possible the lines of the chart when they went through their running plays. But a greater group of individualists never stood upon a field.

The other great so-called machine backfield, the Four Horsemen of Notre Dame, Stuhldreher, Layden, Miller, and Crowley, had its periods of running as wild as so many hawks, out of sheer exuberance and native ability, and, although the regular signal was called when Frank Carideo ran a later Notre Dame championship team, he and Joe Savoldi cooked up the plays in which this great plunging back starred, by thrashing out the idea right on the field in choice Italian. It took a linguist to play defense against that team. Reverting for a moment to the Four Horsemen, Rockne told me one fatal day at Princeton—fatal, that is, for Princeton—"They're out there pulling stuff I never saw before, and stuff that I certainly never taught them."

The best example of this through all the football ages, perhaps, was George Smythe of West Point, who should be dubbed "Fore and Aft" Smythe. As everybody knows, it is a football crime to run back. The exception lies in getting away with it. The times Smythe ran forward it was a parade of demoralization for the opposing team. The times he ran back were nerve-wrackers for his followers. Yet nearly all his forward progress was made after he had run back, and laterally, in both directions. Talking not long ago with Eddie Garbisch, center on that team, this All-America personage said: "You ask where I went on Smythe's runs? Straight up the field about thirty yards where I could get into touch with the deep defense man. And as I did so I said a prayer. That prayer was for a touchdown, because with Smythe lugging the ball, it was likely to be either a touchdown or a safety against us, with George tackled behind his own goal line. As soon as I heard drumming feet behind me I knocked over the defense man and we scored. But I've had many a long walk back."

Captain John McEwan, head coach, it was, who had this human top on his hands. At that time the late Colonel Herman J. Koehler, Master of the Sword, was a power at West Point. On the eve of the Navy game that year he told me in all solemnity, "I'm going to be on the side line tomorrow, with a service revolver, and if Smythe starts to run back I'll shoot him right there on the field, so help me." Sounds crazy? Well, only those who have been close to them know how steamed up these old-timers can get on the edge of a big game. When he said it, Koehler meant it. As it turned out, this same Smythe, with the score against him in the last minute of the Navy game, ran back, and sideways, then back, then forward, then sideways, and finally threw a forward pass for a touchdown and victory. He was just as crazy as Koehler.

I ran into McEwan that night. He pointed to a stack of books on the table. "Freud," he said, and grinned wearily. "No use. I tried it out on Smythe. And now *I'm* nutty. I guess when you have a libido like that there's nothing to be done."

Just to complete the record, I had a little talk with Smythe. "You see," said George, speaking of his convoluted running, "I guess I'm just that way." And it is of men who are "that way" or some other way, equally strange, that the heroes of the gridiron are made, and no machine has ever been devised to take their place.

There haven't been many teams that even looked like machines down Princeton way. The nearest were the great elevens of '89, Edgar Allan Poe's mighty outfit, Doggy Trenchard's '93 team, which sprung the novelty of holding the Yale line men up on their feet while they whirled them down the field, and the famous eleven of 1896, which beat Yale 24 to 6. Perhaps the 1903 team showed signs of machinery to the unpracticed eye. But this eleven was built around John DeWitt, a domineering, at times almost savage personality, unpopular on the campus, but a born leader of the driving type, and one of the greatest football players who ever went to Princeton. DeWitt is one of the truly great who have passed on to the Football Valhalla, along with Alex Moffatt, the individualist who in one of his big games kicked four field goals, *on the run,* two with his right foot and two with his left. Hardly a product of the football lathe.

There is no doubt that Bob Zuppke was a little put out all the time Red Grange was becoming famous. It is true that Zuppke taught Red a great many useful things, and it is also true that he developed Britton and McIlwaine as interferers to clear a path for Grange, but the fact remains that Grange was one of the greatest "shadow" runners who ever played the game. He had one thing I have known no other player to have in equal measure, and that was the photographic eye. That was as much a secret of his success as his foot and hip work. When Grange took the ball there flashed on his retina a picture of the position of every man on the field. Instantly he figured where each man would be at every stage of his run, and charted his course accordingly. No coach can teach that. Somewhat disgusted with the "Grange and me" complex, the lively little coach took his team to Philadelphia (how he loves to beat an Eastern eleven!) and told Grange: "All right, today you're quarterback. I've got a team out there that is all yours. Go out and run it to suit yourself. It's your game." And it was. Grange had never had the generalship responsibility on his shoulders before. Zuppke had put it up to his star and the star came through. After Red's departure, Zuppke said, "Now I got a team without a hundred-thousand-dollar star on it. I got a team without any star." And he had. Not even the great Zuppke can get along without them, painful as it may be to admit it.

And now there is that other myth, that there is such a person as a super-player, the greatest of all time. More and more good white paper has been spoiled in picking teams made up of such players, a dangerous pastime, with the psychopathic ward at the other end.

Even today, ad nauseam, we read of the exploits of the great Jim Thorpe, the Sac and Fox Indian of Pop Warner's days at Carlisle. His greatest fame was made by those who never saw him play. For many years now, Pop Warner has been bleating futilely to the world that Thorpe was not even the greatest player he ever coached. The bleating, of course, has not been very loud, for if one mentions Thorpe one has to mention Warner, and since Pop has become a widely ballyhooed author (he is really one of the greatest of all the coaches) publicity fits him like an old coat.

Jim Thorpe was a great football player. But he has been badly overdone. He made perhaps his greatest reputation running rings around a pair of stationary ends at West Point. (They have changed the system of end play at West Point since then.)

And he passed his way all over a certain Pennsylvania team to the tune of 28 to 0. Digging over my notes of the Carlisle-Princeton game the following week at the Polo Grounds, I find that Thorpe was stopped in his tracks all afternoon, and Princeton won by the score of 16 to 0. A curly-headed Tiger end named Brown, suffering from a lame and strapped-up shoulder, spent most of the playing period throwing Jim Thorpe for many and serious losses. The rest of the time, when Princeton wasn't running with the ball, Eddie Harlan spent in kicking it at the feet of the Indian backs, which early exhibition of good judgment may have had something to do with his turning up in later years as Judge Harlan. This is nothing against Thorpe. He was just one more Napoleon indulging in a Waterloo. In fact, Princeton always made powerful bad medicine against Carlisle, and in all their six meetings was the victor.

So, if any reader wishes to spend a pleasant afternoon with Pop Warner, especially duck-hunting, I advise him to leave Princeton out of the conversation.

As for bad afternoons for stars on the football field, Ted Coy of Yale came away pretty nearly as scot free as anybody, although I remember only one game in which Ned Mahan, the great Harvard star, was thoroughly shut down. To this day Ned refers to it as the "nightmare game." And yet it was not entirely Ned's fault. The Crimson wonder ran into a Cornell eleven in 1910, coached by Doctor A. H. Sharpe, that was all set for him, especially on the ends. Up to that time he had been running against waiting, or at the best, hesitant, ends. This time he found in Shelton and Eckley, the Cornell wing men, a pair that had been coached to go right to him. The game wasn't five minutes old when the pressure these men put on caused him to fumble. Cornell recovered the ball and went over for a touchdown. In further defense of Mahan I must say that he was also the victim of strangely poor scouting—for Harvard. The Crimson was on the crest of the wave at that time, sang about the "bloody crossbar," and was in general very "snooty" as too habitually victorious systems are wont to be. So Reggie Brown went over to Ithaca, took a casual glance at the Cornell tackle play with Charlie Barrett carrying the ball, and opined that it could be stopped easily enough by dropping back the tackles. As it turned out, once these tackles were dropped back, they found it impossible to get up. Also, Mahan was told nothing about Ray Van Orman's system of end coaching. The first few shocks upset him, and a great player was stopped for the day.

Last season Albie Booth, Marchmont Schwartz, Barry Wood, and others had their bad days, and Shaver of Southern California and Stecker of the Army came with a rush. Yet the former were none the less wonderful performers on their season's record.

Joe Beacham, now a Colonel in the Army and through with football, used to say, when any one mentioned a football machine: "Oh yes ["yeah" was not at that time current], suppose we throw some monkey wrenches into the machinery? I'll take my chance with football players and a prayer."

Little by little the football public is being educated up to an appreciation of the work of the players in the line, and they have opportunities today seldom afforded the old-timers, with such rare exceptions as Heffelfinger of Yale, and Rinehart of Lafayette; of Hare of Pennsylvania, and Metzger, the "watch-spring guard," of Notre Dame. It is hard for the spectator to learn to take his eye off the ball long enough to appreciate the work of such men, but if he will do so he will be rewarded with exhibitions of superlative individual effort quite as scintillating as any put on by the ball carrier. For the time being a good offensive or defensive guard has to rely for his publicity on the loudspeaker of the announcer and such idiosyncrasies of personality in action, figure or costume, that may catch the eye. A bare-headed guard, for instance, like Jack Cannon of Notre Dame, is sure to appeal to the spectators, granted, as was the case with Cannon, that he is playing some of the finest football of the year. Evans, of West Point, a great kingpin of defense, stormed the attention of the spectators by the simple expedient of rolling up his sleeves. The rolled-up sleeves were taken as evidence of pugnacity, and so the onlooker began to watch him. Soon they found him hurling the interference back in the face of the Notre Dame quarterback, and his reputation was made. "Watch-spring" Metzger, two years ago, led the interference for many of Notre Dame's best sweep runs, and he was the observed of all observers because of his small size for a player in that post, weighing as he did, 153 pounds.

The tackle has greater range, often making some of the best of his plays well out on the flank. He is much easier to follow. The end, of course, is as much in the public eye as the backs, and needs no artificial helps to fame. Although, if we are to hearken to young Mr. Collins, of Notre Dame, a fine end and now a coach, much of the finesse of offensive end play is often lost to the crowd. "You see," says Collins, "a good offensive end ought to make faces at the defense, and thus cover his intentions when he charges." Any good coach will admit that a first-rate back ought to be something of an actor, and it was only a few years ago that a great Dartmouth team was piloted to thorough satisfaction by the president and leading man of the Dartmouth Dramatic Club. I doubt if acting or making faces could be taught in a thorough machine manner, even by a Gil Dobie, who today is about the last of the Old Guard machine-minded coaches. But there are times when even Dobie's machine gets away from him, and he is also ready enough in the event of a smashing defeat to put the blame on individuals. "What can you expect from a lot of students?" queries Gloomy Gil.

"We are dependent, of course," an old-time coach told me one day, "on these individual upsurges. But they are to be ranked with Napoleon's 'imponderables'—you can't tell just when they are going to materialize."

In the last analysis it is pretty safe, I think, to agree with Bob Zuppke, when he says the best touchdown producer is desire. And that is hardly a product of machinery. "I don't know," says Zuppke, "who this Sui Generis is you fellows are talking about, but he sounds to me like a good Swedish halfback. Tell him I need him." They all need him. Fortunately for coaching reputations there are quite a few of him.

The Babe

By PAUL GALLICO

Paul Gallico is sports editor of the DAILY NEWS *(New York) and contributes regularly for the "Sports and Games" section of* VANITY FAIR.

THERE is, in all Christendom, no other figure quite like the great, ugly baseball player, christened George Herman Erhardt, who is now known as Babe Ruth; and there is no other nation on the face of the globe better fitted to harbor him, cultivate him, and for that matter, actually bring him into being, than these goofy United States of America.

In France they might call him something like *Le Gros Bébé*—but, then, he never could exist in France, because the Gallic temperament is not suited to baseball. The Frenchman could never stomach a close decision around second or home plate without beating someone over the head with a gold headed cane.   In Germany, he would be known as *Der Starke Ruth,* and his tremendous and overweening personality would be resented or misunderstood. In England, where nobody would ever call anybody Babe, he would probably be known unhumorously as Georgie Ruth.

The rise, the existence, the *being* of Ruth is purely an American phenomenon, like those other phenomena—crooners, Andy Volstead, the Valentino funeral, million dollar prize-fight purses, skyscrapers, peanuts, chewing gum, and the freedom of the press. Ruth's nickname, "Babe," is so much a part of our national consciousness that the strange message spelled out in letters six inches high across the top of any afternoon paper, "Babe Conks No. 36" or "Bam Busts Two," is not, as an Eng-

From *Vanity Fair*, May, 1932. Reprinted by permission of the author and *Vanity Fair*.

lish or French cryptologist might imagine, a code for "Come home, all is forgiven," but a very simple presentation of the news that Ruth has hit his 36th home run, and that he has made two homers in one game.

Americans called him Babe because he looks like anything else but and the sports writers re-nicknamed him the Bambino—also for no good reason, as there is no Italian in him—and then characteristically they shortened it to Bam.

The Sultan of Swat, the Colossus of Clout, the Behemoth of Bust, the Bambino and the Slambino, all mean one and the same person, Ruth, a ball player owned by the New York Yankees, whose extraordinary co-ordination of eye, brain, and muscle, coupled with an enormous frame and the most powerful wrists in the game, enable him to hit more home runs than any other man in the world. . . .

Ruth is an American Porthos, a swashbuckler built on gigantic and heroic lines, a great athlete, a Golem-like monster, a huge, vital, vulgar fellow in whose bosom surge all the well-known elementary emotions and whose tear ducts lie close to the surface. He lives—ye gods, how he lives!—wholeheartedly, with complete gusto. He is one of the most completely alive men I have ever known. He loves to eat, to sleep, to royster and horseplay, to drink beer and play cards with companions, to play ball, to play golf, to swear and shout and laugh. Everything about him is big—his frame, his enormous head surmounted by blue-black curly hair, his great blob of a nose spattered generously over his face, his mouth and his hands—only his ankles are strangely slim like a woman's.

He talks in loud tones, he laughs uproariously, his voice is a basso-profundo and rumbles forth from the caverns of his chest like Kilauea. His greeting to all is "Hello kid," and his conversation is ripe, rich, and bar-roomy. He talks like a sailor whose every third word is an oath and to whom oaths are so completely idioms of conversations that they are no longer oaths.

Ruth is a beloved figure and the greatest single attraction in the entire world of sport. Dempsey simply isn't in it with him, a statement that will disturb the cult of Dempsey worshipers no end, but the fact is too patent to call for proof. In one baseball season, Ruth draws more people through the turnstiles of the ball-parks than Dempsey has drawn in his lifetime. The Yankees play steadily to fifteen and twenty thousand patrons a day during the week, and over Saturday and Sunday, against opponents high in the League standing, to crowds of sixty and seventy thousand. When Ruth is removed from the line-up for one reason or other, the crowds are cut in half.

The Babe is the only man I have ever known as spectacular in failure as he is in success. His home run is a magnificent thing, a poem of rhythm and timing. The bat meets the ball with a distinctive and peculiar sound all of its own—veterans will say "There she goes," just from the sound, and the ball, a diminishing speck, soars from the inclosures over the top tier of the farthest stands. A strike-out is just as impressive. Ruth is not constituted to do anything unimpressively. When he misses the ball, the force of his swing whirls him around until his legs are twisted like a German pretzel. Sometimes he swings himself clear off his feet. Every miss is its own guarantee of honest effort.

Nobody ever strikes the Babe out with his bat on his shoulder. He takes three healthies at the ball, *andante furioso,* each one more vicious and murderous than the last. Each miss draws a delighted roar from the crowd, or rather a grand and public shudder at the might of this man, and a sigh for what would have happened if he had connected.

The effect of a home run upon an immediate cross section of any part of the audience is curious and inexplicable. The ball has fled the park. The Babe trots around the base paths with his arms close to his sides, taking little mincing steps on his small feet, and occasionally tipping the peak of his cap to acknowledge the roar of approbation and the patter of applauding hands. Look at your nearest neighbor. You find him acting in a manner that under any other circumstances would call for a spell at Bellevue under close observation. He is grinning from ear to ear, shaking his head from side to side, making strange noises, and thumping the nearest person to him on the back. He is acting like a man who has just been told by the nurse that it's a boy. He looks into his neighbor's face to make sure that there is equal appreciation registered thereon. He lights a fresh cigar and settles back in utter contentment.

There are some men to whom has been given the faculty of living all of their lives in newsprint. They have a natural attraction for headlines. These are very apt to become our heroes. Sometimes, like Lindbergh or Tunney they object to the hot spotlight we turn upon them night and day, upon their private lives, their ills, their triumphs, their personal and domestic problems, an illumination which does not even spare the obstetrical chamber. Then we are liable to be impatient with a modesty which we feel is obtuse and selfish, and which denies satisfaction to our besetting sin—curiosity—not minding our own business.

There has never been any complaint about Ruth's modesty. The only walls he has ever known have been the parallel columns of the newspapers. Even his sins are public and certainly his expiations have been notably so. In 1925 at Asheville, North Carolina, he fell victim to the gluttony that has beset him for years—the gluttony one is liable to find in a poor boy who has never had enough good things to eat and suddenly finds himself with money to eat all he wants. Now gluttony with Ruth is not your stuffy napkin-in-collar, bring-me-a-steak-smothered-in-pork-chops kind. The beginning of the tummyache that was felt around the world was engendered by a wayside collation consisting of nine or ten greasy railroad-station frankfurters mounted on papier-mâché rolls, and washed down with some eight bottles of green, red, and yellow soda pop. Anyway, they shipped him up North on a stretcher, and the whole nation trembled with every turn of the wheels that brought him home. He was tucked into a cot in St. Vincent's Hospital, in grave danger of relinquishing his hold upon his great, mortal body, and hung between life and death for many days—on Page One. Bulletins were issued from the sickroom. Little boys brought nosegays, or congregated outside the high walls of the hospital, and looked up at the window of the room wherein lay the stricken hero. The presses lay in wait with pages of obituaries, and editorials announced the impending catastrophe as a national calamity. Even in England, the penny papers watched at his bedside. That IS fame. He recovered, he convalesced, and the nation sent a great sigh of honest relief up into the ether.

Back in 1922 Babe had a bad year. He was untractable, he drank, he fought with Judge Landis, the high priest of baseball, he abused umpires, he committed the gravest sin in baseball, that of chasing a fan up the stands. Also, he played poor baseball, although he had just signed a contract for five years at $52,000 a year, the largest salary ever paid a player up to that time.

At the annual dinner of the Baseball Writers Association, Ruth met Senator Jimmy Walker. The Senator was a baseball lover and an admirer of the Babe. He told Ruth that he owed it to the boys of the nation to behave himself. Later when Ruth was called upon to speak, he arose, gulped, and then with tears rolling down his enormous face he solemnly promised the kids of America that he would reform. He swore off drinking (in large quantities). He reformed.

The scene, the speech, the promise, the great reformation rang through the headlines. Here was a great and touching thing, usually seen only in the privacy of the parlor, where the prodigal son breaks down and promises that he will sin no more. Ruth became everybody's son. Everybody forgave him. Everybody went out to the ball yard the following year to see how his repentant prodigal was making out. He made out very nicely, hammering out 41 home runs, increasing to 46 the following year, then dropping to 25, due to his shortened playing year (the Great Tummyache), and then increasing his output again until in 1927 he had amassed the amazing total of 60.

The man is a hero out of Horatio Alger or Burt L. Standish. He rose from Rags to Riches, Sink or Swim, Do or Die. He is the prototype of every hackneyed hero of juvenile (and adult) dollar literature come to life. The Alger books used to tell us that a poor boy could eventually triumph over temptation and adversity and acquire wealth and position, but nobody ever knew of anyone who really did.

Ruth came from the slums of Baltimore. He was an orphan. He went to a reform school. At St. Mary's Industrial School in Baltimore, he played baseball. He was a natural athlete. At the age of 20, Jack Dunn, the owner of the famous Baltimore Orioles, took him out of the school on the tip of one of the brothers. Dunn sold Ruth to the Boston Red Sox where his rise to fame was almost instantaneous, curiously enough, as a pitcher and not as a great slugger and outfielder.

Thereafter he began to amass folder after folder of news clippings, and photographs, the surest gauge of success. There are fourteen envelopes stuffed with clippings, and seven folders of pictures, seventeen inches deep in The New York *Daily News* Morgue alone. Run through these clippings and you will find no single item of his life omitted, no matter how trivial, from the appearance of a boil on his neck to the mystery that enshrouded the birth of his daughter by his first wife. (He claimed the child was born in February, whereas his wife declared it had happened in June.) Everything is there, his contract squabbles with his owner, his trials with speed cops and the demon rum, his every physical ailment from chipped ankles to flu, pneumonia, and tonsil snatching. You find him in the movies, on the stage, engaged in fights on the ball field, suspended by his manager, barnstorming against Landis's orders and suffering punishment therefor. You witness his grief at the grave of his first wife, his courtship, and his marriage of his second, his yearly struggle with avoirdupois, his casual winter golf games, his lawsuits, his sentimental journeys to the bedsides of sick youngsters.

The Babe has become a member of every family in the country that cares anything about Sport, and a great many that don't. No one goes to see him play ball impersonally. No one can look impersonally upon a public figure about which so much is known. British athletes are presented in the glossy print weeklies wearing blazers and smoking pipes, and that is that. The Frenchman makes a fuss over his athletic hero while he is on the scene, but promptly forgets him between games or matches. The Germans react coldly towards their own world's heavyweight prizefight champion, Schmeling. A professional athlete relegating political and national news to page two in Europe is simply unthinkable. But snoopiness is a national disease with us. We are a nation of gossips and Walter Winchell is our prophet. Snoopiness, our unceasing thirst for information about people in the public eye, and the activity of our press in supplying this information have built up an orphan boy and a reform school graduate to a high estate where he receives as large a salary as the President of the United States, and far more sustained publicity. It could only occur, we are told, in a democracy, hence we are a democratic nation. It is about the only remaining proof left to us.

A Herring for My Uncle

By ALBERT HALPER

Albert Halper was born in Chicago in 1904. He now lives in New York. His first novel, UNION SQUARE, *appeared February 15, 1933.*

M Y FATHER came from a family of many sons, but only two of them reached America. Of the others, one took root in faraway New Zealand, another was swallowed up in British South Africa, and two or three more settled down somewhere in Northern and Western Europe. There were sisters, too, but my father lost track of them.

Twenty-two years ago, when I was a very small boy, a letter was forwarded from the Census Bureau at Washington to our home, and when my father opened it, he found it came from his brother Herman, whom he had not seen since they had separated as young men in Europe. The letter came all the way from Wellington, New Zealand, to Chicago, and I remember the excitement it caused in the flat. We looked at the post-mark and saw it had taken six weeks to make the trip.

Uncle Herman wrote that he had arrived in New Zealand a long time ago, after wandering about for a while in Eastern Europe. He said he had married early and now had a large family, mostly girls. He was in the butcher business and was doing fairly well.

He wrote in a large, strong hand and he must have used a pen with a stub point, for the lettering was firm and flowing and fairly marched across the page. All of us crowded around; I jumped up on my oldest brother's back to get a peep at the postage stamps, and the letter was read over many times.

From *The American Mercury,* November, 1932. Reprinted by permission of the author and *The American Mercury.*

Then something fell out of the envelope, and when we picked it up we found it was Uncle Herman's photograph—a small picture about the size of a post-card, showing his head and shoulders. My father stood looking at the photograph for a long time, then passed it quietly among us. We saw the likeness of a man of fifty, a wide-shouldered fellow with a big, square head, iron gray hair, and a heavy mustache. He was a fine looking man, he looked straight at us from the photograph.

"That's Herman," said my father, and took the photograph in his hands again and stared and stared at it. After a while, because he knew all of us were watching, he turned around sharply, blew his nose violently and wanted to know why we weren't eating our supper.

Just before we went to bed, when my father returned from the store, he took the letter out once more and sat in the old rocker in the front room. He was a man who rarely showed his feelings (I speak of his younger days), but the arrival of this letter broke down all his barriers. I slept in a big, hard bed between my youngest and an older brother, and as I lay I could see, by lifting the upper part of my body, that my father was still sitting in the chair; he was rocking gently, holding the post-card in his hands and staring at the picture. The gaslight in the front room flared, making a hissing sound, and my father had to frown a bit because his eyes were just beginning to go back on him.

The next day, after the first excitement died down, my oldest brother was told to take out pen and paper and answer Uncle Herman. My oldest brother, about seventeen then, had just finished an evening course at a business college, and he sat down and wrote a letter to our relatives far away in New Zealand.

At first, my father told him what to write, but after a while he found himself dictating the same words over and over, so at last my oldest brother tore the sheet up and started on another. We sat around in a circle quietly until the letter was finished; then my brother read it over, we all listened, and my father insisted on putting ten cents in stamps on it, so it would be sure to reach New Zealand.

The next day I heard my mother talking to my father. "Why don't you tell Gustav?" she asked. "You haven't seen him for a long time now."

My father started; he had forgotten all about telling his older brother about it, the other one who had also come to America.

So my mother stood in the store while my father got ready to call upon his brother. At the last minute he took me along; I had been wearing a hand-me-down from my bigger brothers, and my trousers were patched on the seat and at the knees. I was about five years old and was very small for my age then, and my pants were always dragging around my ankles. My older brothers once made up a little rime about my sloppy appearance, but this has nothing to do with the story.

"All right," said my father, looking at my mother's pleading eyes. "I'll get him a suit, but even an iron one won't last on him."

So I followed him out of the store, keeping a pace behind. We rode the Lake street trolley to Halsted and transferred south to Maxwell street. The big outdoor market was there and for two dollars my father picked out a suit for me. A tall, skinny merchant argued hotly for a long time and finally, placing the garment against my body to show what a perfect fit it was, he at last convinced my father, who handed over the money.

Then we walked off and I had a hard time carrying the package, because the string was thin and cut into my fingers. I kept thinking of the nickel-plated buttons on the new jacket and made up my mind to spit on them, and then rub, thus working up a better shine.

When we came to a busy crossing I reached up and took my father's hand. Car tracks cut across in all directions, the iron rims of wagon wheels struck the cobbles with a jarring bang. Running southwest was a crowded diagonal street, one of the old Indian trails, which I learned later was Blue Island avenue. But though the streets were heavy with traffic, the neighborhood had a dead and desolate appearance. There were plenty of buildings about—it was an old settlement—but many stores were empty and there were old chalk marks on the filmy windows.

At the corner we went into a fish-store where my father bought a herring, and when we came out he handed it to me. Now both hands were full and I didn't know what to do. The string cut into one palm while I felt the juice from the herring soaking through the newspaper into the other. Beside this, my nose had just started running. I kept walking fast, my pants dragging, and tried to keep up with my father.

My Uncle Gustav, every time I saw him after that, was fond of telling me how I looked when I came up with the new suit and the herring.

In the middle of the next block we approached a small cigar factory. I stopped to watch two Cuban men rolling tobacco in the front window, but was called away.

"Downstairs," said my father, and we went down a flight of old wooden steps.

At the bottom, inside, hung long rows of tobacco leaves. There was a small gaslight burning because of the darkness, and the cellar had a damp and musty smell. From a table in a corner some one stood up and smiled our way. It was Uncle Gustav. I put down the package and the herring and wiped my juicy palm against my trousers.

"Shake hands with Uncle Gustav," my father said and I stuck my dampish hand out.

I was glad to see my uncle, but I turned my eyes aside. He held my hand for a long time and when I looked up I saw him smiling at my father. His palm was soft and had a gentle sort of pressure to it. Then he smelt the herring and chuckled softly; he knew my father had brought it especially for him.

"You carried it?" he asked.

I rubbed my palm against my pants and nodded.

"Ech, ech," he said and opened up the package.

Uncle Gustav was my favorite relative. He was smaller than

254

my father and did not have my father's broad and robust build, and many times I heard my parents talking together, saying that Uncle Gustav was a very sickly man. He had a short, brown beard and always wore a low, black hat, and now when I recall him I think of a little Jewish rabbi going meekly through a field.

We all sat down at the small tobacco table and Uncle Gustav cut the herring equally into three parts. He watched me with a smile as I tore into it with my fingers and when I turned to look at him I saw him nibbling gently like a rabbit.

My father cleared his throat, felt his inner pocket, but did not come directly to the matter. He asked his brother how he felt, if he was making more by working piece-work, and when Uncle Gustav started coughing my father looked the other way. He was younger than Uncle Gustav, but because he owned a little grocery and was a healthy fellow he treated Gustav like a younger brother.

"And how is Selma?" asked my father. "Does she still plague you, does she still think I'm hoarding all your savings?"

My uncle began coughing again, placed his handkerchief to his lips and slowly shook his head. Then he turned to me and his little, mild, brown eyes began twinkling. For the hundredth time he asked me how old I was, what I wanted to be when I grew up, and he also inquired if I still ran after laundry-wagons. Every time I saw him he asked the same questions, yet they did not bore or grate upon me.

My father cleared his throat again, and frowned. "Herman—I've got a letter from Herman."

Uncle Gustav gave a queer gurgle and for a while could not talk; he began coughing, clutched at his mouth, and finally fought the fit down. Looking important, sitting strong and stocky on a packing case, my father brought out the letter, showed the photograph, and told his brother all about it. While they talked I wandered around the basement, poking into dark places. I heard the talking and saw that Uncle Gustav was excited and liked the way he sat there meekly near the gaslight. He called to me and began telling me about his brother Herman, how Herman was a devil of a fellow but not so bad at that.

Before we left he pressed a coin into my hand, when my father wasn't watching, and gave my head a pat. He stood there smiling at the bottom of the stairs as we climbed up into the light and for some reason or other I had the feeling that he was crying; he crinkled up his eyes so strangely.

We rode back to the store in silence. Every time my father saw his brother he would feel sad for days afterward. He used to tell my mother that Gustav was the best of all his brothers and yet was weak and ailing and married to a witch.

Later on, when I grew older, I learned my uncle's story.

In Europe Gustav was a student, the scholar of the family. When the break-up came he remained home alone while all the others went their ways. My father went to England and struggled on in London for three years, and because he was having a hard time of it wrote to Gustav to stay at home and finish up his studies.

Then my father came to America, lived in a few cities, tried his hand at several jobs and at last settled down in Chicago just before the Columbian Exposition. He did not hear from Gustav for seven years.

Then one day he received word from him—Gustav was coming to America too. He had been tricked into a marriage, but of course made no mention of it in his letter, and when my father, who knew nothing about it, met Gustav at the railroad station he found his brother accompanied by a small, wiry woman and two children. Gustav stood there smiling meekly. I can picture every detail of the scene. I know the way my father frowns, how he wrinkles up his brows. I know the way my uncle used to smile, the goodness shining from his little eyes. There they stood, my father short and stocky, my uncle small and slight.

My father clears his throat, I know that rumble.

"Gustav," he says, and stands there frowning, scowling at his older brother.

A HERRING FOR MY UNCLE

"Ech, Isak," says my uncle, surrounded by his family and the baggage. He still smiles faintly, standing meek and mild.

The immigrants arrived over the Baltimore & Ohio, pulling in at the old Polk street depot. I know that station. It has a wide, smooth floor, old-fashioned arches, and the draught from off the railroad yards whistles into the waiting room.

There they stand, the little woman hard and tight-faced. She knows my father, she was already a widow with two babies when my father left the town. "Selma?" he says and still he stands there frowning.

Then, without another word, he picks up my uncle's bag, turns around darkly and is followed by the woman and her kids. They carry their own bundles; my father will have nothing to do with them.

Later on, the truth came out—slowly. One of the woman's relatives gave a small dowry, another promised to take the children, and so a bargain was struck. In the end the relatives of the bride took up a further collection, bought steerage tickets, and shipped the whole family over. Selma was older than my uncle and was known as the village shrew, and everybody was glad to be rid of her.

And so my uncle married, and so he came to America. He took a flat a mile away from my father's place and stumbled about the brawling city, trying to learn the language. My father, through a friend, got him a job in a stock-room, but the hours were long and, beside, Uncle Gustav was not a muscular man. Then Selma stepped in. She went sniffing about the city and finally found a relative who was a cigar-maker, and so Uncle Gustav learned a trade. The hours were long, but there was no heavy lifting to do; he had small, quick hands and in a short time was firmly settled.

All this happened just before the turn of the century, about six years before I was born. My father rarely talks about his brother Gustav now. His hate for Selma was a long time in dying; he never could stand the sight of her. She had the small, sharp head of an alert weasel. She never came over to visit us, but went about the town, telling everybody Gustav

257

was giving a part of the wages he earned at the cigar factory to his brother, stinting his own children, hoarding money in secret. When Gustav came home from work, all tired out, fatigue etched deeply in his face, she used to shrill at him, then stick her bony hands in all his pockets. She bore him no children.

Sometimes, in the long summer evenings, Uncle Gustav used to come over to my father's store before going home. He worked on a piece-work basis, and if he labored especially hard was able to get off an hour earlier now and then. I remember how they used to stand in the rear of the store, where my father used to keep the big kerosene barrel, their hands clasped behind their backs, not talking much, staring toward the front windows and the street. The structure of the Lake street elevated threw thick shadows into the store and across the way; if one looked through the first row of shelves, one could see the tops of the swaying trees over in Union Park.

Business was always quiet in the evening, and if a customer came in my father used to wait on her, ring up the sale, then go back to stand near Uncle Gustav, his face heavy, his short, strong arms behind his back again. I was too small to understand a lot of things, but I sensed the tragic mood of both of them. It must have been apparent, to an older person, that my father's brother was slowly dying.

And each time, before he left, he'd call me over and shake my hand, giving it a gentle pressure.

"How about the herring?" he would ask me, chuckling softly. "Ech, ech, have you got a little herring in your pocket?"

My father, unmoving in the rear, would stand frowning toward the windows as his brother gave my head a pat and left the store. Working in the cigar-shop, down in the damp of the basement, was the worst thing in the world for Uncle Gustav. To save money he used to bring his lunch along and at noon would go out for a five-cent bottle of pop to wash the dry sandwiches down. The carbonated water caused him to belch for hours, little belches which relieved him but left him weakened. My mother talked to my father about him late at night, but there was nothing my father could do. He himself was a poor man, with a big family on his hands. He couldn't go over to visit Uncle Gustav in the evenings because of Selma, and he was unable to see his brother very often because of the grocery. But my mother used to stand there crying, and in the end, leaving her cooking and her washing, she said she'd mind the store and wait on the trade.

So every few months or so my father went over to Blue Island avenue, and after a while he began taking me along. I believe his brother told him to. We would cross the tangle of car tracks and I would reach up for my father's hand, and at the corner fish-store we would stop to buy a herring. Walking along, keeping a pace behind, the juice would go soaking through the newspaper, until my palm was wet.

"You carried it?" Uncle Gustav would say.

And I'd rub my palm against my pants and nod.

"Ech, ech," he'd whisper and then would open up the package.

Each time I saw him I had grown a little taller. Each time I left him I had the feeling, as we climbed up the stairs into the daylight, that he stood there smiling and crying to himself. My father's face was always set as he climbed the stairs. We came outside, out upon that dead, desolate section near Blue Island avenue, and as we reached the car tracks we had to stop until a line of wagons drew away. The thoroughfare was used by the farmers on their way to the great Randolph street markets and I remember how the horses had prairie flowers in their manes, because coming to market with a great load was something of a festive event. And there were small, bare-footed kids, who sat on top of the heaped vegetables and fruit, and if I hollered one or two of them would throw an apple or a peach my way.

All this while we had been exchanging letters with Uncle Herman in New Zealand. He had some grown-up daughters and they too wrote, sending photographs and asking for ours. So one Sunday afternoon we all went over to a studio on Madison street and had our pictures taken. My father acted strangely about it. He went over to Blue Island avenue a day before and talked to Gustav, and when we were ready to go to the studio, the door opened and Gustav came in, his low, black hat upon his head.

"Gustav wants to send Herman his picture too," my father said, and we all walked the six blocks to Madison street.

In the studio we were posed by the photographer, my father sitting in the front row beside my mother, one fist on his knee, the other out of sight. My kid brother sat upon my mother's lap and the photographer had to talk soothingly a long time to make him sit quiet and reserved.

When it was all over my father went up to Uncle Gustav. "You sit alone," he said. "You get a picture taken by yourself."

"Ech, Isak. Why should I do it?"

"I'll pay for it," my father said, and so my uncle posed. He sat there with his low, black hat on and meekly stared toward the camera.

Then we all went from the shop and walked the six blocks home.

A few months after the photographs were sent away we received a letter from New Zealand, a letter with a black border around it. My oldest brother was the first to read it, and did not want to give it to my father. Uncle Herman had passed away while undergoing an operation for appendicitis.

As soon as my father learned the news he closed the store early and came over to the flat. It was winter time and both coal stoves were going. When he reached the flat we were already finished with our supper and our mother had warned us beforehand not to talk or move around.

My father came home and didn't eat the meal. He stood with his back toward the flat in the kitchen, staring out at the snow in the backyard and the alley and cracked his fingers, one by one. His face was heavy, his eyes were clouded. Later on, he read the letter over and over, slowly and in a quiet way; his lips moved a little, forming the words to himself as he read. Then he took out his brother's photograph and stared and stared at it.

"He was the strongest of us all," he told my mother, and that was all he said.

In the night, once again in the big, hard bed, I raised myself and through the bedroom doorway had a view of the parlor. I was seven years old then. My father rocked gently, working up a sort of rhythm, and as he rocked he whimpered quietly to himself. I could hardly hear it. He sat rocking like that for a long time.

Months later he told Uncle Gustav about their brother's death, but Uncle Gustav had noticed my father's mood and was prepared for the worst of news. They stood at the rear of the store near the big kerosene barrel, not talking much, and when Uncle Gustav left he asked me, so as not to break the habit, if I had a little herring in my pocket; but now I saw that he was really crying, he did not try to hide it as he gave my head a pat.

And three years later Uncle Gustav died. My mother cried the hardest. She cried so much that my father put on a stern and surly look and acted sharp around the flat.

We sat about all evening, my mother with her puffy, reddened face, my father staring dully at the stove.

Then we went to bed, everyone except my father.

And once more, for the third time, I raised my body and turned to look through the doorway toward the parlor. My father was rocking there. His face was stern and heavy, I could see the set muscles in his jaw. He rocked up and back, working up a sort of rhythm, his feet firm upon the floor.

How long he rocked I do not know. I grew tired holding my body rigid and had to rest a couple of times. But I did not go to sleep. I lay stiffened in the dark, listening to the flare of the gas flame in the front room. And pretty soon I heard my father; his whimpering sounded like a kind of humming. I raised my body more.

Now his face was slack and flabby. He was holding Gustav's photograph in his hands and stared and stared at it. The tears were pouring down his face. He moaned softly, one fist holding the picture, the other resting heavy on his knee.

I sat up rigid in the dark, between my two sleeping and un-
caring brothers, and heard my uncle's voice.

"You carried it?"

I rubbed my thigh under the quilt and nodded.

"Ech, ech," he chuckled and opened up the package.

Portrait of a Celestial

By FLORENCE BENNETT ANDERSON

After being graduated from Vassar, Mrs. Anderson was honored with a fellowship at the American School of Classical Studies (Athens). She has taught Greek at Vassar and at Hunter College, is a student of anthropology and physics, and a critic of art and literature. Her versatility is shown by two titles from her published work, RELIGIOUS CULTS ASSOCIATED WITH THE AMAZONS *(1912), and* SPINDRIFT, *a collection of poems.*

SURELY his ghost—brown, nimble, spare—will haunt these grounds, peering on a moonlit summer night to see that the sprinklers' duties to flower-beds and lawns have been performed, zealous in the Halloween frosts that leaves be well raked and bulbs bedded, anxious for the cleanliness of walks and driveway from winter snow, wistful over proper tendance of spring mysteries. The new man will never be growing celery as crisp and white as his? Ho! What fool had charge of the asparagus bed? "Pletty soon him learn cauliflower no grow all a same place where him put him. Too much alkali." Forty years and more of loving fidelity to the soil of these few acres about the house—indeed, they will bind his spirit, even though his bones may be earthed, as he wished, in sacred China. His hands created the admired spot in the front garden: the island, cleverly buttressed with stones, in the little brook, where there are sequent glories of iris and sweet alyssum and columbine against the lustrous dark background of English ivy on the farther mainland bank and of Oregon grape, starred in season with great yellow blossoms. And on an inferior islet, beneath the bridge that prolongs the gravel walk to the front gate, he set a natural tangle of woodland ferns. The crooked runway of the brook until it comes to a second span, floor to a trellised summer-house, he lined with stones, concealing art to the very semblance of nature.

And when my Fong arranges flowers for the house—a prime delight, in which he scarcely tolerates the slightest rival interference—he has cunning of eye and hand for color combinations and coquetries of symmetry.

Invading any province of his activity is hazardous. To introduce a new plant in a garden bed is to elect the complete task of watering and trimming. A lazy master thinks twice before assuming such a vigorous routine. There were two clippings of Greek acanthus magisterially set to grow, with a Hellenist's enthusiasm for their ancestry, in the triangular plot near the east porch. It required subtle diplomacy to transfer them to Fong's expert guardianship. And later, when master took it upon himself to snip away the gigantic and withered leaves to give light and air to the tender new growths, gracefully outlined as should beseem the prototype of the Corinthian capital, there was some ado to find a willing brown hand to the wheelbarrow for trundling the defunct out of sight. A family of willow slips that traveled from the neighborhood of Napoleon's first grave at St. Helena by way of another island, Nantucket, died of thirst. Master and mistress went on a holiday. The care had not been formally assigned to the person who should have been accorded choice of site and privilege of planting.

But you must not misread my Hue Fong. He is the friendliest grig, and the most patient and ready of response, in all the cosmos. But there are very sensitive feelings at his core.

A gnarled little gnome he might seem in his out-of-door work clothes, blue-jacketed in denim, widely and conically-hatted against the summer heat, sweatered and capped in cold times. How to characterize him for the indoor solemnities? For verily he is gardener, cook, and housemaid. His first assumption of the splendors of white coat and apron for the task of handing the dishes at table was the investiture of shyness, and he carried the garb for a while with shamefacedness. He might be heard clearing his throat—wetting the whistle of his courage—just beyond the pantry door. And he would startle guests by a nervous chuckle as he presented a vegetable or a plate of bread. But underneath he was vastly elated. Great social progress this was: that the gardener of long service was now the house-boy. At first, while accepting the apron as appropriate vestment, he balked at the white coat except for the grandest occasions. "What for you no put on your coat when my sister-in-law eat a lunch here?" asks mistress, reproachfully. "Before I know him," is the explanation, firmly offered as adequate.

Curiously enough, when one considers his many years of very different activity, he showed immediately a genuine aptitude as cook, disconcerting to the novice-mistress who instructed by the method of object lessons. Book-bound she was. But that which he saw done once he could duplicate, and improve presently on the model. How exultant his polite humility of reply to compliments! "Not much cook." How encouraging to boa-constrictors would be his joy in seeing his viands appreciated! He has a passion for urging his delicacies on guests; indeed, if left to his own devices, would pour to the brim every cup of tea or coffee and lavishly apportion each helping from a dish with his own hand. If he could feed us individually by spoon, like the courteous Indians of La Salle's encounter on the lower Mississippi, he would be in his element. Yes, but be sure that, if you refuse a dish once, he will list you personally as never desiring that again. Also, if convinced of a diminished appetite, his economy will ration you accordingly. And you will make your purchases of meat and groceries, knowing that a stern monitor at home will point out to you by ocular demonstration how grossly you have been cheated. If master leaves a bulb wastefully burning in some dark closet or attic haunt, he will hear of the lamentable lapse from the watchful fidelity that has corrected it.

Expect no guests whom you can not accurately define of habitat and profession before or after their departure. The known caller is announced with glee; of the unknown, the query is, "Who come? Before no see him." There is no stone of anxiety about possessions in the bosom of *dominus* on a long absence from home. Jim knows better than the owner what the treasures are. Not a piece will be missing when you return. Your only fear will be lest his scrupulous and numerous house-cleanings will have rubbed off the gilding from the picture frames or introduced soap and water as ministrants to articles that can not brook such ardors. A sustained frenzy of hard work possesses him when he is left alone. Union labor would find him the arch-incorrigible. "You go country"—a journey to New York or London from our provincial *metropolisette* is "going to the country"—"I work all a same you stay here. Work more." New England at her Simon-purest could not produce a conscience of superior driving power. No extra in the way of parties or house guests daunts him. Rather he exults in hospitality of every description and is likely to chide a socially delinquent mistress. A late-lingering caller, if it be one of his pets, he will of his own accord bid to stay for dinner.

There is the other side to this picture of boundless energy. It is extremely difficult to find satisfactory help to ease at times the labors of the beloved gnome. In the seasons when he must be assisted in the garden, how he mourns of the young academicians who run the lawnmower, roll the lawn, rake leaves, prune trees! "Collegie boy, him work very easy." The fear is that master is squandering money on American laziness. There was on a time a "collegie boy" who came up to the grim requirement of efficiency pretty well, but who had not properly, in spite of warnings, sensed the dignity of the major-domo. *Domina* for some days was go-between for the transmission of orders, until she persuaded young America to offer China the respectful words due to eld, and ability, and fidelity.

He has long been "Jim" to all the ramifications of master's family. Correctly he would be called "Fong," his individual name, which by Chinese custom follows the gentile name. "Hue Fong"—so his pay cheques are made out in English script, and so he endorses them in Chinese character in the exact middle of the reverse. He can read a little in his own tongue, but not a word in that of the country where he has lived some fifty years. But you would find it hard to trip him in a calculation in our values, whether of money or miles or acreage. Arabic numerals he knows accurately.

For thrift he could not be excelled. Regularly his wages, often intact, go home to China when the exchange is most favorable in the medium of Mexican dollars. When he retires— God retard the day, prays *domina,* selfishly perhaps, but with deep affection—if buffeted China has not then been torn to shreds, he will be an esteemed elder in his village of Shui Po on the Hoi River, fifty miles from Canton. There his wife and a daughter live. He has a married daughter in a settlement not far off, and a son, sole male offspring of two marriages, is now also, not very happily for all concerned, in the ancestral hamlet. A man's son, in that land above all others, should be his best pledge for future honor and comfort in death as well as life. But Occidental influences are not always favorable to a Celestial's rearing. My merry brown gnome, after the self-denial of a lifetime, has a harassed look in his patient, deep-set eyes when he speaks of Hue Junior, long a resident of the United States.

Paterfamilias has gone home for a sojourn three times during his many years in America. Perverse law that we have, whereby such a man can not bring wife and children to share his days! On the last occasion of his return, this timid and guileless soul had a sore trial. Some sharpster at the immigration office confused him in his answers to questions, so that there was a weary and mysterious wait somewhere, and a fear so deeply ingrained that this paragon of uprightness walked from southern California to eastern Washington. Yet there was absolutely nothing wrong with his papers.

I saw a gorilla mother once in Dresden, whose eyes were set under a brow much like Jim's and had a similar expression of tender wistfulness. But he can laugh well enough. Indeed, laughter is a constant sauce to our routine. It registers delight and a general affectionate readiness of response to all contingencies, but chiefly it covers embarrassment for insufficiencies of English vocabulary. It requires some patience and a kind of intuitive perception in linguistics to talk with him in our tongue. Picturesque dialogues we have. The trick is to understand when his contribution to the conversation is on a subject which has not been anticipated. However, that is the crux of all dealings in a foreign language, not so much to know your own ground as that of the adversary's unexpected maneuvers. Show the least irritability, and he is hopelessly lost. Fear stops the English action of his mind. He will helplessly repeat each last word of your phrases and gather not a shred of meaning. But hear him in his own tongue with a compatriot and you will see another man: calm, mildly oratorical of gesture, reticent at intervals, with a shrewd smile, master of his nerves. On occasion, when there is some matter that demands thorough comprehension on both sides—as, for instance, when his beloved householders plan a long absence, during which Jim is to look after everything about the place—the head man of the local Chinese colony comes up as interpreter: a bland, stout man, a money-maker, well educated, our faithful friend. In such conclaves, the other Fong, the quietly poised, is seen at his best. He must take pride in the sesquipedalian measure of the words which explain him. "Will he be afraid to sleep in the house alone for so long a time?" "He desires to assure you that his sole reason for trepidation is anxiety lest some marauder enter the mansion and remove some object."

On a midsummer day—and a wheat valley of the Northwest gives genially ripening temperatures at a hundred degrees and upward, but mercifully dry—my conically-hatted sprite was on self-appointed garden duty, which he denoted "easy work." In the shade of the birches by the brook he was cutting away withered leafage of plants that had long since bloomed. His regular habit of labor is an object lesson for races teased by high blood-pressure. Steadily, without hurry, he pursues each task in the routine which he has mapped out for every day. So much of this, so much of that, and an orderly resumption of this and that left for tomorrow. He has not an ounce of superfluous flesh, and his muscles at upwards of seventy have not only elasticity, but that iron-like fiber seldom encountered out of heroic fiction. Squatted beside him as spectator was one of his Oriental friends, haranguing with controlled passion, his umbrella-shaped hat far back on his head. From time to time he dipped into the brook with a paper cup, from which he sipped tiny draughts at wide intervals. The intense light of a cloudless day drew heat waves into an almost palpable veil of magnifying properties between the tree-shadows by the rivulet and the house whence an amused spy peeped. The pantomime was acutely staged. Jim, for the most part little disturbed in the rhythm of his work, now and then stood erect, while the orator was in sipping mood, and gave grave responses, impressively punctuated with sweeps of his sickle, a Chinese incarnation of Cap'n Cuttle.

But my Celestial, as guileless in his loyalties as that marine-flavored "Ed'ard," is no sentimentalist. His thick-shod feet are planted on earth, and no rosiness of cloud obscures the vision of the eyes which nature has established in the airy medium. He would make a good exemplar of Meredithian doctrine. But I gather that common sense, salted with humor, is a known characteristic of his race. Yet without a pinch of the condiment can my paragon at times reveal that other native endowment. There had been a notable funeral in town among his people, with rites both Christian and Chinese, as befitted the dual faith and social importance of the deceased and her husband. We ate an early and rather hasty lunch that Jim might be in street garb at the appointed meeting place in good season. Master, present at the service out of friendly respect for the bereaved man, reported at home certain stately details. Mistress, thus informed, saw fit to pass a few words of general compliment while we were being served at dinner time: "I hear, lots of flowers, lots of people ride in automobiles to cemetery." "Willy Sing no buy flower. 'Nother people send him. And Chinamen ride, everybody pay fifty cents."

The street habiliments are a low-crowned derby hat, honorably turned brown from black by use, a dark business suit, of which the whimsical amplitude is probably due to the fact that the smallest stock size for men would more than clothe my meager gnome, a stiff white collar. But to be without necktie is *de rigueur* apparently, for mistress, although affectionately esteemed, has never seen any of her gifts of such adornment worn. The collar button shines, a golden disc. An overcoat is tolerated only in the most austere weather. For a raincoat, presented brand-new one Christmas by master, there is peculiar regard. But it requires a veritable deluge for its assumption, along with other panoply against moisture, umbrella and overshoes.

Winter pavements can rarely be too icy to keep this nimbleness at home of an evening. An inflexible ritual, self-imposed, sees the last dish washed and all made tidy in dining-room and pantry. Then the faithful one eats his copious dinner in the kitchen with leisurely enjoyment and clears away those remains. After that comes the departure in street-clothes downtown. The convention sits regularly in one of the China stores. Its maximum attendance is on a Saturday night, when garden Chinamen can get in from out of town. In warm seasons there will be a great bowl of tea on a table, into which each dips at will with his handleless cup. In winter several teapots are in service near an urn of hot water, and the tea caddy is also at hand so that fresh supplies may be delicately brewed. In days when Chinese labor was more plentiful in the Northwest, before the severities of the California-made exclusion law, these conclaves were large even in a small city. Few well-to-do households lacked a Wong or a Yin or a Wu in cuisine or garden. Over many a tobacco pipe and cup of smoky Suchong, sucked hot through a slit between lid and container, would have been seen Oriental features, composed, with unsmiling humor, to the likeness of the individual "bossie at home." The President of the Pioneer college, the fortuitously affluent Professor, the Banking Plutocrat, the Big Merchant, prosperous Lawyer and Doctor and National Senator—each would have sat in counterpart in that group, his character acted to the life by these sagacious mimics. A neatly adjusted scale determined prestige according to kind and place of employment, and stipend too. In bicycling times, before queues were abolished by Celestial rulers, our streets were streaked with swiftly pedaling young Chinese, whose pigtails floated on the mild valley wind.

That long wearing of the ornament of hair has made my Fong resemble a tonsured monk. Around a shining brown baldness grows a circle of grizzled floaters, fine and unsubstantial, like a doll's hair. I think he does his own clipping. Sometimes the stragglers are delightfully uneven of cut. A breeze in the garden lifts them fantastically, but always that suggestion of a downy halo persists. Stepping about the lawn in the hot months at the endless task of changing sprinklers in a dry climate, this little figure that has the look of a religious will rather incongruously be spied now and then with a pipe in his mouth. One of the few relaxations of methodical decorum! If he catches sight of authority, the pipe is whisked into a pocket. Mistress has often turned behind a shrubbery that she might not make him lose his face in one of these moments of expansiveness. Nor does she invade the kitchen when she hears him softly lilting in his own tongue at his work. But she wishes she had ear and training to note on paper that melody of Oriental intervals.

He loves the movies. Largess of a Sunday takes him weekly to his prime delight. Talkies, I am sure, have added little to his pleasure—probably contribute rather to confusion of mind, for he gets little from sustained English, unless it be in his jargon. But he is a swift interpreter of a scene presented to the eye. Usually he is in his seat in good season to see the film through twice with attentive gravity. The devout of our family circle have wondered whether the urgency of a tip should not be directed church-ward rather than cinema-ward. But to dictate to a soul expert in the virtues of Christianity seems to overtax our zeal. At least, he has been exposed to our religion more than forty years. His eagerness to have us regular in church attendance is exemplary. Illness, unless severe enough to make the patient bedfast, is small excuse with him.

Illustrated magazines are also a staple of quiet enjoyment

in the sparse leisure of an evening when he returns from the nocturnal gossip of Chinatown. If the bosses, male and female, are to be out for a whole evening, the lure of that conclave of compatriots is sometimes ignored and the ingle-nook at home holds a close student of the *Geographic* or a magazine of travel. Or he may choose from the shelves a book of Florentine views, a special favorite, or perhaps a tome filled with illustrations of sculpture or painting. He is joyous when he identifies the same picture in different volumes. On these occasions he likes to sit in his cap, much as a priest shelters his tonsure against drafts. His spectacles are large and horn-rimmed. When you return, if he is still up—his hours are wholesomely regular and rather early—be sure that he will not open the door for you. You must use your key, and he will greet you with loud chuckles. Prudence knew there was a slim chance of its not being you, but some dangerous interloper. He has been known to parley through a locked door at night with intimate friends a-calling. But, cautious although he is according to the sober dictates of reason, I am certain that he would lay down his life in defense of an object of his devotion. Nothing could surpass his delicate chivalry toward *domina* when she is alone in the house. Returning from down-town, he makes considerable noise before he enters from the kitchen quarters. He wishes her to know that this is no intruder. He comes in for a moment, and they exchange frivolous remarks on the state of the weather, and then he withdraws. She may be sure now that there is a protector in the house.

His studiousness once when he was laid up with lumbago for several days was a quaint sight. It was mild weather, and he was persuaded to spend the days in a *chaise longue* on an enclosed porch, with an electric pad to his back, a device of which he had great fear at first, but to which he became almost indissolubly wedded. It grilled his pride as well as his sense of decorum to be waited on by his venerated employers. And yet how comfortably he settled back after meals, be-capped, be-spectacled, with a paper-bound Chinese volume and numerous American magazines in the receptacle attached to the chair-arm and with a rug over his knees! You would have thought him a Chinese savant touring the world by steamer *de luxe*.

In case of need the doctor must be sprung on him unawares. He has a tender affection for the family practitioner as guest at table or ministrant to the august ones, but here is a mental objection to all of that profession when personally required. "Melican doctor good, China doctor very good. China doctor give medicine, sometimes eat him, sometimes shine him. Melican doctor, very quick him cut." Some of our own breed have tasted that lurking fear of the inevitable knife. But Jim was cemented to a novel respect for the art as practised in Melica when our physician, called for him at an anxious time, used the stethoscope. "Telephone?" I heard Jim's crescendo chuckle through a closed door. It was amply apparent that he had a new angle of appraisal for one who could hold converse by 'phone with the department of the interior. And the findings were completely reassuring.

He is devoted to every member of master's family in all branches of kindred and in-lawness. But naturally among the revered there are favorites. A chosen few receive gifts at Christmas. Master and mistress are always generously remembered by Santa Jim, and at China New Year—old style, a little later than our beginning of a twelvemonth—a China lily is a regular token of regard. Very cheering at that bleak season, this pretty fragility, incredibly rooted among smooth stones in a bowl of water! Candy is frequently one of these festive offerings, and it is always of a good make. Sometimes there are silk handkerchiefs and gay pieces of transpacific embroidery, or there may be lichee nuts in a fair exotic box, or jasmine tea in a lacquered caddy. Or again affection materializes in a Cantonese dish or a potted plant purchased after the jealous scrutiny of an expert at the florist's. And in the midst of our ordinary routine, if mistress chances to be alone at a meal, particularly if she seems a bit ailing, peanuts are brought to her as a surprise treat. A little trying at times digestively! But who could resist such solicitude? Among the favorites in the intimate circle are those whom Jim has watched in their growth from babyhood. You should see him hail an infant born of one of these! He has the connoisseur's touch with children. Even tiny creatures smile and stretch to his eager demonstrations.

Yet one might think his odd face would be frightening. Narrow, with high cheek-bones, deep-set tilted eyes, a large mouth twisted to one side, a great cleft in the middle of the forehead from some terrible misadventure in boyhood, a wen above the left brow, leather-toned skin, great yellow horse-teeth, random grizzled bristles about the chin. One day a new piano tuner was at his work. Celestial curiosity hovered, unsuspected, just above him on the dusky stairway. Suddenly delight in these unwonted manipulations evoked a chuckle. The stranger almost shattered the delicate mechanism of the "action" as he looked up into that goblin face bending over him.

Invariably, when carpenters or plumbers or painters are at work about the place, my Fong contrives a duty which will give him a good view of proceedings. And later you will find him wielding brush or hammer serviceably in some corner, putting into practice the lore gleaned of observation. "Can do." No possession in the house has lacked his thorough examination. Timidly but exhaustively, he handles every appurtenance in a new automobile.

This *doer* will never be at rest. He resisted the alluring invitation to the wedding of one of our best-loved relatives until he bethought him to tuck coat and apron in a bundle under his arm. Thus armored for helpfulness at the breakfast, although he had been bidden as a guest, he braved social terrors. Arrived with master and mistress on a holiday visit to another of his adored ones in a sylvan camp among the Thatuna Hills, he was observed, on alighting from the motor car—in which he had sat politely on the edge of the back seat for some two hundred miles—to have apron strings dangling from a coat pocket. Instantly he was in array of service, cannily treading the rustic path between cabin and impromptu refrigerator— a bucket set in a shady nook of a rill. Those apron strings, pendent of tied ends as he flitted domestically in the virgin forest, surely symbolized an ancient and tranquil civilization. He sympathizes with all your woes and those of all whom you love. But he tempers commiseration with laughter. The perverse spirits of ill health and mischance are probably best driven away so. I have heard that at a certain point in the ritual of a funeral among his folk every one present laughs aloud. News of a painful accident is likely to arouse involuntary mirth. "Spoil him leg? Ha, ha!" But he is grave in a moment and very sorry. In a crisis of illness that befell his boss, he sat down and wept.

Yes, he is a happy exile. Indeed, I wonder whether his race does not, by innate habit, best of all savor the Pauline doctrine of contentment with existent conditions. Profoundly peace-loving, industrious, honest, cheerful, humorous—such a Cantonese coolie is not unfairly an epitome of national character.

War in general is an abomination to him, a senseless interruption to the proper rhythm of life, a costly, unthrifty nightmare. His hereditary patriotism has been like an ancient Greek's devotion to a tiny fatherland, a city, or, more largely, a district, a compact unit of which the dust of his ancestors forms part. The first news of the Japanese hostilities in Shanghai awakened a sickening fear that Canton would be the next objective. An American acquaintance, either for the joy of hectoring or because he had mis-read a newspaper, informed him one day that Hong-Kong was under gun-fire. *Domina,* by good luck hitting on a similar place-name in the Shanghai region, Hong Kew, persuaded him that thus the mistake had come about. After this there was avid inquiry each day for news. Of course, meanwhile, much talk on home politics went on at the nightly sessions of the expatriates. From that ingrained provincialism has emerged a patriotism that darkens his eyes when he speaks of Shanghai and Manchuria. "China say: Japan stop, China stop. No stop, fight. Before Jap think everybody scare. China not much gotta gun, not much gotta ship and airship. Jap all gotta heap lot. But China no scare. Chinamen now, everybody mad inside." He touches his midriff emphatically. We cannot have failed to be aware in time past of an anti-Japanese prejudice in him. Cups of that island manufacture used to vanish in the washing. Small wonder of such dainty, perishable fabric! "No strong him. Jap make him. No good." The conception was of that as an upstart folk, facile in imitation. But even present resentment, added to this bias, has not bereft him of perspective. "Some Jap no like a war. But head man tell him fight."

Perhaps some day, among friends and relatives in sight of the Kwangtung rice-fields along that Hoi River, he will be drawing our portraits conversationally. A Celestial Ulysses truly! We have never asked him how he came by that bone-deep scar in his head, fearing to stir an intolerable memory. And we have been mystified by the fragments revealed through his English speech of early experiences in British Columbia, where he first touched America. He seems to have been then for a time astray in the mountains. "Some Injun good, some heap bad." But what can not that lifetime of shrewd and exact observation of alien men and places tell when the leisurely days come? A great linguist he will be, haled in as interpreter when an English or American tourist chances upon that hamlet. And suppose among those wanderers he should some day spy out his old American bosses, at the errant game of catching glimpses of foreign lands? Suppose then a turning of staid Occidental heads by a worshipful greeting from all the Hues of Shui Po!

But this is not a *vale* to a beloved pensioner, but a grateful *ave* to the incomparable diligence and versatility of a Celestial paragon.

Alice and the Aquitania

By CHRISTOPHER MORLEY

Christopher Morley was born at Haverford, Pennsylvania (1890), and it was at Haverford College that he matriculated for his B.A. degree. After winning a Rhodes scholarship, he spent three years at New College, Oxford, and published his first book, THE EIGHTH SIN (a book of poems), while he was there. Upon his return to the United States, he sought experience in the publishing business and in newspaper work. His column "The Bowling Green" first appeared in THE NEW YORK EVENING POST. When Morley, Canby, and Benét founded THE SATURDAY REVIEW OF LITERATURE, "The Bowling Green" went along with its author and has remained a distinctive feature of THE REVIEW.

In addition to being a columnist, Christopher Morley is a poet, a short-story writer, a novelist, and an essayist. The Haverford Edition of his works was published in 1927 in twelve volumes. His autobiography appeared in 1931 under the title JOHN MISTLETOE. Mr. Morley calls it his "personal statement."

SHIPPING business is bad; it is grievous to see so many good vessels laid up in the Erie Basin and in the alcoves of the Gowanus Canal. But *Alice M. Moran,* "of 29 net tons measurement," says her certificate, still puts in a lively twelve-hour day.

We were talking to Buck McNeil at the Battery Pier. If you have ever fallen—or jumped—overboard from the Battery seawall, you know Buck. He is the fellow who pulled you out. In his 26 years as boatman at that pier he has rescued 290 people. At least he has been credited with 290; the number

From *The Saturday Review of Literature,* November 21, 1931. Reprinted by permission of Christopher Morley.

is really more than that, for Buck has a habit of walking away when he has got the pessimist ashore. He keeps in his pocket the certificate of the U. S. Life Saving Medal of Honor, "for acts of Unusual Heroism," and on his watch-chain is the gold medal of the Dock Department, given him by Mayor Hylan. But in spite of hard times, people don't seem to go off the deep end so much nowadays. Buck hasn't had to go into the harbor for anyone in the last two years. He's just as pleased, for he says there are occasional twinges of rheumatism. We wanted to ask Buck whether the Carnegie Medal committee knew about all this, but just then *Alice M. Moran* came steaming across from Jersey City with a bone in her teeth. This was the Club's first chance in many years to go tugboating, and we hastened aboard.

We are not the first to raise a small chantey of praise in honor of *Alice,* for her skipper, Anton Huseby, proudly showed us an admirable article written about her by Roy Crandall in *Gas Logic* of last September. No one could improve on Mr. Crandall's excellent story, which Captain Huseby keeps in the pilot house, and which includes also a lifelike photograph of *Alice's* snug galley with the skipper, and Mr. Banks, the mate, and Mr. Anderson, the chief, and I think also Selverson, the rope-artist on deck, sitting down to chow, with Bill Paton, the Scotch cook, in the background. The deckhand is the lad who can toss a four-inch hawser so that it loops itself right round the big iron cleat when *Alice* comes alongside a pier. And Bill Paton is still a leal Scot though he admits it's a long time since he tasted haggis. We apologize to Bill for having thought he said he came from Canarsie. It wasn't Canarsie but Carnoustie, which is near Dundee. This record of the Three Hours for Lunch Club's visit doesn't attempt to compete with Mr. Crandall's narrative. But all days on a tugboat are different, and this one happened to be our own.

We were remembering that it was just 45 years ago this month that the Lords of Committee of Privy Council for Trade granted to a certain Conrad Korzeniowski his "Certificate of Competency as Master." For that reason I was the more interested in Captain Huseby's own license. It reads that he "can safely be entrusted with the duties and responsibilities of master of freight and towing steam vessels of any gross tons upon the waters of bays, sounds and rivers and to Dumping Grounds off Scotland Light, and Pilot of any Steamer of any tonnage upon New York Bay and Harbor to Yonkers, Staten Island Sound, South Amboy, Newark Bay and tributaries of the East River to Stepping Stones." The commander of a tug is a more important navigator than a lubber perhaps realizes. He is a seaman to his finger-tips, and performs dexterities of maneuver that astound any lover of craft. And when he takes a steamship in or out of dock he climbs to the big fellow's bridge and takes charge up there. Even if she's as big as the *Aquitania,* it's the tugboat captain who is up aloft giving the word to his leash of soft-nosed whelps, nuzzling like beagles under her tall side.

Alice had already done a good five hours' work when we boarded her. She left her berth in Brooklyn at 6 A.M. First she went to pier 57 North River and brought the *Jacques Cartier* to Pier 3, Army Base. Then she docked the steamer *Tergestea,* and the transport *St. Mihiel* just in from Honolulu. Then she took the barge *Dwyer* 17 across to Pier 7, Central Railroad of New Jersey. It was there, I suppose, that she got the surprising news from her home office that four members of the Club had received permission to come aboard. In older days the owners of tugboat fleets sometimes signaled their captains by intricate codes of waving from the office windows in Battery Place. Perhaps there still is an emergency signal that means Visitors for Lunch.

We were hardly in the roomy pilot house before sturdy *Alice* was again about her affairs. The first thing one noticed was that tugboats, by old tradition, steer backward: unlike social craft the wheel preserves the old theory of the tiller. When the wheel is turned to starboard, the tugboat turns to port. So the ordinary merchant seaman or yachtsman is a dangerous fellow at a tugboat helm until he has learned this difference by instinct.

We went down past Governor's Island, which seemed empty and peaceful. A solitary officer was riding on a horse beside the big polo field. Captain Huseby recalled with some amusement a thing that happened (but not to his own clients), a few years ago. A big cattle-barge for the Union Stock Yards was rounding the Battery when someone hit her amidships, "right in the belly." She began to founder and the nearest safety was the army pier at Governor's Island. She was got alongside just in time and drove off several hundred terrified steers and sheep who fled in panic among barracks and parade grounds, putting major generals and polo players to flight. That day Governor's Island's dignity was badly shaken. It must have looked like a Wild West show. We had always wondered at the origin of the name Buttermilk Channel for the strait between Governor's Island and Brooklyn. Did it imply that mariners of softer temper kept in that sheltered reach while men of strong gizzard plowed up the main slot? No; Captain Huseby thinks it was named when the Brooklyn shore was all farmland and there was a rustic refreshment stand for thirsty boatmen near where the Hamilton Avenue ferry is now.

At Erie Basin and along the Gowanus Inlet one observes the curious transition in the naming of ships. There we saw old-timers like the *Buccaneer,* romantic names like *Silver Sandal, Western Ocean, Munamar,* alongside the *Commercial Guide,* the *Bird City,* the *Commercial Trader,* the *Cities Service Empire.* The *Eastern Temple* is a sulphur trader from Louisiana. The *Gibraltar* of Glasgow, a sturdy British tramp with salmon and black funnel, showed an active riffle of steam from her escape. The *West Isleta* was canted far over to starboard so we supposed she was loading. Among many idle bottoms it was encouraging to see these signs of activity. The *Cities Service Empire* was evidently very much on the job, but some of her neighbors lay rusting and forlorn. What a setting for a mystery story, one of these grim idle freighters.

We lay off Owl's Head, an old mansion on the hill at Bay Ridge, waiting for the *Alaskan.* Two old wooden hulks are on the beach there, surely a disgrace to the pride of New York Harbor. They have been there many years, and boatmen are sensitive about these things. Why doesn't the Port Authority destroy them?

In the sunny noon, which seemed more like April than November, we tarried for our client. The great heights of Manhattan showed faintly through soft haze. Along that Brooklyn shore one is aware of the enormous auxiliaries of power and service that lie behind the tall frontages of the office world. The Bush piers, the Edison plant, the Long Island Railroad freight terminal give one plenty to think about. The incredibly vast warehouses of the Army Base add a vibration of anxiety. Then the *Alaskan* of the American-Hawaiian Line came striding up the Narrows, in light from Boston. We had thought she might be the original *Alaskan,* whom F. R. had met years ago in the Straits of Magellan. But she must be a younger vessel, and her bow showed traces of a previous name, *Wheaton*. It was fine to see *Alice* slide alongside of her, running parallel and at exactly the same speed, and gently edge in with hardly a creak from the log fenders. Bill Banks took the wheel, Captain Huseby ran up the tall green ladder *Alice* carries at her side. With unbelievable address she was swung and pushed to her berth. Her neighbor there was a well-known Bermudian friend, the *Fort St. George*. Not far away were the handsome *Eastern Prince* and *Japanese Prince* with their emblems of the Prince of Wales's three feathers. Just above was the pier of the Brazilian Lloyd, and a very handsome ship the *Niel Maersk* of Svendborg. A few hours round the waterfront make geography very real.

Now it was time for lunch. Tugboat meals are a noble tradition, and Bill Paton, even though four guests had been put upon him unexpectedly, was ready for the test. No one ever tasted better corned beef and cabbage, boiled potatoes, spinach, coffee with condensed milk. The bowl of apples had been polished until they glittered. Bill's doughnuts, little balls of crisp fluff, compare to the average doughnut of commerce as Bacon's essays to a newspaper editorial. When we asked him if he ever gave his crew a Scotch haggis he replied that there was hardly enough room to compound one in that galley, where the stove warms the backs of the eaters as they sit. But I think he could do it if it were laid upon him. His eyes shone as we recalled how Captain Bone has the haggis played in with pipers aboard the *Transylvania,* and the cook is honored for his art with a tumbler of neat Highland elixir. The next time *Transylvania* comes up the harbor I think if Bill Paton happens to see her he will look out from his galley, see her commander high aloft in gold stripes and yellow gloves, and say to himself "Yon's the skipper wha kens aboot a haggis."

What's our next job? we asked, already feeling that for one day *Alice's* affairs were our concern. We were to take out the *Ashburton* of London, said Captain Huseby. We had noticed her at Pier 2, flying her Blue Peter, and her house-flag, with the emblem of a swan. "The Hungry Goose they call it in the Old Country," said Bill Paton.

But the *Ashburton* wasn't quite ready for us yet, so we tied up and lay comfortably in a warm drowse. Grey gulls were squealing, New York shone faintly through a yellow veil of sun. The radio in the pilot house was turned on, and through peaceful siesta some humorist from Newark was singing hunting songs about view hallos and gentry in scarlet "galloping, galloping, galloping." We ourselves felt more like snoring, snoring, snoring. Another member of the *Moran* family, *Eugene F.,* sidled in and lay alongside us with calm brotherly affection. One member sat on the stringpiece of the pier, sketching the pair. Others walked along beneath *Ashburton's* comely stern, watched the last of her cargo going aboard, learned from her mate that she was bound for Newport News and then Australia. A Diesel barge called *Corning* went buzzing fussily in and out of various piers, carrying only one huge case which looked like a crated automobile. It was like a small dog with a bone he hasn't decided where to bury. *Corning* barked every now and then with a loud and very unshiplike-sounding horn. From *Alice's* pilot house we heard the radio cry "This quaint minuet is redólent with the atmosphere of bygone days."

Then suddenly there was a hail from *Ashburton's* stern. We woke from our drowse on the pierhead. *Alice* and *Eugene F.* sprang to life. One of the Club's own members, master mariner himself, cast off *Ashburton's* stern lines from the big iron cleat. Water boiled under her counter. We took her out and swung her toward open sea, feeling we had done well. But our greatest adventure was still to come.

We came up harbor again in the pink light of late afternoon, too wise even to try to match words against that cluster of stalagmites that will never be described by deliberate intention; only, if ever, by accident. Perhaps James Bone came as near it as anyone: "The City of Dreadful Height." It is a much steeper view from the deck of a tug than from the high terraces of a liner. We steered for the deep notch of Broadway, as the big ships do, and rounded the bend of the island. F. A. remembered that the last time we had come up the bay in a tug was the night President Harding died, when some great building in Battery Place had left its lights burning toward sea in the pattern of a huge cross. "I'm afraid they wouldn't do it again for poor old Harding," was someone's comment. Yet no man need be grudged whatever light he can get as he heads down those dark Narrows.

We passed the *American Farmer* at her pier: a merchant man of letters in spite of her bucolic name. The other day she brought over from London the new edition of Sir Thomas Browne; and is it not her commander, good Captain Myddleton, who told us long ago that he always keeps the General Catalogue of the Oxford University Press in the chart-room, for momentary relief during hours of fog or soundings? But our minds were on other matters. The *Aquitania* was now at Quarantine and would be up shortly—a full day late, after a bad voyage. *Alice* was to help dock her.

At Pier 42 is a little rendezvous where the *Moran* family and their friends the *Barretts* wait for the prima donnas to come in. We tarried there in a plain, undemonstrative family group. From the various errands of the day these stout work-women of the harbor came puffing in. They seemed to wipe their hands on their aprons and sit rocking gently on beamy bottoms to talk things over before the big job. They filled water coolers, the men took a sluice at the fresh-water hose. There was *Joseph H. Moran,* bigger than ourself; and *Helen B. Moran* with a small white dog on board, very alert and eager of eye, much aware of his responsibility as the only dog among so many informal human beings. He stood up with front paws rigid against *Helen B's* bulwarks and watched the other kinsmen arrive with critical attention. Oliver (who notices everything) says the small white dog was furiously annoyed when in the middle of his supervisions one of the men sprayed him humorously with a mouthful of drinking water. Certainly it was a liberty, and the more so if it was done by someone on the *Howard C. Moore* or the *Downer X,* who were not *Morans* or *Barretts.* But I did not see this myself, for at that moment · F. R. was telling me of his excitement in reading Defoe's *Journal of the Plague Year* and asking me (so it seemed to my morbid mind) why none of us could write as well as Defoe.

We lay in a knot, haunch to haunch, at the end of Pier 42. *Eugene F. Moran* had followed us faithfully from Brooklyn. *Grace Barrett* was there, and *Richard J. Barrett,* and *R. J. Barrett.* It must be fun to have a big family and a tugboat to name after each of them. *John Nichols,* however, kept a little in the offing. He was too proud to join our little gab, for it is *John Nichols's* captain who goes aboard the big liner and commands the whole fleet of tugs. The rest of us sociabled our soft noses together, our upward poking bows muzzled with the big fenders that look like a brown bear climbing aboard. Above the soft aroma of the North River was a good smell of cooking. We lay in an eddy of it, for all galleys were busy.

Aquitania loomed up in the haze. Only someone very important could arrive so quietly, so steadily, so sure of herself. We had the oblique profile of her, best for both women and ships. Every slant of her seemed to accept homage. She took it as her due, yet not wholly unconscious of it, for she was still a little sore from discourtesies outside. At sea, alone with gray trigonometry, she is only a little thing. Here she was queen. In that soft light she did not come, she grew. But these were the thoughts of lubbers. The urchin tugs (I am sorry to switch metaphors so often) have no time for awe. They swarm about her skirts and hustle her with sooty grasp.

Our little fleet throbbed into action. It was like letting a pack of well-trained beagles out of a kennel. No one needed to be told anything. The routine has been perfected in every detail. *John Nichols* turned downstream to meet her. *Joseph H.* and *Helen B.* shot up ahead of us with a scurry of froth. *Grace Barrett,* pirouetting on her solid heel, twirled across our bow and took the inside track along the pierheads. Behind this interference *Eugene* and ourself and *Howard Moore* followed upstream. There was a very strong ebb, Captain Huseby had told us. But there was no difficulty of wind, a gentle breeze from S.W. It was pink November dusk at its mildest.

Alice and *Eugene* went outward to join her. She came huge above us, steadily increasing. Now we had no eyes to note the movements of the other tugs, only to study this monstrous nobility of a ship. It must have been a bad voyage, for she looked dingy, rusted and salted from water-line to funnels. High on her sloping stacks were crusts of salt. Her white-work was stained, her boot-topping green with scum. The safety nettings were still stretched along her steerage decks, even high on the promenade we could see them brailed up. Passengers at her rails looked down incuriously as we dropped astern. Just one more landing, they supposed.

We passed the notice board—*Propeller 8 feet beneath surface, Keep Clear*—and with *Eugene* slid in under her magnificent stern. Her bronze fans, turning unseen, slipped her cleanly along; we nosed busily into the very broth of her wake. Almost beneath the overhang we followed, dipping in the great swelling bubbles of her shove. It was like carrying the train of an empress. AQUITANIA, LIVERPOOL! Only the sharks have followed her closer than that. She was drawing 33½ feet at the rudder-post. The smooth taper of her hull, swimming forward ahead of us, made her seem suddenly fishlike. Beneath that skin of metal you could divine the intricate veinings and glands of her life: silvery shafts turning in a perspiration of oil, hot bulbs of light, white honeycombs of corridor, cell-like staterooms suddenly vacated. All the cunning structure of vivid life, and yet like everything living so pitifully frail. Then Bill Banks the mate went forward with a boathook. He stood under her colossal tail with his rod poised like a lance. "My God," said Oliver, "he's going to harpoon her." We looked at *Eugene F*. and there, too, stood one with boathook pointed. Like two whaleboats we followed *Moby Dick*.

She swam steadily. A uniformed officer and two sailors looked down at us from the taffrail far above. There was superiority in that look. But *Alice M*. takes condescension from none. "Give us your rope," she cried. They said nothing. We continued to follow. A breath of anxiety seemed to pass over Captain Huseby and Bill Banks. For now we were almost abreast of the pier. Perhaps that ebb tide was on their minds. To deal with that ebb was our affair. They repeated the invitation. "Wait till we get word from the bridge," replied the officer calmly. The devil with the bridge, we could see *Alice* thinking. Her job is to get hold of a line and the sooner the better. At last it came, snaking downward. Bill Banks caught it, partly on the boathook and partly on his neck. The big hawser drooped after it, five inches thick of new rope. There was fierce haste to get it looped on the towing bitts astern. It was *Alice* who took *Aquitania's* first line, from the port quarter. "You've got to be careful taking a rope under way like this," said Captain Huseby spinning his wheel. "These big ships have a powerful suction."

Eugene F. took the second line. The next thing we realized a quick hitch-up had taken place, and we were towing in tandem. *R. J. Barrett* was coupled ahead of *Alice, Richard Barrett* was in line with *Eugene*. The quartet headed diagonally upstream. The big hawsers came taut and creaked. *Alice* trembled. Up at *Aquitania's* port bow were three other tugs pushing downward, side by side. Seven of us altogether on the port side. There must have been half a dozen to starboard, but what was happening there we couldn't see.

Alice shook with life. The churn from *R. J. Barrett* boiled past us. The mass of *Aquitania's* stern plus the flow of the whole Hudson watershed hung on a few inches of splice hooked over the bitts. The big ship stood unmoved as a cliff, while our quartet strained and quivered. *Morans* and *Barretts* dug their twirly heels into the slippery river and grunted with work. Steam panted with hot enjoyment. *Aquitania* didn't seem to care. She wasn't even looking at us. Her port side was almost deserted. Passengers were all to starboard looking for someone to say hullo to. Lights began to shine from the ports. One was blocked with a wooden deadlight, proof of smashing weather. A single steward looked out calmly from the glory hole. It was all old business to him. For several minutes nothing seemed to happen. In midstream a big Socony tanker, almost loaded under with weight of oil, stood by to bring in fuel as soon as she was docked. John D. ready for business, we thought. There was no time to lose: she must sail again only 31 hours later. And in this, the very stress of the battle, they asked us, "How about some supper?" *Alice* had hold now. Apparently she could do practically all the rest of it herself. Captain Huseby was surprised when we said we were too excited to eat.

Gradually the big hull swung. The downward sweep of the tide crisped in a smacking surf against her side as she straightened out across the river. Her great profile brightened with lights in the thickening dusk. Now she was straight onto the opening of the pier. She blew once, very short, a deep, mellow rumble. Thanks! We all answered in chorus, with equal brevity. Sure! Our quartet slackened the pull, wheeled off at wider angles to safeguard her stern as she warped in. She had pivoted round the corner and was slowly easing against the camels, those floating rafts that keep her from rubbing. Captain Huseby now did his steering from the wheel at *Alice's* stern. The rest were at supper.

It was blue dark, 5:10 P.M. New Jersey had vanished except for the bright words LIPTON'S TEA. *Aquitania's* stern was flush with the outer end of the pier. Her ensign came down. We could hardly believe it was all over.

Bill Paton was a little disappointed we could not stay for supper. But we had seen too much—and eaten too much lunch—to be hungry yet. "Next time let us know a day ahead," he remarked, "and we can really give you a meal." We tried to compliment the deck-hand on his sure skill with a hawser. He was embarrassed. "I'm glad you were pleased," was his modest reply. They put us ashore at the end of the pier.

Why do people build or buy big steam yachts, we wondered. Surely a tugboat is the perfect craft. They build them on the Great Lakes—Green Bay, I think they said, was where *Alice* came from. You can get one like her for something like $100,000. A maiden voyage in a tugboat from Green Bay to New York would be a good trip to take.

Aquitania lay there, a blaze of lights, stewards busy carrying off baggage. *Alice* backed off with a curtseying motion, and vanished into the dark. She sleeps in Brooklyn.

Five Points of Illusion

By WALTER LIPPMANN

Walter Lippmann, born in 1889, has won a most enviable place for himself as editor, philosopher, journalist, and political scientist. He is America's most brilliant political observer. His column of judgment appears daily in the New York Herald-Tribune. *He contributes regular monthly articles to* Vanity Fair *and provides the London weekly,* Time and Tide, *with a monthly supplement covering American affairs. A* Preface to Morals *(1929) is his most widely read book. "Liberty," according to Mr. Lippmann, "is not so much permission as it is the construction of a system of information independent of opinion."*

IN THE midst of trouble it is the memorial habit of men to look for a scapegoat. They feel that if things go wrong the reason must lie in some specific blameworthiness of particular men and not in a general failure of the mass of men to appreciate, and then to adjust their affairs to, a radical change in their environment. The scapegoats are, of course, easy to find. The American nation is passing through one of the greatest changes in its whole history. Within this generation its basic position in the world has been transformed and the consequences are affecting the life and labor of all its inhabitants. The change is not generally understood. It is not reflected in the nation's policy. It is not realized by the mass of the people. Therefore, events do not conform with expectations. Therefore, the promises of leaders turn out to be ludicrously wrong. Therefore, the mood of the people is not to say "E Pluribus Unum" but "Oh, Yeah?"

It is, of course, easy to compile an encyclopedia of errors committed by diplomats, politicians, bankers, employers, and everyone else who has had a hand in guiding our destiny in recent years. It is a healthy thing to have the errors pointed out. But as the process of pointing out errors goes on, as committees pile up the testimony, as the books of criticism are written and published, it must, I think, gradually come home to a reasonable person that so much error and so much miscalculation must have some deeper and more general explanation than the greed, the wickedness, or the stupidity of particular individuals. Something must have been going on beneath the surface which caused nearly everyone to miscalculate, something which created unusual opportunities for folly. For let us not be over-righteous and suppose that things could have gone so much askew without implicating pretty nearly every adult person in the process.

I am no admirer of President Hoover's policies or of the Republican Party's conduct in the last ten years. It is possible, I think, for individual Democrats to say honestly that they criticized specific acts and have been justified by events. But I do not believe the Democratic Party can truly say that it foresaw the outcome or that in any clear and resolute way it warned the country about the inflation and its results. The truth is that practically everyone participated in the illusions which have now collapsed.

If we are to assume, as I think we must, that Congress fairly reflects public opinion, then we must conclude that as a people we are still at the stage of recrimination rather than of understanding. If Congress had its way, it would, I believe, stand on this platform:

1. Non-intercourse with foreign nations.
2. The uncompromising protection of American rights abroad.
3. The collection of the last red cent of all foreign debts.
4. Prohibition of imports.
5. Prohibition of loans to foreigners.

This is, I believe, an accurate summary of what Congress genuinely believes that the American people now desire. It would be admitted that each item in the program cannot be pursued to the bitter end, that there has to be a little intercourse with foreign nations, that all imports cannot be stopped, that some credit has to be granted abroad. Nevertheless, the Five-Point Program I have outlined faithfully conveys the present intentions of the prevailing majority.

On all but one point the program expresses the real direction of American foreign policy during the whole post-war era. The exception is in regard to foreign lending. During the decade of the Twenties we abstained from diplomatic co-operation with the outer world. We insisted upon our vested rights. We obtained agreements designed to collect the utmost it was believed our debtors could pay. We revised our tariff twice for the purpose of excluding from our markets goods which could compete with our own. But at the same time we made gigantic loans to foreigners. That was the one breach in the wall of the defenses we erected to attain isolation and self-sufficiency. Now Congress would, if it could, close that breach. In spirit, at least, it is in the mood to condemn, not merely certain imprudent or corrupt practices in the making of some of the loans, but all foreign lending as such.

Broadly speaking, it may be said that the degree and the permanence of our recovery from the existing crisis depend upon a popular understanding of the contradictions and the impracticability of the Five-Point Program. We may, and probably shall, recover somewhat by purely domestic readjustment. But it is inconceivable that we can recover and hold steadily to a high level of well-being as long as our national action is confined within the contradictory limits of the isolationist's creed.

No nation can be secure in an unstable world. Vested interests cannot be protected by any one nation's power alone. Great debts cannot be paid unless the debtors can earn the means of payment. It is impossible for a nation to sell more than in the long run it buys. These are axiomatic truths, as fundamental and as certain as anything that can be declared about human relations. They are not yet understood by the majority of

American voters and those who stand upon them are regarded not only as mistaken but as subtly dangerous and not wholly patriotic. The fashionable way to abuse those who dissent from the Five-Point Program is to call them "internationalists" and to suggest by that odious term that the national interest is not safe in their hands.

When you examine the isolationist's creed you will find at the bottom of the whole argument, beneath all he has to say about not co-operating with foreigners, not buying from, and not lending to them, the simple fallacy that it is possible to get something for nothing. To get security without giving it, to sell without buying, to export without importing, to receive gold dollars without giving up gold dollars: these are the impossible fantasies which control the minds of the irreconcilable isolationists. It is precisely as difficult for them to grasp the fact that international relations are an exchange of goods and services as it was for our forefathers to believe that the flat earth they saw about them was actually a globe. It took centuries to convince the mass of men that the earth is round; after two centuries of international capitalism they are still unconvinced that trade is an exchange. There is nothing farfetched in this analogy. If a man has not grasped the fact that relations are exchanges, he is as helpless to understand what is going on about him as a mariner who tries to navigate a flat ocean.

There is a very good reason why this adult generation of Americans has had such difficulty in grasping these axiomatic truths. In the formative years of this adult generation the United States was still a debtor nation. It paid its debts by the export of its surplus raw materials. Thus it seemed that there could be no trouble about selling more than was bought. The United States had to sell more than it bought in order to pay its debts. In the war this position was reversed. The United States became the creditor of the rest of the world. But it still wished to sell more than it bought. For ten dizzy years it succeeded in doing this by the process of lending the world the gold dollars to pay the world's bills and the world's debts. That epoch has come to an end, and the day is at hand when the American people have to adjust their minds, their laws, their policies, and their daily actions to the wholly new fact that henceforth they must buy and lend if they are to sell and be paid.

In its historic significance this change of position is one of the great moments of history: it marks a change in the relationships of two continents. That the process of adjustment is marked by confusion and punctuated with outcries is not to be wondered at. The great transitions of history are never smooth. When they have to be effected as suddenly as the one in which we are involved, they are full of pain and trouble, and, except in the long view, they are excessively bewildering.

If I Were Dictator

By OSWALD GARRISON VILLARD

Grandson of William Lloyd Garrison, the Abolitionist, Oswald Garrison Villard has always expressed the view of the left wing, or extremely liberal viewpoint, in American politics. He has spent his life as a newspaper man, having been editorial writer and president of The New York Evening Post *until 1918, and, from that time until recently, editor of* The Nation. *His position is now that of contributing editor of the latter journal.*

IF I were dictator? Well, I am sure that what I have to say will disappoint many readers who look for far more radical and violent changes than I have to suggest. I am conscious that the immediate remedies that offer themselves to me will seem lacking both in originality and in thoroughness, perhaps because I have not lost faith in democracy or the workability of our institutions, provided that these are adjusted to modern economic, social, and political conditions. The fault, in my judgment, has been less with the economic and political system under which we have lived than with the men that we have chosen to work it. But the evolution of capitalism has given ever-increasing opportunities for the selfishness and greed of the average human being in industry and politics, and these traits are bringing down the structure. We in America have learned the bitter lesson that uncontrolled individualism, whether rugged or otherwise, leads but to despair.

If I were dictator I should begin in the field of international relations, since it is in that field that we are today most menaced by conditions which not only threaten the peace of the world, but make an early recovery from the economic chaos impos-

From *The Nation*, January 20, 1932. Reprinted by permission of *The Nation*.

sible. I should first of all muster out the fleet, laying it up as did Thomas Jefferson when President, and reduce the regular army to the police force of 25,000 men which it was at the outbreak of the war with Spain. I should retire every single one of the talking generals and admirals and send them all to Guam with the direction that they put that island into a state of 100 per cent preparedness and play at war maneuvers to their heart's content. Resuming the historic American attitude of being unarmed and unafraid, I should say to the rest of the world: "See how genuinely pacific we are. We have done away with the arts of war, have ceased to teach our soldiers how best to disembowel their fellow-men or how to kill innocent women and children by the use of aerial bombs and poison gas, which are not selective in dealing death and destruction. We are ready to take the risks of peace. We have faith not only in our own moral strength; we know that in modern war there are neither victors nor vanquished, but that all suffer alike, and that less than ever can one be assured that the heaviest battalions and the best generals will be on the side of right."

If I were dictator I should abolish every tariff because I know that the rapid rise of the three great industrial nations of modern times has been due chiefly to the fact that within their respective empires it has been free trade that has made them powerful and prosperous. Particularly I should say that this is true of the United States; that if tariffs are the blessings they are said to be, then we should surround every one of the forty-eight States of the Union with those magic walls which are supposed to raise the standard of living and bestow prosperity upon all inside their circle. I should put an end to the abomination that we must protect all trade within purely arbitrary geographic lines. I should first of all abolish the sugar tariff against Cuba, an island almost within sight of our shores, whose sugar would come into our country free and untaxed if the American flag floated over Morro Castle in Havana; instead of which, merely because Cuba is outside of our national lines, we raise the price of sugar to every man, woman, and child, and destroy the value of great American investments in that island. Also we help to reduce the working masses in that country to misery and despair, and help to render them the helpless and hapless victims of a ruthless dictator—merely in order to insure profits for some of our citizens who unnecessarily entered the sugar business at home.

If I were dictator I should serve notice upon Japan that if she did not withdraw within her former lines in Manchuria I should invoke an international boycott to compel her to do so, and, to demonstrate that I meant what I said in all sincerity, I should withdraw every last American soldier from Haiti, Nicaragua, Cuba, Samoa, and the Philippines. I should free the latter before their inhabitants had time to petition me for this action and so live up to our plighted national word. Then I should offer to China every possible help in the way of financial aid and expert advice and service to enable that harassed country to constitute a strong and honest central government. I should immediately recognize the Russia of the Soviets with every gesture of friendship and goodwill to the Russian people. I should not be afraid of communism because I should set out really to constitute an honest and efficient government for the United States, one responding to the will of the American people as expressed through the initiative and referendum, and I am bold enough to believe that if I could have my way, our own system of government as reconstituted would not only challenge comparison with the Soviet program, but would seem infinitely more desirable so long as the Soviet Government is a bloody-handed class dictatorship.

To accomplish this I should do everything in my power to bring about economic equality, and equality before the law. As I do not believe in prisons as they now are constituted, I should relegate to prison farms every single American official— and their number runs into thousands upon thousands—who violates the law, believes himself superior to it, and connives at the abuse of personal liberties by men in the garb of police officers or in that of civil authority. For I believe that the chief explanation of our being the most lawless civilized nation is to be found in the fact that we have more lawless officials sworn to uphold the law than any other nation on earth.

I should remove from the statute books by one stroke of the pen every law regulating the private morals of individual citizens. I should declare that, however men and women behaved in their relations with one another, it was their own affair, save where the public peace was disturbed. I should, however, continue and increase the control of the sale of narcotics, and my government would be as rigid as that of the Soviets in preventing the exploitation of the bodies of women for the gain of individuals. Censors of literature, art, or the theater would be my special game. I have long wondered where would be the proper place in which to exile the censors and snoopers, and then it came to me—the Virgin Islands! I should seek to find a method of dispensing liquors and wines in a way rigidly to control the drink habit, so that men should not profit by catering to that appetite of their fellow-men which undeniably has done more than any other one thing to fill our jails, our hospitals, and our asylums. I should appeal to my subjects to join me in treating alcohol from the same standpoint as that from which we treat the abuse of drugs, believing that unlimited use of alcohol is almost as much a danger to the race as is unlimited use of opium.

I should at once tackle the disgraceful statistics which reveal to all the world that the death-rate in childbirth is higher in the United States than anywhere else. I should follow the policy advocated by Governor Alfred E. Smith of New York when he asked the legislature to see to it that every community in his State received adequate medical and nursing care, and I should make it possible for the poor to have not only adequate medical care, but the dental service of which they are today deprived because it is beyond their means. And, of course, I should make free for all the necessary information as to birth control. I should free our schools from the domination of all the politicians and all the priests. I should introduce self-government not only among the scholars, but among the teachers, and I should not only guarantee absolute freedom of teaching but see to it that every new or old ism was carefully explored within the classrooms of school and college. One of my first steps would be to make impossible the control of our colleges by boards of trustees comprising wealthy men devoted chiefly to the old order of society and to the prevention of the teaching of new doctrines and new theories of economic and political life. I should read to each board of university trustees the famous words of Patrick Henry: "Give me liberty, or give me death," and then give them their choice. I should ask them not to come to me to explain that there are "certain things" that must not be laid before the "immature minds of undergraduates," and that there must be some limits to liberty and free speech lest they degenerate into license. If anyone sneaked through into my audience chamber and began to address me with the words: "I believe in liberty and freedom, but there are limits," I should immediately sentence him to twenty-five years on my most northern Alaskan prison farm, in company with all those benighted citizens who might appeal to me to continue intercollegiate athletic contests under present conditions. William Green and Matthew Woll of the American Federation of Labor I should designate as Governor and Deputy Governor of the Aleutian Islands. For Mr. Hoover and his Cabinet, and other talkers of economic nonsense, I should reserve the Island of Yap with the requirement that morning and evening they should meet together to inform one another that prosperity is just around the corner, and that every day in every way things are getting better and better.

Then I should give my attention to the revision of our own government, to vital alterations in our Constitution, a noble document, admirably constructed for the use of thirteen struggling States along the Atlantic seaboard when they did not know their own hinterland, when not one citizen had yet crossed the continent overland. I should change the Constitution so that the state should take over and operate, either directly or through some government corporation like the Mississippi Waterways Corporation, the railroads, the pipelines, the telephone and telegraph, the radio, the mines, the oil wells, water power, and all other natural resources, thus making enormous savings, closing avenues to the making of excessive fortunes, and destroying the foothold of many masters of privilege. By income taxes and inheritance taxes I should make impossible the transmission from one generation to another of swollen fortunes. I should enormously lighten the burden of taxation by having the profits of public utilities go into the pockets not of stockholders, but of the communities which operate them, or into a general treasury. In other words, I should endeavor to create social control of institutions as a source of funds for a progressive social policy. I should further reduce the expenses of government by saving almost entirely the $750,000,000 now devoted to the annual upkeep of the army and navy. I should seek in every way to redeem my country from the stigma placed upon its common sense by the present Secretary of the Treasury, Mr. Mellon, when he twice declared in his annual reports that 85 cents out of every dollar raised by taxation now goes to wars past and future.

With the money so saved and earned and raised, I should rebuild our cities so that every slum would disappear. I should frankly and boldly imitate the Russian government in that I should stress above all else the welfare, the prosperity, and the happiness of the plain people of Abraham Lincoln. Instead of making this a government by and for the well-to-do and rich, I should make it a government primarily concerned with the welfare of the toiling masses, and I should let the rich go hang. The ablest men that I could find I should set to the problem of the farmer, gradually and voluntarily bringing about the creation of great co-operative farms, and working out the problem of large industrial agricultural enterprises versus individual farming. I should find some way of eliminating the middleman so that the farmer living within forty miles of our greatest cities would no longer get between three and five cents a quart for the milk that sells at around fifteen on the streets of the metropolis.

Turning to the States, I should so devise their constitutions as to abolish the bicameral legislatures along the lines of a plan suggested by Senator Norris, creating a single chamber of some twenty-four members, more in the nature of a governor's council, to be elected without benefit of party. I should take every office now bestowable by a politician and put it under rigid civil-service rules. So with our municipalities, I should eliminate politics and make the office of mayor a scientific job to be held by professional mayors freed from all political control, precisely as is the case today in Germany, instituting local referendums that the people might vote upon policies. Judges I should put to work, real work, and I should make them simplify the processes of law so that they would be humanized and speeded up, as is the case in England; and, as is the case in Russia, I should abolish the death penalty, and go farther than Russia by abolishing it for political offenses as well. Divorce would be, as now in Spain and in Russia, by mutual consent, and as in both those countries, there would no longer be any distinction, legal or social, between children born in or out of wedlock.

As for the immediate emergency, I should at once introduce the five-day week, and remove from industry all children under the age of eighteen. I should institute a scientific system of unemployment insurance, and make the system of old-age pensions recently adopted in New York State nation-wide. To take care of the existing unemployment, I should immediately sell a bond issue running into the billions and utilize the proceeds for great public works, and especially for the rebuilding of our cities so that no city dweller should remain in dark and unsanitary quarters. Planning? Of course. Not only for caring for the unemployed today but for a general overhauling of the economic system in the belief that it is not overproduction but underdistribution which is troubling us and especially to prevent the recurrence of depressions like these. Naturally this would entail first of all planning to end the enormous waste of the competitive system in such an industry, for example, as that of the makers of rubber tires or of the producers of oil. But the most important means of ending the existing economic crisis would be those measures for the regulation of international trade, including means of putting an end to the hurtful heaping up of gold in this country, which I have already outlined, the abolition of tariffs, the forgiving of debts and reparations, complete disarmament, and the ending of the rule of fear and suspicion and hatred among peoples—at least so far as our example could bring this to pass.

By this time, I am sure, more than half the people of this Republic would have risen against me; the generosity of my dictatorship would be too much for them to stand. But one last thing I should strive to do before I was led off to the guillotine. I should close two-thirds of the churches of the country, allowing only those to remain open that were absolutely dedicated to peace at any price, whose ministers agreed that they would go to prison—our present type of prison abomination if you please—for life before one word of approval of mass killing should cross their lips. They would have to promise, moreover, to preach but one sermon a year dedicated to abstract theological doctrine. The rest of their time they would have to give over to social endeavor, to true spiritual leadership, according to the teachings of Jesus of Nazareth, preaching sermons directly connected with the problems of society and the practical welfare of those about them. Finally, just to show that I was human and therefore extremely inconsistent, I should once more turn censor myself and abolish lipsticks, high-heeled shoes, silk hats, all remaining Ford cars of the original model, the Navy League, the Civic Federation, and the Protective Tariff League, not to mention *Ballyhoo, College Humor,* the tabloids, and the *Saturday Evening Post.* I should send Henry Ford himself, with his humbug reputation as a model employer of labor, to join the heads of the American Federation of Labor in the Aleutian Islands.

If these things that I have outlined seem inadequate to some, too radical to others, as well as inconsistent, please remember that I have none the less stressed liberty in all the relations between human beings, and that I have had no other object in view than social, economic, and political equality. In other words, I have suggested nothing which does not seem to me in keeping with the true spirit of American institutions, with democracy and the desire for life, liberty, and the pursuit of happiness. Sometime, soon it is to be hoped, we must come to some such recasting of our governments—city, state, and national; if we do not, then we may be sure that a totally new system, whether that be communism or something else, will have to be devised to insure equality of opportunity and of life, to curb and restrict greed and appetite for wealth, and to end all the special privileges which have been established under our modern industrial system and our government—as it has been perverted from the control of the masses into the hands of the dominating few.

Ten Years of Hitler; One Hundred of Goethe

By WILLIAM HARLAN HALE

In the following short essay, Mr. Hale meets his question with the same confident honesty that he portrays in his book CHALLENGE TO DEFEAT: MODERN MAN IN GOETHE'S WORLD AND SPENGLER'S CENTURY. *Mr. Hale is only twenty-one but in turning his back upon futility puts many an older man to shame.*

Berlin, February 15

NO ONE dares remotely prophesy what may happen in Germany in the next months—or even by the time this article comes off the press. Everything hovers in a state of suspension; one minute it looks as though a Nazi Government and an ensuing revolution were inevitable; in the next it looks as though the radicals were being discredited in the face of a soberer majority. Nobody can tell today how the political powers are matched. Everywhere is subterranean secrecy or unbelievable propaganda. And there is not one newspaper in the entire country that makes a sincere attempt to cover dispassionately the news or help reveal the truth.

A decade of Hitler's storm troops, street-fighting, and fanaticism concludes in this 1932. And the same year marks the hundredth anniversary of Goethe's death—the conclusion of a century of his influence. Germany is celebrating both facts, both men. And that is, indeed, the central meaning of the Germany of 1932. After ten years of yearning for a Messiah, whole sections of the country are surging as never before to Hitler's banners.

And the hundredth anniversary of Goethe is no mere liter-

From *The Nation*, March 16, 1932. Used by permission of *The Nation*.

ary memorial; it is not just another case of publishers' boosting in order to clear out the stocks of Complete Works (in seventeen volumes). The year is a sort of milestone for the German thinking mind: it stops to make self-inquiry. First it asks: Is the meaning of Goethe dead for today? In other words, has that historic idealism, the studied spirituality and philosophic temperament, of the Germans now become obsolete? Has Goethe been displaced by modern artistic movements such as expressionism, and has the old type of intelligent German who lived so much in the realm of removed ideas, Schubert's songs, and long-stemmed pipes been entirely thrust aside by the new type of German who lives in the realm of nudist-athletic clubs, Kurfürstendamm jazz, and cigarettes?

This year Germany is taking stock of itself: What is the validity of the political radicalism which Hitler typifies; and what is the validity of the spiritual conservatism which Goethe has traditionally typified?

Both heroes have their cults, and it is difficult to say which goes to the more lamentable excesses. The process of making every German acutely Goethe-conscious has been carried on in a completely American manner. The poor old poet who could barely sell 500 copies of each new work he published is now being stuck on every placard wall, in proud portraiture, as an advertisement to lure you to Come to Germany, Come to Frankfort, Come to Weimar, and be sure and spend lots of money. Everywhere there are Goethe calendars and almanacs; there are memorial plaques, portraits, busts, silhouettes, reliefs, and other beautifully graven images to suit every pocket-book. There are collections of his sayings, in which some casual remark to Eckermann is multiplied into millions of pamphlets, brochures, souvenirs, and gift-books. There are luscious tales of Goethe the lover—of women, or of birds; there are whole books containing nothing but consecutive pictures of Goethe. The scholarly world has done its share in adding to the literature—here are some recent titles: *Goethe and His Relations with the Swiss Cotton Industry* (almost none); *Goethe's Visit to the Deaf-and-Dumb Institute in Leipzig* (only one); *Goethe's Toothache* (very bad).

He is being used in anthropology, to show the rise of man: at one end of a series of pictures is the ape, at the other end is—Goethe. He is being used in hygiene, to aid the sale of health pills: on one side is a photograph of a charming young girl, on the other side is—Goethe.

Austria is observing the anniversary moment of his death by a minute of silent reverence; performances of his early (and very inferior) plays, recitals of his less-known songs, and reprintings of his most-forgotten prose stuff up Central Europe. Suspender buttons and toothbrushes rest their appeal on some Goethean epigram; every scholar of any standing has discovered some new and very crucial fact about him, and is revealing it over the radio; and as for the Weimar festival—everyone will be there. It has been remarked that the only stocks worth buying in this depression year are those of the Weimar hotel industry.

One of the few happy moments in this vast humorless struggle toward Making Goethe Pay was a burlesque performance given by Munich students during the historic annual *Fasching* carnival. Its title was taken from the most famous footnote ever made by an editor to the poet's works—namely, Professor Düntzer's correction at the bottom of a page of Goethe's autobiography: "Hier irrt Goethe"—Here Goethe is mistaken.

The Hitler cult may be more serious; certainly it is more humorless. Hitler himself is the traditional type of fanatic—a speaker of unquestionable hypnotic power, a leader of undoubted force and ability, a man utterly lacking in any sort of intelligence. The persons he has around him are a strange collection of heavy doctrinaires and helpless neurotics; their newspapers rage, roar, and rant day after day until they become practically unreadable. The yelping anti-Semitism of the *Völkischer Beobachter* and the *Angriff* is only another confession of that lurking sense of inferiority to the Jews and that continuing obsession of being persecuted which animate the whole movement.

The world pretty well realizes by now that Hitlerism has become the haven of all the malcontents of Germany—all, that is, except the Communists. To say that the party is "radical" is of course a dubious assertion; actually it harbors thousands and tens of thousands of men whose ultimate aim is only to get their old officers' pensions back, or to see the monarchy restored. Hohenzollern, Wittelsbach, and Hapsburg are more powerful Nazi slogans than is often believed. Then there are the university students, the majority of whom are "radical" only in their methods: untold numbers of them want nothing better than the old Prussian system, and armies, and a great clanking of steel. The truer radicals of the movement are the men with a definite economic program; but every minor leader seems to have worked out his own private system—each as complete as a Kantian cosmos—which he sees as the country's only salvation.

Hitlerism is the rush of exploding political emotions; it naturally appeals to the citizens of a country that is treading along the brink of collapse. Its strength lies in its hold on youth; and that same fact will be its weakness. The Hitler cult proper is centered in the howling agitations in the universities and the nocturnal exhibitions of the storm troops. It is a game of war; it is a trial at battle. Its adherents are a mass of high-strung, nervous, and tragic young men, whose very education condemns them to unemployment, who feel they will never gain anything from the present republicanism. They are in despair, they want to get out and march in the street, sing songs and shoot guns, and hail some new Messiah. Through some hundreds of years Germany was the land of the best troops and the most ever-present princes; suddenly the whole structure disappeared. It is not so easy to strip a country's youth of its central heritage

So the nation may be said to live between two poles—the balanced, studious, and essentially conservative Goethean point of view, which tries to make the best out of present possibilities; and the reckless, fanatical, political points of view symbolized by Hitler but ranging through the entire catalogue of opposition from Prussian ex-cavalry colonels to Schwarzwald stable boys.

Certainly "balance" has been the essence of the policies carried on by Stresemann and Brüning: both men have seen the impossibility of isolating Germany from the rest of Europe, of turning it into a self-sufficient and unfriendly island. They worked always toward a rapprochement, toward some show of internationalism. With masterly leadership Stresemann struggled to appease the insatiable maw of France; Brüning struggled until at last the strain became too great. But still the state of mind which the present Chancellor represents is for co-operation, a belief in the communal settlement of disputes. In this hour, confronted by an implacable France, an uncertain England, a blind and witless Washington, by a growing disharmony between all nations, his difficulties seem almost insuperable. And besides these outer enemies he has the inner enemies to fight—all the natural German desires for revenge against oppressors, for freedom from restraints. To Tardieu's far-repeated cry for *sécurité d'abord,* the German nationalists answer with the trumpet-call of *Deutschland, Erwache!* And that is far more appealing music to the country than a new emergency decree from the pen of its monastic Chancellor.

It is difficult for anyone not directly in Germany to recognize how stern and profound this tension at the moment is. On the hundredth anniversary of its presiding genius's death, the nation is made to remember once more Goethe's antagonism toward the violent and revolutionary, his constructive fusion of imagination with reason, his great ideal of communal effort as it reveals itself in the last acts of *Faust, II.* And these are not the isolated notions of a dead philosopher, they are life-blood in the German mind.

But at the same time all possible forces are conspiring to overthrow this clarity of view and sanity of judgment. The very same tendency to look back to the Germany of a century ago aids in this antagonism; thousands think today of the tragic ruined German lands in 1806-13, groveling at the feet of Napoleon. They think of the men who tried to conciliate the French—like the weak and vacillating Federick William III—and of the men who rose up in mighty revolt—Gneisenau,

Scharnhorst, Stein, Yorck, Blücher, the creators of a new army, an independence, a great people. Two splendid motion pictures dealing with the Prussia of those years that are so similar to these state the same case against the French oppressor; they revel in the call to arms; they burst out in Schiller's grand patriotic odes; and when in Henny Porten's *Queen Louise* the tattered battle flags of old Frederick's unbeaten regiments march by in parade, the whole audience begins to cheer—the foreigners, too.

This great confidence in their ability to do everything for themselves, which the Germans have had throughout a century, is the deepest foundation of their radical movements today. Now this traditional force among the Germans seems to have become separated from the government, where once it animated it; has sold out to the Hitlers and the Hugenbergs, and left the lawful leaders in a lonely and friendless position. What was formerly a positive life-giving essence has now become the essence of negation and revolt.

In the course of this crisis period which state of mind is going to win the upper hand—that making for conservative reconstruction and internationalism, or that making for reckless isolation and warring factions? To clinch the question, which—the strength of Goethe-Brüning, or the passion of Hitleritis? The immediate future of Europe seems to rest on this decision. And it is impossible to make any intelligent forecast. This only is certain: day by day there becomes more patent the inability of the Hitler men to form any intelligent constructive program, to see beyond mere party politics and destructive fanaticism. Every day the suffering of the German people becomes more intolerable; but there appears a growth of seriousness and responsibility, a new stress on that famous German industry and devotion which the latter years have tried so hard to extinguish.

Six million unemployed now walk the streets; dozens of large trades and industries are practically at a standstill; the basic Reichsbahn shows a staggering deficit; everywhere state theaters are closing, construction is being stopped, shops are giving up. But will the events of these fearful years alter or dissolve the stamina of the entire people? Somehow one is inclined to trust the intelligence and the courage of this race; one is willing to gamble that it may be able to resist the lure of shrieking soothsayers and clanking militarists. When one sees this precise and friendly nation going about its crippled business, one still has the hope that its vision may be clear. The nation that spoke through Goethe and the great thinkers of a century ago seems destined to survive beyond the nation that rose up in the agitators and revolutionaries of a decade ago. The country that is still the most orderly, the most efficient, the least touched by corruption in high place seems to be guided by too strong a conscience to let itself run into an overturn—an overturn that could mean little less than ruin.

The Forgotten Man to His President

By WILSON FOLLETT

Wilson Follett has been a member of the faculty at Dartmouth College and at Brown University, but now gives all of his time to writing. He is the author of THE MODERN NOVEL, SOME MODERN NOVELISTS *(with Helen Thomas Follett), and* NO MORE SEA *(a novel, published 1932).*

W E HAVE given you what you asked for—our votes. In unprecedented millions we have sanctioned your aspiration to the office which you now assume. Thousands of us who never before cast a ballot for any nominee of your party have cast our ballots for you. Other thousands who never before participated in a national election at all, because they never detected in national politics a contest of principles worth a trip to the polls, have helped swell your majority. Many of the sound, disinterested, incorruptible men of the party lately in power worked against their nominal affiliations to procure your triumph, and brought to your cause the support of all who value the judgment and trust the motives of these leaders. You go to your inauguration bearing the ostensible mandate of all parties, all social classes, all occupations, all sections of the country, in a way and to a degree never granted to any man since America came into her full stature as a nation.

You might pardonably look upon yourself, therefore, as having won, by either the arithmetical or the moral scale of measurement, every plaudit and every tribute within the power of your fellow-countrymen to bestow. Nevertheless, we beg of you not to see yourself in that light. It would be natural enough, human enough, for you to surrender yourself to the elation of the victor in a partisan contest; but we want you to be a little more than human in this one respect, and to feel something less than elation. The glow of triumph, the gusto of an overwhelming and merited vindication—that might excusably be the mood in which you contemplate your success and approach the responsibilities of your office; but to us it seems desperately important that you attain a mood for which no excuse need be framed.

Superficially considered, the circumstances invite you to take your oath of office as a victorious general, the resplendent conquering hero who leads a triumphal procession in his plumed and gilded coach. We can perhaps forgive you if you so feel and act, for are we not human and ordinary folk ourselves, capable of petty exultations and gloatings, fond of a bit of pageantry or dramatic retribution now and then, prone to imagine ourselves with a foot on the necks of fallen enemies, and touched with humorous charity for our own average weaknesses made manifest in the conduct of other men?

At the same time, we should far prefer not to be obliged to forgive you for being even as we are; we have seen enough and to spare of arrogant fatuity in office. We should like to be satisfied with you, satisfied with the choice we have made. And satisfied we shall never be until we have seen you go to your task, not arrayed in self-confidence and pride, not vestured in the illusion of power, glory, and importance to which one of us might succumb in your place, but rather clothed in the sackcloth of an invulnerable humility.

We have given you the votes you asked for; but is there not one other thing, even more important, which you require from us along with them? It seems to us that there ought to be, and that without this other thing your handsome majority will turn out to be worthless to you and to us. We hope you want what goes with the votes; but, whether you do or not, we want you to have it. We have a moral right to demand that you accept it, and even to force it upon you if we can find the way.

What is it that we are so insistent upon your having? Simply an understanding of what we meant by all those ballots cast for your electors.

To whom can you turn for this urgently necessary understanding? Who is going to challenge you with a truthful interpretation of your victory? Not your late campaign workers and managers and backers and their astute lieutenants. These men's game is not truth, but flattery; not wisdom, but tactics. Up to the eve of the election they were busy flattering us, the electorate, in what they thought to be your interest. Precisely at that point their usefulness ended.

An hour after the result was known, most of them had turned to flattery of you. They began with one consent to inform you that we voters had just given a stupendous and crushing demonstration of our confidence in you. There you have the measure of their hopeless remoteness from us plain, non-political folk and our mental posture. It was perhaps an inevitable bit of comedy that they should make you that hollow declaration; but if by clamor and repetition they get you to believe a word of it, then you will have become the victim of tragedy, and we the spectators of tragi-comedy.

The underlying truth of what the country meant by its behavior on election day is not to be had, then, from those interested ones who have the readiest access to your ear. It is not to be had, save in vestiges and glimmerings, from even the most disinterested of political specialists and regionalists. These can help you to some extent with technics and devices—admitted. But for a knowledge of what has really been happening of late in the mind of America, for trustworthy counsel as to the actual basic obligations and policies of your administration, there is only one quarter to which you can afford to turn, and that is the quarter occupied by the inarticulate forgotten man made memorable in the phrase which you borrowed from Sumner for your campaign.

Let us not be technical about whether by "the forgotten man" you mean precisely what Sumner meant. We know what you mean, or think we do; and it is something real. You mean us, the forgotten people of forgotten America, the country nobody knows—us, the plain folk, distrustful congenitally of politics and politicians, us whose votes put the rungs in your ladder. As well as we knew how, we said by those votes, "See here, all you officeholders and interest servers and blind mouths generally, *we* live in America, too. It is high time someone thought of *us* for a change; and, mark you, we mean sooner or later to be remembered."

If, having once really understood that we exist, you are resolved to keep us in mind, to work for the advancement of our legitimate hopes, and to ignore all expert advice to the contrary, then you possess the first and greatest qualification for becoming the President of all the people, and you can have any degree of support from us that you will ever require. If, on the other hand, you lose touch with us among the intricacies of bureaucratic manipulation; if you rest content with the conventional executive ideal of being merely a plausible party leader and industrious fence builder; if you let politicians sell you their political interpretations of our extremely non-political state of mind—then you are primed for exactly the disaster which overtook your predecessor in office. You will find yourself the marshal of an army with a pretentious plan of campaign, an elaborately organized staff, and not a corporal's guard of privates in the ranks.

In the long interval between your election and your inauguration, we hope that you have devoted your time to measuring and collecting your merely human powers against the appalling demands ahead, studying to make yourself a better man than the one your party convention nominated and we elected. We hope especially that you have spent some of it in feeling out the new spirit of the country, striving to penetrate the smoke screen of mere party strategy to the realities of your forgotten man.

Believe, if you can, that the very voice and spirit of that naïve fellow are trying to speak to you from these pages. They have no panacea to offer, no sure cure for the ills which beset us, for the forgotten man has not been educated to the point of believing in the magic of his own words. The intellectual ones will bedevil you more than enough with their pat little formulas of salvation. These paragraphs, then, contain not a hint of anything that could be called a political program. They are merely an attempt to suggest to you, in the most general way, how the masses of us feel about you, our President, and what we meant by that overpowering majority in November, and what manner of service we shall have to receive from you to escape the conviction that once more we have been sold, made to waste our votes.

You will find nothing here which does not faithfully represent the thoughts of unnumbered Americans—clerks and sales persons trying to get along on a third of a job apiece; foreclosed ranchers in the high plains, ruined farmers and planters in the Mississippi belt; newspaper men who privately revile the policies of their managing editors; mechanics in garages, attendants at filling stations, waiters in restaurants; the bankrupt clients of city and country lawyers who cannot collect one fee in seven due; mill operatives and bench hands in towns built on a single industry now idle; fishermen the length of both coasts; folk who have come to the pass of accepting public aid for their children, and other folk who have pawned belongings to help the children of neighbors; tenants struggling to pay rent, landlords struggling to collect rent or to meet their necessities without collecting it; movie extras and librarians and teachers and writers and the mining engineers of mines two years closed down—in fine, *us*.

You cannot say that it is officious of us to wish that we might make you feel and hear us. After all, we hired you, and you ought not to object to knowing what we expect of you. You cannot very well say that our opinion of you has ceased to be worth your hearing since we recorded it en masse in November, when you were so gracefully deferring to it. The fact is, we are about the only ones from whom you have much chance of hearing the astringent truth; for we are about the only ones who ask nothing for themselves individually and expect nothing save in terms of the common good. It seems to us that you must care to know what we think.

Here you have what we think, or some of it. Believe it if you can. Our greatest hope for ourselves politically is that you may have discovered for yourself that the account here given is, in its spirit and essence, true.

To go back for a moment to the beginning:

You must not let your advisers tell you, or believe if they do tell you, that the statistics of the election demonstrate an overwhelming popular confidence in either your party or yourself. The campaign oratory is over now, and all may gratefully forget it and the moods in which it was delivered and heard—heard as often as not, by the way, with a wry skepticism which might have disconcerted the speakers and given them some new ideas about the general acumen of the American people. We have come to the time and the place for a friendly sort of candor; and you will have lost the most salutary part of your self-preparation for office if you do not let us tell you candidly that you must not mistake the vote for a vote of confidence. It was not that, for the simple reason that confidence was not what we voters felt in you.

What we felt, and all we felt, was hope; and the only way for any holder of a national office to capture our confidence is to justify a reasonable fraction of our hope by his conduct in the office itself. The head of the ticket, in this of all presidential years, is no exception. What we have given you is an opportunity to earn our confidence hereafter.

Your opponents elected you. We did not so much accept you as reject them; and we rejected them, not because their campaign suffered by comparison with yours, but because their acts in the preceding twelve years suffered by comparison with any tolerable standard. As one of them, an ostensible liberal, has lately declared, they had taken advantage of every major opportunity to be wrong since the year 1919. Our cumulative realization of that wrongness eventually defeated them. They had conducted the national administration in a way to make it almost a test of patriotic endurance, concentrating at Washington more than were ever seen in one place of the forces which one who loves his country must love it in spite of.

They devoted their campaign to showing that the nation's plight might have been worse. It might; but not, we told ourselves, in any way which the Federal Government could conceivably have affected. We turned them out of office; and with them we got rid of their local counterparts almost to a man. No such general sweeping of political dead leaves and cobwebs has ever been seen on this continent. That it was not, as charged, the outcome of an insensate rage against all present incumbents, a mere mania for change at any price, we showed in a number of scattered instances by retaining in office persons of notable integrity and ability, regardless of their party connections.

You became the beneficiary of our conviction, rightly or wrongly held, that a change of administration might just possibly improve our condition, and could not sensibly be expected to make it worse. You were elected by our almost universal belief that the worst calamity overhanging us in the political sky was four years more of what we had been having.

About you, personally, we have never as yet felt that our knowledge went very deep.

We realize that you are what is called a good fellow; and we are inclined to believe that you are also a good man—one whose heart is in the right place. We can easily imagine that you would go to almost any length of personal sacrifice to relieve misery or promote happiness among your fellow-men. And we are utterly unable to imagine that you would ever use your office for any of the cruder forms of self-interest or class interest. There will be no scandal connected with your discharge of your executive functions—we understand that.

Also, we count upon you to select your advisers from among men of admitted probity, breadth of outlook, and public spirit. If you have judicial appointments to make, your nominations will be beyond challenge. We admire you as a man of really civilized and urbane qualities—a man who confronts his work with the healthy gusto which a good many persons devote only to their play, and who does his work all the better for finding in it an enjoyable excitement.

If you had had the destitute veterans of the bonus army on your hands last summer, we suspect that you would have gone to the Anacostia flats very informally in a White House limousine, talked companionably with leaders and men, had a grand time yourself, and left the whole outfit feeling that you were their personal friend. You would never have put them out of Washington for a reason or by a method that would not stand examination; and if it had become necessary for you to put them out, we conjecture that you would have made it your business to go and tell them why. Your tact and candor would have made them see it, too, and the vast majority—all who were not there expressly to make trouble—would have gone cheering you.

You have, we think, a really fine gift of making it easy for all sorts of persons to like you, to feel your color and reality as a man, office or no office. That is in itself a great gift. It will constantly enable you to profit by doing the thing which is at once politically advantageous and morally genuine. We shall never begrudge you an ounce of that sort of profit. Being nobody's fool, you will probably enjoy a private chuckle whenever the ideally right thing for you to do is also the commandingly popular thing; and, being nobody's fools ourselves, we shall chuckle with you.

Your detractors tried to make us feel last summer that your little cruise in New England waters was a hollow and rather childish bid for publicity; but those of us who are coast dwellers understood perfectly why you chartered that yawl. It was because, loving the sea and sail exactly as so many of us do, you had a sapient little premonition that for the next eight or nine years you might not be allowed to be at close quarters with the sea again except with a good part of the United States Navy in attendance. We American people may be a little thick-witted at times, but when a man is genuinely keen about doing a certain thing we are not so dull as to forbid him because he knows that his doing it may catch him a few headlines and some votes. Such a cruise is an admirable way to spend time, even if people admire it; and you will never alienate our regard by collecting the applause which is due to your qualities.

The question is, not how much support you win by doing the right thing, but rather how many wrong, dubious, or evasive things you are capable of doing to win support. And here, we must admit, is the point at which our actual knowledge of you breaks off and gives place to the high hopes already referred to.

We see clearly that it will take a very great President indeed to bring about any positive betterment in the state of the Union during the next few years. The merely shrewd administrator, the expert party leader with talents for getting himself liked and putting the opposition at a disadvantage, can help us only in the obvious negative ways. That is, such a one can make it fairly hard for government to waste our diminished substance, further dishearten our morale, and interfere with the slender existing impulses toward health and recovery. Frankly, we have not dared count upon much more than that from our next Chief Executive.

Regardless of what anybody has said, we never believed either that the party in power produced the depression or that the party just coming into power could end it. We made the depression ourselves, without even as much help from Europe as some of the bad consciences among us insist; and we fully expect to cure it ourselves in the long run, by revaluation and relocation of the various misunderstood, misplaced things in our civilization.

About all we can really demand of the political system is that it shall stand out of our sunlight. To *make* sunlight for us, our President would have to be of altogether uncommon stature both intellectually and morally. There would have to be a good deal of the seer in him, something of saint and stoic, and possibly a touch of the martyr, all over and above the clever politician and good fellow. He would have to be both the man of the hour and a man for the ages. We have *hoped* to find that paragon in you. (One of the great things about the American political scheme is the way it can keep hope alive by just the perpetual dim possibility of miracles.) But we have certainly not had the hardihood to count on anything of the kind. We do not know enough about you to justify such expectations; and some of what we do know rather tends to discourage them.

Surely you will see how events have worked together to unsettle our minds and muddle them with doubt.

For months before your party convention, it appeared that to get the nomination you were ready to go to any length within the canon of political decency. That appearance dismayed, even staggered us. A man, obviously not insane, who *wanted* to become President of the United States at such a time—that struck us as a bizarre phenomenon indeed, hardly accountable at all save on the hypothesis of a well-nigh pathologic personal ambition. There are plenty of us ordinary forgotten men who, if we had a bear by the tail, would hang on as long as we could (which is why the obstinate campaign of your rival seemed intelligible and human), but not many of us would go about gratuitously seeking a grizzly to tackle barehanded.

Your insistence upon assuming the man-killing task was so prolonged and became so passionate that at last we began to entertain the speculation that there must be in it something quasireligious and dedicated, something of the inspired major prophet. Did you possess a secret fanatical conviction of being the man uniquely provided for the great emergency? That was a thought pretty difficult to reconcile with your suavity, your level-headedness, and your twenty-two years' practice in playing the game. Nevertheless, whenever you opened your lips in the campaign we half expected them to give forth flames and lightnings. It was somehow an anticlimax when, every time, they yielded only the restrained, polished, conciliatory, sometimes slightly evasive utterances of a well-bred candidate who had made up his mind to run no avoidable risks.

We made allowances for you on tactical grounds. We admired your discretion as a master of loyal party team play. We told ourselves—with less and less conviction as time went on—that just as soon as the votes were counted you would dare show us the real caliber of your mind. Now we wait with the same hopeful expectancy for your inaugural message. Sometimes we ask a little wistfully: "Will 1936 find your official spokesmen assuring us that, whereas you have had to spend your first four years subtly working for re-election, in your second term you can afford really to let yourself go?" We are in a comparatively realistic and skeptical frame of mind this year, and less given than of old to counting chickens unhatched.

You see how it is. With all the will in the world to expect of you the great things for which the exigency itself cries out—greater things, we suppose, than have been required of any President since Lincoln—we have been led by the march of events to wonder if there is quite enough sheer power in your composition to meet with inspired energy the stupendous demands of the time. More than we have ever wanted anything from public life, we want to find in you a leader enduringly great by the standards of world history. Only let us see that you are that leader, or even that you comprehend the necessity which calls for him, and there is no length to which we will not follow you and support you. But if, as President, you try too urbanely to please everybody, if you substitute even the highest grade of practical politics and diplomacy for uncompromising courage, if you lose our realities among the plausible and convenient misrepresentations which always so loudly outshout them in Washington—what, then, can we do but heave the same old familiar sigh over our wasted votes?

We shall have asked for the bread of wisdom and leadership, only to be given, not perhaps exactly a stone, but the cut glass of some graceful forensic diction. Is it, after all our hopes, to end so? We are ready, heart and ear, for a savior. Have we him? Or have we, instead, an attractive and facile man, an able politician, a fluent compromiser, whose importance to history in the long run will be that he once called attention to the neglected works of William Graham Sumner?

Probably you have no idea how many substantive errors in

policy we common forgotten people could forgive you, or how easily we could forgive you them, if only we might find you cherishing some broad general convictions akin to our own and fighting with the courage of those convictions. Few errors of policy are irreparable, and we had rather see you arrive at all the wrong answers in the right spirit than at all the right answers in the wrong spirit.

We do not primarily demand to be convinced by the details of what you do about the tariff, or the bonus, or prohibition, or the foreign debts, or farm mortgages, or even the relief of hunger. We quite appreciate the insoluble element in all such problems, and, unlike professional politicians and lobbyists, we do not make your circumstantial agreement with our view a first condition of supporting you. We concede you a really handsome margin for experiment and the making of mistakes—especially if, against all political usage, the mistakes be admitted and, as far as may be, corrected.

The thing that we need from you is not infallibility in practice, but unquestionable generosity and candor in motive. The fact is, we ordinary folk have always understood that the world is not going to be saved by holding the right ideas about political and economic questions. That is where we differ from the intellectual liberals and radicals; and that is why we read their weekly manifestoes rather seldom, and then ordinarily to smile with indulgent irony.

The important consideration about a man, a horse, a dog, or a President, is how he is *disposed*. Man is, it seems, an animal who can be saved, not by great truths about things in general, but by his affections, his desires. Now, the masses of us love our America and desire to see her become in certain ways a better land to live in. It is your privilege as our elected leader to clarify, to crystallize that love and that desire—to reveal to us the essential unity of purpose underlying the apparent diversity of our clamorings, and to hearten us for acceptance of the fundamental lessons which we are beginning to learn and must sooner or later master.

You cannot give us prosperity, but you can help create the

atmosphere in which real prosperity breeds. You can lay the basis for a new and tenable definition of prosperity, which is the first desideratum. Nine-tenths of all discussion of American prosperity is tacitly based on a premise which we do not accept: the premise that everything will be right-side-up as soon as those who were making money four years ago can make it again as fast and as easily, by the same methods.

We not only do not believe that that sort of prosperity is just around the corner, but we do not *want* to believe that it is. Half of this so-called depression is débris from the inevitable explosion of that so-called prosperity. The other half is our open-eyed repudiation of prosperity on those illusory terms—our discovery, better late than never, that we really prefer security, continuity, thrift, and more modest values that will stay put longer. Presumably you share our preference; but we are waiting for the day when everyone in North America will be dead certain that you share it, including all bankers, financiers, wildcat promoters, members of the New York Stock Exchange, and every vendor of insecurities.

Why should the American people be miles ahead of their nominal guides in these matters? Why should it be imagined that the last thing we can bear is the harsh truth about what lies just ahead? We are a patient, a philosophical people—witness the unprecedented good nature and forbearance with which we have stood the pinch of want in the midst of a mocking surplus—and we can go through almost any passage, however long, if shown a chance of coming out at the right end. What we cannot stand much more of is false encouragement. If there is ever a social revolution in this country—which may God forbid, for what we really believe in is individual choice and chance and a lot less government, not mass efficiency and more government—it will not be the product of exhausted fortitude in the national character. It will be the product of unfulfillable reactionary promises made to keep us quiet.

If you want to lead us in 1936, lead us now. Support our morale by justifying the best hopes we have placed in you. Grasp and use the elements of unity, of serenity, underlying the troubled surface of American life today. Keep in touch with us non-political folk who elected you for non-political reasons. Forget all about the Presidency as a drum major's job of beating time to hold the party band together so that it can drown out the rival band. Perhaps someone says that the Democratic Party has a right to count upon you for this and that. Has the Democratic Party (if there is such an entity today) a right to count upon you for anything of doubtful value to the American people?

What a magnificent, what an altogether unparalleled opportunity is yours to be the President of all the people! Elected by the votes of all parties and classes throughout the country, you take office without damaging commitments or entanglements. No President of modern times has been more free to respond to the changing demands of current facts and the fixed demands of his own principles. None has been in a better position to take the country into his confidence, or to talk honest talk to the plain citizen over the heads of political obstructionists. There is not a legislator or a lobbyist whom you could not place in a withering light before his constituency if he were to take the wrong side of a question touching the public interest. In short, everything invites and even commands you to solidify your political position by the ideal method of transcending party politics.

You probably realize that there is a disastrous tendency to over-professionalization in American life today. No doubt you see it operating in phases of life remote from your own. Many professions have become so large that they constitute within their own ranks a body of opinion, the force of which gradually substitutes itself for the opinion of the actual public. You have perhaps observed writers and publishers unconsciously producing books for the impression they will make on critics and other writers. The motion-picture people are industriously imitating each other's dreariest work, on the naïve assumption that it must be what the public wants. Metropolitan journalism has become so exclusively an expression of journalists that you might about as well go to a burlesque show for a true picture of American life and taste as to open your morning paper. Almost any ordinary driver of an automobile could tell the motor-car manufacturer some startling things about his present unsuspected opportunities to serve the public better, to his own incalculable profit, but the manufacturer would not believe a word of it, because he has so largely lost touch with his market. Out of his own technic he has evolved a convenient but fictitious notion of what the public is and wants, and that idea designs his product and tries to sell it.

The man in political life is assuredly not immune from this lamentable tendency. Plenty of Washington politicians do not even see a normal private citizen of the United States from year's beginning to year's end, and they forget that there is any such animal. When they do see one they dread his approach as a potential embarrassment and nuisance. During campaigns they confront him only en masse, not to find out what he wants, but to tell him. In short, they breathe, think, and exist for the approbation and support of other officeholders. The higher the office, the higher the fence separating its holder from the people and their realities. The Presidency itself can easily become a mere catch-as-catch-can bout with the desk work of day-to-day administrative routine. Even a pretty capable executive, unsustained by a broad conception of the trust committed to him, can become snarled hand and foot in festoons of innocent-looking official red tape, like a kitten in a ball of yarn.

You cannot eliminate this tendency, to be sure. But you can resist it. When the knowing ones suggest to you, as they will, that the Presidency is not social philosophy or homiletics or generalizations, however inspiring, but simply the oiling and adjusting of an incredibly complicated machine; when they try to convince you that any appeal to us against them will be disloyalty and cheap demagoguery on your part—why, we hope that you will then remember certain things out of the past. You might remember Theodore Roosevelt, who lives in history just in so far as he crystallized the non-political sentiments of millions by very much that sort of disloyalty and demagoguery. You might perhaps think of Woodrow Wilson, who asserted the non-political moral sense of mankind against all the narrowly political motives, and whose thought is a conserving force in the world today, while the expediencies which he denied are wrecking the world.

And we hope you will think of that immense popular and electoral majority which we gave you. That is to say, we hope you will think continually of *us*. We shall not bother you very much. We are not conspicuously articulate. We do not clamor at our officials or hound them. We shall be so quiet that you may be tempted to wonder sometimes whether we do, after all, exist. We do; we have eyes, ears, hearts, even if we do but little shouting and self-asserting; and, as you have seen, we have votes. We shall be here when you have need of us; we will answer when called upon.

Work for us, and we will stand by you. Let us feel that you believe in us, and nothing can undo our belief in you. Remember the forgotten man, and he will make you a remembered President.

Column Left

By STUART CHASE

Stuart Chase was born March 8, 1888. After his graduation from Harvard in 1910, Mr. Chase became a partner in the firm of S. Chase and Company, Certified Public Accountants, Boston. From 1917 to 1922 he investigated the meat industry under the Federal Trade Commission. Since 1922 he has been with the Labor Bureau, Inc. Mr. Chase is the author of THE TRAGEDY OF WASTE *(1925) and* MEXICO *(1931), and co-author with F. J. Schlink of* YOUR MONEY'S WORTH *(1927).*

UTOPIA-MAKING is good fun, and so is sand sculpture at low tide. I know what path I should like to see my country take, but I can hardly expect her to take it. No prophecy is quite devoid of wish fulfilment, but let us try as honestly as may be to trace the curve of America's immediate economic future as it springs from the curve of her economic past. Thus we leap into space from firm ground. If I read the past aright, the course in the years before us veers to the left, in the direction of an increasing social control of industry. The extent of wish fulfilment in this conclusion I must perforce leave to your appraisal.

The American frontier, according to James Truslow Adams, ceased to exist about 1890. In that year the Bureau of the Census reported: "The unsettled area has been so broken by isolated bodies of settlement that there can hardly be said to be a frontier line." The mental habits engendered by the frontier have continued to this day, however, exhibiting a cultural lag of more than four decades. Mr. Adams describes some of these habits and I have added a few more. They include:

An unlimited optimism as to the economic future. "The United States cannot be sold short." We still feel sure of an infinite frontier of land, minerals, forests, potential population.

The gospel of hard work and getting things done in a hurry. The compulsion of speed.

Engineering ingenuity and mechanical ability.

The worship of financial success. A toleration for the means provided the end of money-getting is achieved. The cloaking of business with moral sanctions (*vide* Bruce Barton), and the seating of the business man at the pinnacle of the Republic.

The gospel of getting by, and of getting away with it.

A gross callousness toward the waste of land and natural resources, and toward the esthetics of land use. Stream pollution, litter, road-side slums.

A sturdy repugnance to all "foreign entanglements." There was more than enough work to be done at home.

The cheerful, nay, determined shoving of government into the hands of third-rate, easily manipulated men. It was assumed in a general way that a country of such unlimited resources did not need a government.

And, finally, a certain cowardice in facing economic realities. The pioneer was essentially a man so overborne with troubles at home that he preferred to take an ax and a covered wagon rather than remain and make a fight on the home front. This is particularly true of the great immigrant population. It chose escape as the easiest way out. The American frontier was the safety valve of popular economic unrest not only for the Eastern states but for Europe as well.

Meanwhile economic facts have been moving relentlessly onward in a direction increasingly at variance with this typical American outlook and ideology. The most explosive fact of all is that the frontier ended forty years ago, leaving us without a safety valve for more than a generation. As Charles A. Beard says: "We are living on the husks of the nineteenth century." Almost as shattering is the fact that the curve of population is rapidly heading into a plateau, and Dublin tells us that along about 1960 we shall probably come to a dead level of one hundred and sixty millions or thereabouts. What with birth control and the restriction of immigration, the ever-expanding domestic market is doomed—certainly on the old gorgeous, automatic basis.

In the third place, the machine has bored so deeply into our economic structure that today a man can hardly do the simplest act—turn a faucet, go for a ride, smoke a cigarette, give a present to his sweetheart, listen to a song—without sending out economic waves which reverberate around the seven seas. We are at last locked into a structure so complicated, interrelated, far-flung, and tenuous, that untold millions of delicate cog-wheels must join if Sam Smith is to eat tonight or Mary Robinson to have a new dress upon her back tomorrow. While Americans still view foreign entanglements with a malevolent eye, and while, theoretically, we could be a nation largely self-contained, the cold facts are that we have loaned some twenty billions abroad in recent years, and come increasingly to depend on exports to keep our wheels turning and our wheat waving. Without a number of key products not procurable at home—such as rubber, nitrates, coffee, sugar—we should promptly be most seriously embarrassed. We could be far more self-sufficient than we are, but the point is that we have never taken the effort, beyond flag flapping and speech making, and are now, whether we like it or not, clamped into a world economy.

The collapse of the frontier was a serious business, but its effects were slow in making themselves felt so long as population increased rapidly, markets were maintained, business opportunities continued abundant, and mechanization was not too cataclysmically complicated. These mitigating factors were in evidence until well into the nineteen-twenties, aided by a wide-open immigration policy, by the fillip to business given by the war, and by the phenomenal passion of Americans to own and operate a motor car.

But at last the day of reckoning has come. Added to the usual downswing of the business cycle—a phenomenon we have known since the depression of 1819—we find ourselves with no frontier to which to escape. (Nor can we even eat on our highly specialized, one-crop farms.) The war fillip has faded out, indeed reversed itself, as the sad realization dawns that we have loaned the money to foreigners with which foreigners have paid for our industrial activity during the past decade. Now the loans are marked frozen, and our mile-high tariff iceberg has helped to freeze them. Our population growth is sluggish and promises to be more so, which brings real-estate values to a full stop if not to a back somersault. The whole theory of such values throughout the history of America has been to tie them to a mounting population curve. The future has already been capitalized and that future, according to Mr. Dublin, will probably not materialize.

We have oversold ourselves on gadgets pumped by the instalment plan, enormously extending an industrial plant for the production of luxuries and semi-luxuries which, in a crisis, people do not need to buy and frequently, in the teeth of the advertiser's psychologist, will not buy. A recent commentator has estimated that the margin of "consumer capriciousness" in the present domestic market is at least twenty-five per cent. No former depression has known such a margin, and the current slump is rendered the more severe by virtue of a huge new element of overproduction in the sense of excess-plant capacity in the luxury trades. Where, for instance, are the Tom Thumb golf courses of yesteryear?

We have oversold ourselves on securities, an ominous percentage of the offerings of the past decade coming under the head of beautifully engraved cats and dogs and foxes. Loans—tremendous loans—have been duly advanced on this menagerie. The whole credit structure has become involved, and sways dizzily, wracked with an alarming internal pain.

Lastly—the technological process having marched to the tune of rugged individualism, no man seeking to guide it or even to understand it—we find that the railroads have become technologically antiquated without our knowing it, and can never take their proud place again; and that the motor car, which gave us such a mighty impetus in the twenties, is destined for a *replacement* rather than a *new* market, never again to furnish a spear-head for prosperity. A day's study would have been sufficient to provide any intelligent person with the railroad curve. He need only have cast up the tonage being torn away by the motor truck, the high-power transmission line, the oil-pipe line, the natural-gas long-distance line, the hydro and central-power station. The handwriting has been on the wall for a dozen years, but it is a script which neither Wall Street nor American ideology can read. In 1925 I foretold the end of the motor-car new market (I placed it a little too soon, not counting on the dying gasp of the two-cars-per-family campaign), but I was obviously a crabbed knocker, untrustworthy and un-American.

How, gentlemen, do you propose to circumvent this bill of particulars? Even if I have erred in one or two of them, enough remain to bring us to a halt. And to a full stop we have indeed come. The business and political captains have tried holding the right thought for two and a half years and the results of their efforts may be found deftly documented in *Oh, Yeah?*

Ruin, disaster, the end of the world? Not at all. At least not necessarily. We have come to the end of the classic American formula, nourished on the frontier, the population curve, the luck of our natural resources, of a profitable world war (for us), of a four-wheeled gadget carrying immense psychological appeal. Our basic physical plant was never in better shape, our fields never more fertile. Our natural resources are growing a bit ragged, but vast quantities remain; our population is still reasonably healthy, ingenious, and adaptable. All that has happened—to be sure it is enough—is that the credit structure has jammed, the guiding formula has collapsed, and we are face to face with reorganizing the nation on the basis of economic stability rather than zooming speculation. For all I know, the Florida boom and the Big Bull Market were the last two great joy rides of an epoch which has ended.

For the first time in our national history since the opening of the West, we have to deal with a roughly static rather than an ever-expanding structure, and, most painful of all, to discard frontier habits, ideologies, and slogans, and begin to think. There is no prairie, no mountain, no forest, to which we can escape; there are no bounding real-estate values to cushion our industrial mistakes; we have at last to face real things in a real world, stand our ground and fight. Our luck has run out. Thinking is good once in a while for men and for nations. We might even get used to it, alien as the process is, and enjoy thinking our way out. We might, for all I know, become enormously stimulated and thrilled—like the Russians—in liquidating a bankrupt economic epoch and building a new and better one. All the raw materials are ready to hand. We have to deal with a slower tempo of economic expansion; with a closed frontier and a closed safety-valve; with a world in which rugged individualism is—and has been for forty years—an anachronism; with the possibility of another orgy of speculation—such as the Big Bull Market—completely outside the picture; with the stark necessity of national and regional economic planning.

I do not happen to belong to the "plan or perish" school—except in a very general way. We shall probably have to do some radical emergency planning immediately to get us through the depression, but a long-swing program inaugurated in the next few months is not, in my opinion, the alternative to a general smash. We can probably muddle on for a few more years with temporary shots of adrenalin and temporary crutches. Planning is not a patent medicine which we must swallow or die, it is the inevitable answer to a chain of economic circumstances. The proponents of planning are under no compulsion to work out a complete blueprint, and, waving it at a recalcitrant business community, cry: Take this or expire! The logic of the circumstances which I have sought to recite above will force the business community, the government, the trade union, the public generally, to accept a new weapon for a new battle-front. Planning will probably make equal, if not greater, progress if its convinced advocates do no more than ask industrialist, banker, politician, merchant: Here are the conditions, what are you going to do? What are you going to do? What are you going to do? Conscious economic control rather than irresponsible drift is the only answer to these conditions. Sooner or later the fact will register in every intelligent brain. We are not necessarily doomed if we allow the registration process a reasonable time limit. Social habits have ever changed slowly.

If we do not plan constructively we shall not necessarily perish—just yet, as Veblen used to say. But we must certainly plan, and that soon, if American civilization is to go *forward*. The goals are already outlined with some clarity. They include:

The creation of national minimum living standards, below which no family, able and willing to work, shall be permitted to fall. The liquidation of economic insecurity on the basis of plain food, shelter, clothing, and education.

The conservation of natural resources.

The use of land for human living rather than for profitable speculation, entailing the end of Megalopolis with its compulsion of speed, noise, dirt, ugliness, and overcrowding. A wide extension of those areas devoted to natural beauty, sunshine, and first-hand recreation. Though the frontier has gone, we have plenty of land.

The education of the consumer to buy *goods* rather than jumping jacks, gadgets, and junk.

To achieve these goals, we shall probably have to experiment with such technics and methods as:

A managed currency. The end of King Gold.

The strict supervision of new investment in order that it may be at once genuinely productive and reasonably safe. In return for safety, the rate must be modest.

A drastic revision in the distribution of the national income to maintain an adequate volume of mass purchasing power. Income and inheritance taxes are the most obvious agents in this connection.

An enormous increase in the endowment for medical, agricultural, and industrial research.

A drastic decline in high-pressure salesmanship.

The declaration that all basic and essential industries are affected with a public interest, subject to public regularization, stabilization, and control. This implies the Interstate Commerce Commission technic extended to power, coal, oil, lumber, wheat, cotton, textiles, steel, copper, chemicals, and other groups.

National and regional planning boards to co-ordinate these activities, and above all to prevent the crystallization of industrial progress.

Who is to grasp these goals and work out these technics? We hear today a great hue and cry over the lack of leadership. Our business men and statesmen have failed us in this crisis. As for our scientists and professional men, nobody has ever expected anything from them. Their only function in the American saga has been to grease the wheels. Well, what does one expect, a psychological miracle? Nature does not act that way; she is not in the habit of producing stars from a vacuum. We have no leadership, because, forsooth, after the opening of the West, we never needed any. We were a self-generating perpetual-motion machine. There was no function for overhead economic leadership; no school in which such leaders could be trained. For about fifteen months in 1917 and 1918 we started a school, and called it the War Industries Board. But the emergency over, that academy was promptly sunk in a sea of normalcy. (Oddly enough, if we are to survive 1932 without a major lesion, it will probably be some of these old pupils who will pull us through.)

New conditions will create leaders. The times will call forth the man. Where the leaders are I do not know—though I could, if pressed, perhaps remove a bushel or two. Nobody knows. But they will come. You, my friend, may be hiding a marshal's baton under your coat at this moment. And the path along which they shall lead us can bear only to the left. No more excursions into the petrified forests of rugged individualism. No more attempts—save perhaps by job-hunting executive secretaries—to keep government and business single and celibate. No more jogging placidly in the middle of the road. No more mass movements to the good old days when the easiest thing to do with an over-mortgaged house was to leave it to the mortgage-holder and take the sunset trail.

Right trails, center trails, are also posted No Thoroughfare. The left road is the only road, and willy-nilly we must take it. Why? Because we cannot ride out this depression without taking it. We cannot cope with the complexities of a machine civilization, we cannot conserve our irreplaceable natural resources, we cannot build up popular purchasing power to buy back the commodities we can so readily make, we cannot get rid of unemployment and overproduction, we cannot keep our banks from freezing periodically, we cannot meet the challenge of Russia, which hour by hour climbs up the eastern sky, we cannot hold a people, some day overborne with misery and disillusion, from turning to the barricades—unless we take it.

Paying the Bill

By H. L. MENCKEN

H. L. Mencken has edited THE AMERICAN MERCURY *since 1924. His editorials for* THE EVENING SUN *(Baltimore) always present a very definite point of view and are expressed fearlessly. Before he became editor of* THE AMERICAN MERCURY, *Mr. Mencken was co-editor and critic of* SMART SET *(1908-1923). Besides contributing to American and foreign newspapers and periodicals, he is the author of a long list of books, among which* GEORGE BERNARD SHAW—HIS PLAYS *(1905),* IN DEFENSE OF WOMEN *(1917), and* THE AMERICAN LANGUAGE *(1918) are most widely known. Mr. Mencken's book on Shaw was the first book to be written about the great Irish dramatist.*

Note—See the essay "The Maverick Turned Bell Mare," page 182.

ONE hears less and less, of late, about reducing the costs of government. The war veterans have been deprived of their bonus, and some of the Federal employees in the lower brackets have had to give up part of their meager wages, but that is about all. The Federal tax bill is actually much heavier this year than it was last year, at least in its bearing upon the average man. And Congress, instead of cutting down appropriations, has been increasing them. At the same time State and municipal taxes are also rising sharply, and many a small property owner who has managed to pay them so far will lose his property to the sheriff next year.

The Federal Government will probably emerge from its present troubles with a net debt quite as large as the debt it was saddled with at the end of the war. The late Andy Mellon, LL.D., between 1921 and the great blow-off, redeemed $8,000,000,000 worth of war bonds, but the accumulated deficit since 1929 runs to more than $4,000,000,000 and Congress will undoubtedly add five or six billions to it before the return of normalcy. The money due us from Europe is gone forever: we'll be lucky if we get even trading stamps for it. And the taxable basis underlying most kinds of Federal taxes is going down almost as fast as the taxes themselves are going up.

Many of the big cities of the country are already bankrupt, and some of the States are but little better off. The condition of Chicago is not, perhaps, quite typical, but it at least shows the way things are going. Every effort to cut down the cost of government there has failed. The town is horribly infested by useless and corrupt governmental agencies, and all the worst of them are so securely intrenched, legally and politically, that getting rid of them is impossible. Thus the only way to meet the current deficit is to hold up the salaries of minor but necessary functionaries, and this is being done. The public school teachers have been paid mainly in promises for more than a year past, and the police have got no pay at all for four months. Until a few weeks ago the poor cops were supported by a voluntary dole from the speakeasies, but now the speakeasy proprietors begin to cut it off. If, in a little while, you hear of policemen taking to the highways as footpads, do not be surprised.

It is easy to put the blame for this appalling condition of affairs upon the incompetent and venal quacks who run the Federal Government and most of the state and city governments, but the truth is that they have been forced into many of their worst extravagances by public pressure, and that this same public pressure prevents them undertaking rational economies today. With a loud voice the people demand that Congress cut down expenses, but with an even louder voice they urge it into all sorts of new and preposterous expenditures. Thus its so-called leaders run in a bewildered circle, and every time they save a dollar they waste two or three.

PAYING THE BILL

What lies under all this is a profound change in the common American notion of the purposes and functions of government. There was a time when the American people thought of government as an agency of narrowly limited powers and responsibilities, and the less they heard of it the better they liked it. That attitude is reflected plainly in the Bill of Rights passed in 1791, which is mainly a recital of what the government may *not* do. But in late years there has been a turn in the other direction, and the government is now loaded with an almost endless list of fantastic duties. Within our own day we have seen it undertaking to drum up trade for business men, to teach farmers how to plant and harvest their crops, to show women how to have babies, to pry into every citizen's private books, to decide what he may drink and not drink in his own house, and to provide capital for all sorts of dubious persons who think they need it, but cannot find anyone to lend it to them.

Such enterprises, of course, cost a lot of money. Each of them must be outfitted with an immense staff of bogus experts, lured away from productive industry. They need elaborate offices in Washington and elsewhere: they use up a great deal of stationery and other supplies: their functionaries travel constantly at the public expense. The service naturally attracts more rogues than honest men, and so there is constant stealing and blackmail. We all know what the Prohibition Unit has cost the country—in money, in annoyance, in turmoil, in crime. But we are apt to forget that many of the new governmental agencies cost quite as much and that some cost even more.

When this madness to be governed to the last place of decimals descended upon the American people, most of them figured, I suppose, that they, personally, would not have to pay the bills. The common idea, at the beginning of the frenzy, seems to have been that the whole cost could be unloaded upon the very rich, or upon some other small class. But it is now seen that this was an error. The rich paid for a while, but then they stopped paying, and now the burden is falling upon the relatively poor. Every American who buys anything at all will carry a heavy share of it this year. And next year he will probably carry even more.

One of the things that fanned the fever was the great rise in prices during the late boom. In those days every third American speculated more or less, and most of them showed impressive paper profits. Thus the notion got about that the country was so rich that no conceivable extravagance could break it. The unearned increment was counted as income, and in large part spent as income, and the government fostered the delusion that it *was* income, taxing it as such. So when the crash came at last the government and the speculators went down into a common bankruptcy. Both had been counting on an inexhaustible mine of wealth that was really not wealth at all.

We are now paying for this folly. Practically everyone is short of money. The national income, which was estimated by the Treasury at $90,500,000,000 for 1929, is estimated at little more than $50,000,000,000 for 1932—a decline of almost half. To be sure, the income for 1929 was largely imaginary, but all private and government expenditures were undertaken on the assumption that it was real, and so we are feeling the pinch now, as we return to incomes that are real all the way through. We are all much poorer than we were. But we have yet to reduce our expenses sufficiently to get them within our actual income.

The private individual, of course, will somehow manage it. Since no one will lend him money any more, he must make his expenditures fit his cash receipts. If those receipts are diminished materially, as they are in most cases, he must learn to do without things that he thought he needed three years ago. And if they are reduced to nothing he must live upon his friends and relatives, or throw himself upon public charity. He can't resort to credit, for he has no credit. There is still plenty of cash in the better sort of banks, but he can't borrow it.

Unfortunately, the government can. Its credit is still relatively good, for when it gets into difficulties it can raise money by seizing it, in the form of taxes, from those who have earned it. So long as such persons confine their resistance to academic protests, it will continue well-heeled, and ready for ever new and worse extravagances. Even when it finds, on trying to shake them down, that their pockets are quite empty, it can still borrow on the security of their future earning power. Legally speaking, they are its slaves. It can dip into their bank account whenever it pleases, and if those bank accounts turn out to be too scanty for its needs, it can mortgage whatever money they seem likely to accumulate tomorrow, or next month, or next year.

The question is, How long are the American people going to submit to this absurd system? In normal times it does not burden them unbearably, but now they are sweating and panting under it in a horrible manner. The less they earn, the more they have to pay. They cut down their other expenses drastically but that one expense they cannot cut down. It hobbles every effort they make to work their way out of the Depression. It is a millstone around their necks that grows heavier every time they attempt to throw it off. How long are they going to tote it? And how, when the time comes at last, will they get rid of it?

I am no economist, but it seems to me that there is a way out. The Bill of Rights gives a long list of things that the government may not do to the citizen in his person. It may not jail him without trial, it may not forbid him to voice his wrongs, it may not quarter soldiers on him in time of peace, and so on. There is only one provision dealing with his property: the government is forbidden to take it without paying for it. It seems to me that there's a hint here. Why not a new Bill of Rights, definitely limiting the taxing powers of the government? Why not a Twentieth Amendment restoring it to its simple and proper functions, and forbidding it forever to collect or spend a cent for any purpose lying outside them?

Young Men in Politics

By WILBUR CROSS

There are few American professors who are genuinely active in politics; Governor Cross of Connecticut is one of the few. Dean of the Yale Graduate School since 1916, editor of THE YALE REVIEW, indefatigable scholar and writer (especially upon the English novel), he has found energy and time to devote to his State's government and now is its first citizen.

WHEREVER I go I find young college graduates intensely interested in the social and political affairs of Soviet Russia. If the subject comes up, as it generally does, in the talk at an informal gathering, the discussion at once becomes animated. Their remarks show that they are reading newspaper reports, magazine articles, and books dealing with Russian issues eagerly and thoughtfully. But when the conversation turns to American politics, the tone, until very recently, has at once changed. The life has gone out of it. Evidently they have not followed the speeches of our public leaders as they have followed those of Stalin. They have been inclined to treat the latest scandals in our municipal governments with boredom or cynicism. "Lousy" has been their word for the whole business.

Why is this so? Why is it that every summer increasing numbers of intelligent, alert young Americans take the fairly arduous and expensive trip to Moscow to see what is going on there and yet show so little desire to learn at first hand what is going on in Washington? I do not for a moment think that it is because they are all converts to Communism—or ever really expect to become converts. The answer is not so simple as that.

From *The Forum*, April, 1932. Reprinted by permission of *The Forum*.

YOUNG MEN IN POLITICS

I believe that behind the enthusiasm among recent college graduates for visiting Russia is, first of all, the fact that they have been assured a warm welcome. Young people have always been peculiarly sensitive about going where they are not wanted, and the youth of our day, for all their confident air and loud talk, are no exceptions to this rule. By extensive and clever propaganda and by special facilities provided for sight-seeing, the Soviet Government makes young foreign tourists feel that they are wanted in Moscow today. And it assumes, apparently quite rightly, that they wish to learn something of the social and political life of the country as well as of its museums and picture galleries.

Again, the young are naturally empiricists, and their school and college training in the scientific laboratories, in the courses in history or economics or sociology, if it has meant anything at all to them, has deepened their interest in experimentation. Now, whatever one may think of it, the fact is that a tremendous political-social experiment is being conducted at this moment in Russia. The whole country is obviously a vast laboratory. Its present rulers lose no opportunity to advertise the novelty and boldness of their effort. The fundamental premise of the entire structure is that this is a changing world and that they are the first to give effect and direction to the new movement of post-war life.

It is easy to see why, from this point of view, Russia exerts a fascination over young Americans fresh from their studies of civilization or science as a process of evolution. Nothing is further from my intention here than to present a brief for the Soviet Government. It may well be that experiments, social or economic, if not political, are now afoot in this country that will have a greater influence on history than anything that is happening in Russia. My point merely is that, if this is the case, they have not been effectively presented to the younger generation as vital or novel issues either in the speeches of our public men or in our conventional party platforms.

And this brings me to another reason for the vividness of the young American's interest in Russia. There is no question

341

that, all superficial signs to the contrary in this year of grace, youth is still a period of crusading. The early twenties are a time of no compromise, of ardent loyalties and equally ardent prejudices. One does not have to be a professional psychologist to detect in the casual indifference or cynicism of many of the remarks one hears or overhears from young Americans the working of a defense mechanism resorted to in order to conceal positive interest or emotion. The attempt at casualness is too pointed. Even the bored and skeptical "Yeah?" which Miss Ferber has pronounced the keyword in the speech of young America may hide a genuine spark of inquiry.

However this may be, the Russian Communists are engaged in a crusade for a program stated in no negative or uncertain terms, for which their leaders are fighting with every ounce of their energy. No one can get the impression that all groups or parties there have much the same middle-of-the-road principles at bottom or that Communist leaders fail to lead. And it is this aspect of Soviet Russia, I think, which most attracts young visitors today. They are made to feel in Moscow that the business of government is alive and serious, and that it is also the business of youth.

How is it with us? Let us picture the candidates who, having completed their courses in economics, history, and social science, come up for degrees each June at our colleges and universities. I have listened with thousands of them to Commencement addresses. The speaker emphasizes the duty of each graduate to take an active and enlightened part in public life. Perhaps he quotes the words of Cicero that the completion of all knowledge lies in its application to the affairs of state. If he does not, he generally expresses the same idea.

What happens as a result of all this? Usually nothing. When the college graduate returns to his home, he finds that the older men whose intelligence and integrity he most admires are "not in politics." They speak of politics as a "hopeless" or "dirty" game. They discourage any incipient desire the young citizen may have to take an active part in municipal affairs, where he would naturally expect to make a beginning. The newspapers bear out their comment. Unless he has a great deal of money which may be tapped for party funds, or some exceptional personal connection with a man in office, no party leader makes any overtures to him, much less seeks him out. And so he goes his way. During a recent state campaign, a number of young college men came to me and said that they would like to do something, but they did not want to "butt in." Rightly or wrongly, they had got the fixed impression that their services might not be welcome. They had no information at hand about the proper way of offering them.

Suppose the young college man is unusually aggressive and tries to push his way into the public life of the community. In that case, he is confronted by political organizations more closely knit than formerly for their own purposes. This is particularly true of state governments. Ordinarily the chairman himself holds no public office; but his control of his party's organization is absolute and undisputed, and sometimes relentless. He must be shrewd and astute; but beyond that he need not be overintelligent. His job is to win elections, not so much in the interest of the public welfare as in the interest of his organization, which is held together by patronage, large and small, extending downward into towns and boroughs, wherever his arm can reach. Members of legislatures may engage in hot debate over the business that is permitted to come before them. But they really initiate nothing of importance on their own motion. At the proper moment comes a crack of a whip and all talk ceases. The bill under consideration passes or the bill fails, as determined by the organization that has a majority in the legislature.

An omnipotent oligarchy, wearing perhaps the face of benevolence, may thus get into the saddle and popular government be reduced to a gesture. The young college man is not obtuse. He has a quick eye and sees exactly what the situation is. He is too independent to submerge his will in the will of a party leader. If he has succeeded in getting into the legislature, one term is enough for him. Again he steps aside and finds his occupation elsewhere.

I have said that young people are by nature and education empiricists. It is well that this is so, for without experimentation there is no possibility of intelligent advance, and the life goes out of any enterprise. Now, we are all constantly repeating the phrase that the world is changing before our eyes. The generation that has been growing up since the war has seen tremendous changes take place in the map, in government, and in social and economic organization. Naturally it looks to find some of these changes reflected in the political language of the day.

Too often what it actually finds is a restatement of timeworn ideas in slightly altered phrasings. Every four years the tariff planks and the other stocks in trade of the political orator are brought out again with little attempt to adjust them to current facts. Real issues are obscured by ambiguous terms. Prohibition is, of course, one of the great social issues now before the country. It has been rightly described by President Hoover as an "experiment," and, if one may judge by the discussion and the polls on the subject in our colleges, the younger generation takes a keen interest in this experiment. Yet the campaign speaker naturally treats it in such a way that his friends among the drys can prove that he is dry, and the wets can claim him equally well for their own faction. How can we expect to awaken young people to activity in American politics while such a state of things persists?

If a natural tendency is blocked in one direction, it will turn in another. Denied or discouraged on the political and social side, the desire of American youth to experiment and reform has lately found an outlet in the arts. I am told that in centers such as Hull House, once devoted to social crusading, the crusading is now being done more in music or painting or literature. In Yale's iconoclastic journal, the best-written article so far published dealt with the subject of architecture. It is heartening to see new blood being injected into the arts. Yet our democracy cannot but feel seriously the loss to the public business of the best minds among its rising citizens. And on their side, these same minds are losing the chance of enrichment offered by participation in social and political causes.

I have remarked that youth is the time of strong loyalties. These tend to center around personalities even more than around causes. Yet this country has had since the days of Roosevelt and Wilson no pre-eminent political figures that appealed especially to the imagination of the young. Today no party leader commands from them the esteem and admiration in which they hold, for example, Mr. Justice Holmes. American college students read with no little enthusiasm about the unbroken line in England of fine and able men who have gone from the great universities into high positions in the state, each generation training its successor in the art of government. But they do not see ahead of them any such line of men who have gone to Washington from their own campuses.

Lately we have not only had an unfortunate lack of men in the highest public offices with the gift of arousing the respect and support of the young, but we have had worse than that. The record of the Harding administration with its pitiful slogan "Back to Normalcy" after all the terrific sacrifice of the war, and the recent disclosures of abuses in such cities as New York and Chicago, have tended to shake all faith in the integrity and intelligence of public officers. These are unpleasant matters, but they cannot be avoided if we are to understand the political psychology of the Americans who are growing up with the present century. In the circumstances, there can be small wonder that most of them have preferred to look on at the spectacle of government from the side lines.

There was a time when it was otherwise. Once it was the ambition of young college graduates to bear a hand in building up the nation. They were given a fighting chance. Jefferson, a graduate of William and Mary's college, was elected to the Virginia House of Burgesses at the age of twenty-six. He was but thirty-three when he wrote the Declaration of Independence. Madison, a Princeton man, was only twenty-five when he was elected a delegate to the Revolutionary Convention of Virginia in 1776. In the next decade, he and Hamilton, a Columbia man six years his junior, were writing the Federalist

Papers and laying the political and economic foundations of the new Republic. Washington, who at the age of twenty-three had been placed in command of the military forces at Virginia, made Jefferson his Secretary of State and Hamilton his Secretary of the Treasury, while Madison was reserved as an unofficial adviser, later to be elected President. Our government was then a young man's business.

Although I do not see any young Hamiltons or Jeffersons on the political horizon today, there are some hopeful signs. A number of gifted young college men, following the distinguished lead of Walter Lippmann, are exerting social and political pressure through editorial work in our dailies or weeklies. There is a sprinkling of them in our state legislatures and even in Congress. One of my colleagues among the state governors is just thirty-four. The organization known as the Crusaders has a good representation of men in their twenties and thirties among its members.

How can more of them be brought actively into our public life? This might happen at any moment in either of two ways. It might come about through the rise to political eminence in one of the great parties of some leader with the force of personality, mind, and speech that draws youth like a magnet. Failing the appearance of such a leader, it might still come about through the adoption by one of the parties of a bold, unequivocal, and progressive platform on the major issues of the day, and a serious effort by its organizers to recruit them into its ranks. If neither of these things happens within a reasonable time, we must be prepared for the possibility that intelligent young voters now aroused will cut loose from the old parties and form a new party, and make it one to be reckoned with, as has been the case with the Labor party in England.

There can be no doubt that among the more recent college graduates, who are feeling it sharply, the present depression is acting as a spur upon interest in public affairs and their conduct. For the first time in many years, young people are beginning to recognize that national policies directly affect them.

Lacking other jobs, they may now do well to go further and look around for any jobs in municipal or state offices that may be open to them. Badly paid as these usually are, they now contrast favorably with many business positions, and the experience to be had in them cannot but prove rewarding.

This brings up the classic objection to politics as a career in this country—that men or women of integrity without private means cannot afford to embark on it. For the majority, certainly, I can see no way around that objection from the purely financial point of view. The number of positions is small indeed, even including the foreign services, in which there is today any reasonable certainty of tenure or any reasonable chance of promotion. Still there are a few such positions. Those in the consular service especially have attractions for adventurous minds beyond the salary, and many others offer training for short periods in the handling of men and affairs that may be turned to valuable account in business.

Those who have jobs but because of the slow pace of business now have also an extra amount of leisure on their hands, and those who because of financial independence need not seek for paid positions at this crisis, I advise to give politics a trial as an avocation. Party organizations do not always prove to be as tight as they look when they are approached by resourceful persons. The thing to do is to crawl in through some loophole, and then, if you find that you are in the wrong crowd, crawl out again and find or form your own crowd. One is no longer born, as in Gilbert's day, either a little Liberal or a little Conservative. Once an educated man who knows how to deal with his fellow beings is inside the right fence, he may exert influence, and with skill, patience, and zeal may win his way to some position of leadership. In any case, active-minded, observant young people should find the experience worth while in itself as an opportunity to put to the test theories that they have studied inside college walls.

Usually a long road must be traversed by the young man who enters upon a political career before he can reach a conspicuous post in the national government. He may never arrive at the goal of his aspirations; but there is a field for him in local and state governments, where the problems, though much simpler, are equally economic. Consider, for instance, the question of taxation as it affects the welfare of a town or a municipality. In that one question is involved the organization of the local government, the prosperity of business from the manufacturer down to the small storekeeper, the maintenance and extension of roads and streets, adequate support of public libraries, public schools, and humane institutions, along with a multiplicity of other details necessary for the material and spiritual prosperity of a community. Nowhere else do the people receive so little for what they pay. With some notable exceptions, town and municipal governments are run primarily in the interest of the party in power. Offices are created to the fullest extent possible for political heelers. When the citizens threaten to revolt, then an attempt is made to appease them by shifting the burden of taxation to the next generation through bond issues, which are mounting higher and higher every year. This process has been going on for a long time until now scores of municipalities in the United States are on the verge of bankruptcy. Some have already gone over the precipice. Here at his door the young college man has a rare chance to perform a service which his fellow citizens are not likely to forget. It is one that should challenge both his intellectual powers and his public spirit.

I believe that never before have American college graduates had so good a preliminary equipment for public office as they have today. I am aware that the newspapers, with lurid reports of their dissipations and cocktail parties in a land of prohibition and steady habits, sometimes give the impression that college students haven't the stamina for politics or anything else that means getting down to hardpan. It is, of course, true that there are too many wasters and drifters among them. Yet the great majority, as one who has long lived with them well knows, are really interested in a good deal of their work, including history and social science.

They have immense advantages today over former generations. Comparatively speaking, the college training of Hamilton and Jefferson was very meager. It consisted of hardly more than elementary mathematics and some Latin and Greek, with a smattering of ancient history. The great universities now provide, under the ablest scholars in the world, studies in political science, economics, sociology, government, and public law, and the political, social, and economic history of the United States and other countries. It is a wide sweep of knowledge, which embraces, beyond literature, the natural and physical sciences and the new psychology developed within the present century, all of which have important bearings upon the problems of government.

In my undergraduate days, college students as a rule were but little interested in public questions. We rarely discussed them. Not until my senior year at Yale, when William Graham Sumner spread before us the great issues in political and social science, did we come to know much about the complicated economic problems of the modern world. Then it was too late to specialize in them. Go now anywhere you please among groups of students and you will find them debating the financial crisis here and in Great Britain or Franco-German relations. They talk about war debts, reparations, and the Far Eastern situation. Some of them understand the political and economic ideas lying behind Italian Fascism, and most of them know the latest news from Russia. Partly through the exigencies of our national depression and partly through this interest in foreign affairs, in which it is clear that we are daily becoming more entangled, the attention of students and young graduates is being turned toward American political and economic questions. The next step should be to translate intention into action. This is the moment to make the experiment—with the most exciting election since the war nearly with us.

Such a deadlock as now exists between the older and the younger generations in the field of politics always looks hopeless until some able man or able group rises to break it. The present situation is in the nature of a direct challenge to the older generation. If the seasoned leaders are wise, they will take account of the political and social awakening which the current crisis is producing among the young, and they will turn it to constructive use by speedily placing before them candidates and issues that will rouse them further from lethargy.

The present situation is a still stronger challenge to robust American youth. I should emphasize the word *robust,* for the political scene is no place for the anæmic dilettante, who is unwilling and unable to learn how to meet hard blows and stubborn opposition. But the opportunity is already in the hands of our muscular young citizens to take the initiative, to make up their minds what our democracy needs, and to use all their educational equipment and organizing powers to get it. From my brief experience in state government, I have learned one thing that our democracy needs today above all others. It is the energy of intelligent, aggressive, and well-trained young men and women in practical efforts for the public welfare. For their own full and vigorous development as much as for that of the country, I have no hesitation in saying to those who can stand a cold plunge: Come on in—the water's fine!

The Voter: His Rights and Duties

By *JAMES TRUSLOW ADAMS*

James Truslow Adams was born in Brooklyn, New York, October 18, 1878. After being educated abroad and at home, he was graduated from the Brooklyn Polytechnic Institute in 1898. He went into the stock brokerage business for fourteen years and at the end of that period gave himself completely over to his life's ambition, the study of history. During the war he served with Colonel House on the commission to prepare data for the Peace Conference, and later acted as special agent to the Peace Conference at Paris. In 1922 Mr. Adams won the Pulitzer Prize in History for his book THE FOUNDING OF NEW ENGLAND.

Besides many other noteworthy historical works, Mr. Adams is the author of THE EPIC OF AMERICA, *published in 1931.*

IN SOMEWHAT more than a century and a half the two great English-speaking nations, the British Empire and the United States, have passed from a firm belief in representative government to the practice, at least, of an almost pure democracy. The change has been coincident with a vast extension of the suffrage which has given to nearly all but children, a few selected criminals, and such idiots only as have been unlucky enough to have got themselves certified as such, an equal voice in the selection of the overseers of their destinies. It is conceivable that such a vast increase in the numbers of the electors might have occurred without a change in the theory of *representation*. A group of ten thousand might just

---

Reprinted from the Autumn, 1932, *Yale Review,* copyright Yale University Press, by permission of the Author and the Editors.

as reasonably have elected a man who was to be a representative, and not an errand boy or a rubber stamp, as the earlier group of a few hundred in the same borough or district. Indeed, theoretically, as the size of the electorate increased it might have been considered that the importance of representation as contrasted with direct participation in legislation of the individual elector might also have increased.

For the most part, the Americans who framed our Constitution certainly believed so, and nothing was further from their desires or hopes than that every Tom, Dick, and Harry who could vote would have a direct voice in Congress and other law-making bodies. Times, nevertheless, were already changing, and the freshets which were to swell the stream of democracy had begun to rise. In addressing the men who had just elected him to Parliament from Bristol in 1774, Edmund Burke made what has become the classic speech on the difference between representation and direct democracy.

"Your representative owes you," he told the men of Bristol, "not his industry only, but his judgment; and he betrays, instead of serving you, if he sacrifices it to your opinion. . . . If government were a matter of will upon any side, yours without question ought to be superior. But government and legislation are matters of reason and judgment, not of inclination; and what sort of reason is that, in which the determination precedes the discussion; in which one set of men deliberate and another decide? . . . To deliver an opinion is the right of all men; that of constituents is a weighty and respectable opinion, which a representative ought always to rejoice to hear; and which he ought always most seriously to consider. But *authoritative* instructions, mandates issued, which the member is bound blindly and implicitly to obey, . . . these are things utterly unknown to the laws of this land, and which arise from a fundamental mistake of the whole order and tenor of our constitution. Parliament is not a *congress* of ambassadors from different and hostile interests; which interests each must maintain, as an agent and advocate, against other agents and advocates; but parliament is a *deliberative* assembly of *one* nation, with one interest, that of the whole; where not local purposes, not local prejudices ought to guide, but the general good, resulting from the general reason of the whole."

On those terms Burke was allowed to retain his seat for six years, but at last he was defeated, as was also to be the doctrine he so manfully and lucidly set forth. What a "congress of ambassadors from different and hostile interests" may do in the way of legislation our own has shown all too often. Last spring the good of the whole, which was obviously the passing of a tax measure to balance the budget, had to wait on the miserable tactics of the "ambassadors" from the hostile interests.

For months Congress reeled in its course like a drunken man while the clear good of the nation was made subservient to the interests of this or that group. This inability of Congress to act was due in largest measure to its abandonment of the doctrine of representation and its complete yielding, even in a crisis of the first magnitude, to the pressures from direct democracy. The Babel in Congress itself but echoed the Babel in the electorate, organized, to a great extent, into pressure groups—copper, ex-service men, timber, agriculture, cheap money advocates, wets, drys, and what not. The congressmen, unlike Burke, seemed unable to use their own minds and act for the best as the representatives of the whole people; they considered themselves incapable of doing anything opposed to the direct mandates of their constituents; and, their constituents being a mob, Congress has become a mob.

All this is hackneyed commonplace, although the situation has long been of appalling and increasing seriousness. Much, but not too much, has been written of the effect on governing bodies of the substitution for the old representative idea of the more modern one of the legislator as receiving his mandate direct from the electors on every topic which he may have to consider, yielding, often against his own better judgment, to the balance of ayes and noes in a barrage of telegrams and postcards or other more gross or subtle means of influence.

A point which has troubled me, however, and I believe many

others, with regard to the effects now showing themselves of the abandonment of representative government is quite a different one. It has to do with the effect of the mandate-rubber-stamp-messenger-boy theory not on the governing bodies but on the members of the electorate itself. It is not what we may be doing to the character of legislation enacted by representatives whom we no longer regard as such, but what we are doing, by forsaking the old doctrine, to our own private lives. For a moment, let us turn from the horrors of legislation as performed by demos and pressure groups, to the individual life of that citizen whom American doctrine proclaims a king, and whom democratic doctrine insists upon giving a direct voice in all public affairs.

"Public affairs"—the old *res publica,* republic, of the Romans. Until comparatively recently we were quite free, ethically, to give our time and thought to them or not as we chose, except on the small stage of village, parish, vestry, or town, where our daily occupations and contacts afforded us all the information needed to act wisely. Public-spirited citizens of such so-called democracies and city states as Athens, Florence, and others were in this happy condition. They could get tremendously excited and take their part in politics which were purely local and in which they knew all the chief actors as fellow members of a small community.

In greater states, such as the Oriental despotisms or the European nations which gradually emerged after the Middle Ages, the individual had practically no share in the central government. That government might impinge on his private life most unpleasantly at times, just as the weather might ruin his crops, a fire destroy his house, or the soldiery of an invading army assault his family. These were all, more or less alike, acts of God. But outside his small sphere of local interests he had no responsibility for running the state any more than he had for running the universe. His leisure time was his own to do with as he would. He could sing, dance, idle, dream of the Virgin, walk under the stars, carve utensils, recite poetry— in fact, do anything which his own errant instincts and tastes might lead him to wish to do.

Even with the growth of the modern concept of "liberty" and the rise of representative government, he was as yet free to do as he would and remain a good citizen, so long as he obeyed the laws and chose his representatives, if he were allowed to do so, as wisely as he could. The representatives did the rest, and the ordinary citizen did not need to trouble himself overmuch as to what they were doing save when he was faced with the final result of their deliberations.

With the passing of the representative idea and the advent of modern democracy, however, a new situation has come about. When citizens decided that representatives could no longer be trusted and that they themselves must dictate legislation, they assumed tremendous responsibilities. As Burke said to the electors of Bristol, "To be a good member of Parliament, is, let me tell you, no easy task." As the pressure of the elector on the member of Parliament or Congress became more and more marked, it meant that the conscientious citizen had to assume more and more of the duties which had belonged to his representative. In other words, in addition to being a farmer, a doctor, a mechanic, poet, or shopkeeper, he had also to undertake to perform the duties of a congressman.

As it was impossible that he could perform this double duty successfully, the ship of state began to wallow. We were told that the cure for the ills of democracy was more democracy. The past generation saw the rise of the initiative, the referendum, the recall, the direct primary, and other experimental methods of making the individual citizen more of a legislator and the representative less. In some States, the inroads on the time of the citizen merely to cast ballots at all sorts of elections and referendums became serious. Far more serious, however, for the conscientious citizen, have become the inroads on his time and thought if there is to be well-considered and worth-while opinion back of ballot, telegram, postcard, or other effort at law-making by the democracy at large.

Let us take, for example, a few of the problems on which the citizen in a democracy which has abandoned the representative idea must have an opinion arrived at with as great knowledge as possible. These include farm relief, private or public ownership of power plants, international trade, regulation of banking, inflation or deflation of the currency, taxation, the bonus, disarmament, the Far Eastern situation, prohibition, tariffs, the League of Nations, education, reorganization of the government departments, and a host of others.

It may be pointed out that there is a large and highly technical literature on all of these topics; that specialists in them disagree as readily as the proverbial doctors; that there is nowhere an "authoritative" opinion to be had for the seeking; and that the public press, as well as private propaganda, frequently does its best to mislead the inquirer after truth.

The so-called "opinions" of the ordinary man are usually a mixture of the veriest smattering of information and misinformation, with a large injection of his favorite newspaper's attitude and the influence of his personal environment. But obviously if legislation is to be based on no better foundation than that, we might as well install a sandwich boy from a drugstore counter as president of General Electric or United States Steel. We pride ourselves on saying that this is the age of the specialist, and that there is no longer place, either in science or business or education, for the untrained. Clearly then, if we are to have democracy and not representative government; if John Doe and Richard Roe in Richmond and Seattle are to settle the legislation in Washington, Doe and Roe will have to sit up nights studying the problems on which they are to legislate. If they do not do so, or if having done so, they and all the rest of us have not been able to form sound opinions on all the topics, what possible hope is there for even reasonably sound legislation?

Again, I return, however, to the point that I am not thinking at present so much of the *legislation* as of the *legislator,* that is, of all of us who are being forced to take on in addition to the more than arduous task at present of making a living the complete duties formely assigned to our political representatives; in other words, of our having to be doctor, salesman, janitor, or portrait painter, *plus* congressman. Burke was right. It is no easy job to be a legislator. It is also no easy one to be a private citizen and to bring up a family in decency and comfort. To combine the jobs is impossible.

Most of us, when we have work, have little leisure time except evenings, Saturday afternoons, Sundays, and occasional holidays—even when we have all of those. Such time is none too much, after we have taken out of it adding up the grocer's bills, writing checks, doing odd jobs, attending committees, and so on, for us to devote to our families, general reading, exercise, the enjoyment of the hobby every sane individual should have, and certain other things. Such disposition of it as we chose to make we could make before the days when we were kings and democracy did away with the representative function of the legislator. There might be things going on in Congress of which we highly disapproved, but we were not called upon to do much about them, at least not until election time. The issues in the older days, moreover, were comparatively simple. The sphere in which a national government functioned was rather limited, and the rest was local politics which we could understand without sitting up nights to read volumes on finance and currency, on what the League really is like, on whether the theory of the Farm Board's operations has been right or wrong, and all the rest of it. In 1824 Andrew Jackson stated that "the duties of all public offices are, or at least admit of being made, so plain and simple that men of intelligence may readily qualify themselves for their performance." This was true, at any rate in so far as the tasks may be compared with those of today.

At present the conscientious citizen finds himself in an unpleasant predicament. Under the old representative system, there was no more perfect justice meted out to all classes than there ever has been, or probably ever will be, under any other system. Because of the perennial dissatisfaction of certain classes whose noses were not quite close enough to the trough, an effort was made to bring the millennium nearer by controlling the votes of the representatives. Under the old system, there had been "pressure groups" of the landed interest and what not. Under the new system we have added numerous other pressure groups to these—the tariff-favor hunters, American Legion, Anti-Saloon League, and the rest of the two thousand who, it has been stated, maintain lobbyists at Washington.

Under the old system, however, the conscientious citizen could curse the government and go for a walk, shoot rabbits, or read his favorite author. Under the new system, if he *is* conscientious, he should spend laborious nights studying the problems of legislation, and does not know whom to curse.

What is he to do? Theoretically he ought to use his influence to bring about wise legislation. To do that, he must know his subject. Practically, he knows not only that, according to the theory of democracy instead of representation, it is his duty to make the congressional rubber stamps register his opinions but that his fellow citizens by the hundreds of thousands are trying to do the same thing, either singly or in powerful groups.

If he is conscientious and wishes to have really considered opinions, the study of one topic after another—if undertaken seriously and if his opinions are not to be cribbed from newspapers and a weekly or two—will occupy his entire leisure time. Even if he spent all of it on the complexities of the modern world and the topics before Congress, he would not be a tithe as well posted as a congressman can be who has his entire working as well as leisure hours for the task. If anyone wants to try it out, let him take one or two of what are considered minor problems, such as the administration of our dependencies or the administration of the Indian Department, and see how long it will take him to decide on actual conditions and wise measures.

The ordinary citizen simply has not got the time for all this. But there is another point. Even if he spent all his time trying to be a wise legislator, would he even then achieve good citizenship? The problems of the moment at any time are largely problems of organization, of how to form a structure within which to lead a sane and balanced life. How sane is it to devote all one's working hours to making a living, and then devote all one's leisure ones to studying the problems of organizing life, and never really to live, that is, to savor life itself and to enjoy the best possible which it may afford, whether in literature, art, or other pleasures according to personal inclination?

What, after all, is the end of government? Aristotle claimed that it was to permit of a happy and virtuous life on the part of the citizens. Our Declaration of Independence stated it to be the securing of the rights of "life, liberty, and the pursuit of happiness." Is not the result of the modern theory of democracy much the same as that of the modern theory of mass production: that man is a consumer who must buy goods chiefly for the sake of keeping the machinery of trade turning, not for his own enjoyment? The citizen, under modern conditions of complex problems in an unrepresentative democracy, would appear to exist for the sake of keeping the government functioning rather than to enjoy his private life.

I have perhaps exaggerated the situation, and yet I do not think I have. If my member of Congress is not to have any mind of his own but is to vote only in response to the mandate of his constituents; if it is considered the duty of the constituents to issue the mandates by sending telegrams; and if all the constituents except myself are considering the problems and sending telegrams, am I a good citizen if I get fed up with it all and read the classics in the evenings instead of articles on farm relief and cancellation of war debts? Or can I be eighteenth-century, decide that I have elected a man to go to Washington, whom I pay for the express purpose of wrestling with these national problems as I wrestle with those of my own job, and chuck the whole thing? I cannot be omniscient. I cannot have a real opinion on all the congressman's problems without giving all my small amount of spare time to it, and may not have a real opinion then. Am I to allow my short remaining span of private leisure to be absorbed entirely by the problems of the day so that I may bring my small pressure to bear on the member from my district, like the other pressure-bringers; or become a bad citizen, selfish, and un-public-spirited? Does modern democracy expect us to issue mandates to our ex-representatives hypocritically without real knowledge of the subject, or does it expect that we shall merge our private lives wholly in our service to the state, and lose our humanism in our citizenship?

Nor can we lose sight of the fact that in this complex modern era, with government impinging on every side of our private lives, it has become almost impossible to disentangle the public from the private interest. It is not only a question of the age-old power of government to drive us to war or to take our property in taxation. War debts, farm relief, bonus legislation, a thousand things which the people now undertake to decide, affect us powerfully as individuals, while in minor ways the government, whether merely recording the sum total of pressures brought by various groups or not, enters our homes at a hundred doors and tells us how we must keep our personal accounts, what we can drink at our tables, what books we can have on our library shelves, what knowledge we may obtain and impart. It has become almost impossible to separate ourselves as citizens from ourselves as individuals.

I am beginning to suspect that the decline of the representative theory, like the fall of earlier forms of governing, came because some groups wanted the extra pickings from the government trough that other groups had been getting. From that quite simple and human desire sprang the theory that I must not consider my congressman as a representative but that I must send mandates in the interest, theoretically, of liberty and, practically, of spoils. Eternal vigilance, we have been told, is the price of liberty, but eternal vigilance is a frontier or a war condition. It cannot be expected of peaceful and civilized generation after generation. Neither the frontier nor the war develops the finest qualities in the private life. A man who sleeps with a gun to protect his family from savage or civilized enemies is not in the best situation to become a contented, happy, and cultured human being.

Life, that moment of self-consciousness which we enjoy between the mysteries of two unknowns, is extremely brief. As we grow older, it appears briefer with every fleeting year and month. For hundreds of thousands of years, man has slowly advanced while paying but scant attention to the *res publica,* the public things, as contrasted with the affairs of his own private interests. The world is immensely interesting, but many of its most absorbing interests lie remote from the problems before Congress, whether our own are golf, motoring, the excavation of Sumerian ruins, the study of Chaucer, or any one of a million things as far from politics as is Hindu philosophy from the splitting of an atom. Each human being must find his own interest, find that which fascinates him most in a transient world of marvels. Some will find theirs in the handling of public affairs, but why should all the rest suddenly be turned into unwilling and unaccomplished amateurs of legislation?

The progress we have made has come largely from the division of labor. Why reverse the process now and make us all members of Congress? It is to be hoped that as many able and honest men as possible should find their private ambition coincide with a career as a politician or statesman, but why should those who do not find this to be so have to sacrifice their whole leisure to a study of problems which do not interest them when they themselves would be far more valuable members of the great society by devoting themselves to other pursuits? Forms of government continually shift and are innumerable. Under all of them, some groups or classes or individuals will probably always get somewhat more than their rightful share of the favors going round. This is certainly still happening under democracy in the year 1932.

It is needless to say that nothing in this article need be taken as detracting from the supreme importance of the right sort of men entering on political careers as representatives of the people; or from the duty of the citizen to encourage their doing so, and to try to choose his representative with care as a man of honesty, courage, independence, and knowledge. Such men would be far more likely to enter politics to serve the state under the old formula of Burke than under the threat of instant dismissal from office if their acts displeased demos at any moment. Such a system would relieve the individual citizen of much of the pretense of being capable of expressing an opinion on subjects in which the accumulated mass of learning and the complexity of problems have become infinitely great as compared with days of a Bacon or an Erasmus. We are supposed to know a great deal as contrasted with our grandparents; but in fact, as any dinner table conversation will most lamentably prove, ninety-nine per cent of our chatter about the problems of the world is nothing but high-class gossip. To base a sound Oriental policy for the nation on what the average intelligent citizen really knows about the rights of the Sino-Japanese question, would be as sensible as to base it on the peeping of bullfrogs. Yet theoretically and to a great extent practically, that is what has to be done today. The effect on the individual is to make him hypocritical, or if not that, to lead him to believe that public affairs can be run without a tithe of the thought and knowledge which he knows are essential in his private business. The moral and intellectual effects are disastrous.

The democratic theory which had rejected the theory of the legislator as a representative has brought us only to the point of the present Congress, and to parties and platforms which dodge every real issue so as to return rubber stamps to seats in the next Congress, and so on year after year. The complexity of governmental problems will increase and not decrease in the future. If we are all to assume the functions which ought to belong to our representatives, either our hypocrisy must increase or our private life will disappear. We must either try to force Congress to vote as we wish without having given adequate consideration to the legislation, basing our wishes perhaps on our selfish interest as we see it without thought to the good of the whole; or else, if we try to play the rôle of the conscientious legislator, we must devote our leisure life to the study of problems about most or all of which we shall never, in any case, gain more than a very amateurish knowledge. Is he who declines to accept either of these alternatives, and tries instead to be a rounded and sane human being, a bad citizen?

It is worth pondering, and the answer may be found in what we consider the values of a humane life and the functions of a government.

There is, perhaps, one possible and practical way of escape from the present demoralizing and increasingly difficult situation. Human nature being what it is, we cannot look for any immediate diminution of the mass pressure brought to bear on those who are in high office. If we cannot at present diminish that pressure we may, however, consider the alternative possibility of increasing the resistance to it on the part of those against whom it is brought. As our central government has waxed in power and prestige, both nationally and internationally, there has been a marked falling off in interest in the local governments—town, county, and state. It may as well be confessed that power and prestige are the two goals of the ambition of most Americans. It has been these and not money which have kept men toiling at amassing ever more tens of millions as they have grown old, and have already possessed every other gratification which money can buy.

As the nation grows older, however, and the prizes offered by economic exploitation, and the chance of securing them, become somewhat less, we may come to regard the work which is good in itself as of satisfying value to us. Few of us have the ability to play a national rôle in politics or statesmanship; just as few of us can become billionaires. If there is less glitter about working for the good of the nation in a state legislature, for example, than in the halls, not to say lobbies, of Congress, the work to be done in the former, as also in town and county, is of national importance. Our national political system, whether controlling men in office or a nominating convention, goes straight down through the hierarchy of bosses to the local unit. At the bottom of all is the ability of the small bosses to deliver given quantities of votes, from groups of individual voters, boards of aldermen, or state legislatures.

Down in this now neglected part of our political life, the average man can find himself, if he will, more in the position of the old voter in Greece. He can know the local leaders and the local issues. The voter may not see or be able to learn all the intricacies of national problems, but he knows, or can know, whether the men of his community whom he is placing in office in town board or state capitol are honest and able. This is not so easy, of course, in a great municipality, like New York or Chicago, as it is in a rural section or a smaller town or city, but even in the greatest of all there are still the lesser units of wards or other divisions.

I do not wish to be understood as advocating that we should not take as active and intelligent an interest in national affairs and policies as our time and knowledge will permit. All I wish to warn against, for the effect on ourselves quite as much as on the government, is the vain and absurd effort on the part of all voters to legislate themselves on such matters before Congress simultaneously with, if not prior to, discussion by that body. It may well prove that in largely abandoning the good old Democratic doctrine of States' Rights, the greatest danger which we have incurred is that of forcing the individual citizen out of a sphere in which he can be useful into one so large that his usefulness is destroyed by ignorance—and ignorance that can be overcome only at a price in time and energy which he is both unable and unwilling to afford. By shifting the whole of our interest to the national government, we have done nothing to improve that, and much to ruin the entire structure by neglecting to think of the foundations. If one wants to make a plant thrive, one waters the roots and not the topmost branch.

The point I would make is that if, instead of keeping our minds mainly on national problems, with the results which I have already suggested, we would undertake to make ourselves familiar with the local ones of our own States, we should be attempting something within the limits of our leisure and ability; and not only that but we should be rendering a service of incalculable value to the national life. A body of informed opinion on local matters, a large addition to the number of voters insistent on honesty in administration and on high quality in local officials, and a group of men in every state legislature large enough to affect legislation, backed by a similarly extended section of an interested and informed electorate, would all have enormous influence on the ability and character of the candidates for office all the way up the line to Congress itself. Much narrower limits would be set to the power of the bosses, and even if we could not, as I have said, diminish the pressure brought to bear on national officials, we could in that way increase their power of resistance. If we became more sure that they would not supinely yield to the pressure of one group or another, we would not remain under the same necessity as we are now of trying to make our own pressure felt, either with or against some other body of citizens. In other words, we could get back more to the old idea of the representative. We could lessen the difficulties which this article has pointed out, and could once more combine a private life with the life of a conscientious citizen in a community.

The day may come—there are signs it has already come—when more men may be willing to enter public life for the sake of rendering service on the stages of our smaller political units. The desire for the spectacular may give place to a saner valuation of what is worth while. We may also as individual citizens come to the conclusion that it is just as important to seek to have an honest and able administration in each of our forty-eight commonwealths as it is to try to direct the solution of all the problems before the national government from the country store or the club smoking room. When that day comes, we shall have gone far toward settling one of the greatest of our national problems—how to get able, fearless, and independent men to administer the government of the nation, with or without postcards or telegrams. Meanwhile, whether this is an impossible ideal or not, there would seem little hope of improving national conditions politically, or of reconciling the citizen's rights with his duties, by merely bringing more and more pressure to bear at the top of the political system while leaving all the local fields to take care of themselves, allowing every evil force to entrench itself. Good citizenship, like charity, should begin at home. If enough of us acted on that belief, the result might well be that we could once more in peace balance the demands of the public and the private life.

A Bibliography of Outstanding American Essays Published in American Periodicals

FROM JANUARY 1, 1932 TO JUNE 1, 1933

Adams, James Truslow.......*America's Real Job*
SCRIBNER'S, April, 1933

Aiken, Conrad...............*What I Believe*
NATION, July 27, 1932

Anonymous ....*So You Want to Write*
SATURDAY EVENING POST, April 15, 1933

Austin, Mary................*Life at Santa Fe*
SOUTH ATLANTIC QUARTERLY, July, 1932

Barnard, Eunice Fuller.......*College Girl: 1932-1933*
SCRIBNER'S, January, 1933

Betts, T. J....................*Chinese Public Opinion*
FOREIGN AFFAIRS, April, 1933

Boyd, Ernest.................*Business—As Usual*
AMERICAN SPECTATOR, June, 1933

Brown, Rollo Walter..........*The Crime Against Youth*
ATLANTIC, June, 1933

Burke, Kenneth..............*The Poet and the Passwords*
NEW REPUBLIC, August 3, 1932

Bush, Douglas................*Pale-Eyed Priests and Happy Journalists*
BOOKMAN, November, 1932

Cabell, James Branch.........*The Breast of the Nymph*
BOOKMAN, March, 1933

367

Calkins, Earnest Elmo....... *Hobbyhorses*
    ATLANTIC, May, 1933

Calverton, V. F.............. *The Liberation of American Literature*
    SCRIBNER's, March, 1932

Cather, Willa................. *A Chance Meeting*
    ATLANTIC, February, 1933

Chase, Stuart................. *World Without Money*
    SCRIBNER's, February, 1933

Colton, Arthur............... *Longfellow's Reputation*
    BOOKMAN, February, 1933

Cowley, Malcom............. *War in Bohemia*
    SCRIBNER's, January, 1933

Craven, Thomas.............. *In Behalf of Boors*
    AMERICAN SPECTATOR, April, 1933

Davis, Elmer................. *Notes on a New Bible*
    HARPER's, February, 1932

De Voto, Bernard............ *New England, There She Stands*
    HARPER's, March, 1932

Eaton, Walter Pritchard...... *A Squire's Complaint*
    ATLANTIC, June, 1933

Edman, Irwin................ *Salute to To-morrow*
    FORUM, January, 1932

Fosdick, Harry Emerson...... *Morals Secede from the Union*
    HARPER's, May, 1932

Frank, Waldo................. *The Universe of T. S. Eliot*
    NEW REPUBLIC, October 26, 1932

Franklin, Jay................. *American Independence: 1932 Model*
    VANITY FAIR, July, 1932

BIBLIOGRAPHY

Fuess, Claude M.............*Debunkery and Biography*
ATLANTIC, March, 1933

Gallico, Paul ....*The Texas Babe*
VANITY FAIR, October, 1932

Gauss, Christian.............*The End of Nationalism*
SCRIBNER'S, May, 1933

Gavit, John Palmer...........*The Passionate Pilgrim*
SURVEY-GRAPHIC, October, 1932

Goldberg, Isaac...............*Sousa*
AMERICAN MERCURY, October, 1932

Grattan, Hartley.............*What the Younger Generation*
Thinks
NORTH AMERICAN REVIEW, March, 1933

Hackett, Francis..............*Why Travel?*
HARPER'S, January, 1932

Hale, William Harlan.......*So Many Doomsdays*
VANITY FAIR, December, 1932

Halper, Albert...............*My Brothers Who Are Honest*
Men
AMERICAN MERCURY, April, 1932

Hansen, Harry...............*Fashions in Fiction*
FORUM, March, 1933

Hawthorne, Julian...........*Nathaniel Hawthorne's Blue*
Cloak
BOOKMAN, September, 1932

Hazlitt, Henry...............*Programs for the Jobless*
SCRIBNER'S, June, 1933

Hibben, John Grier..........*The Turning of the Tide*
FORUM, February, 1933

Hicks, Granville.............*John Dos Passos*
BOOKMAN, April, 1932

BIBLIOGRAPHY

Hutchinson, Paul............ *The Future of Religion*
    FORUM, April, 1933

Johnston, Alva.............. *Twilight of the Ink-Stained*
                               Gods
    VANITY FAIR, February, 1932

Jones, Howard Mumford..... *Betrayal in American Edu-*
                               cation
    SCRIBNER'S, June, 1933

Krutch, Joseph Wood........ *Art, Magic and Eternity*
    VIRGINIA QUARTERLY REVIEW, October, 1932

Lewisohn, Ludwig............ *The Crisis of the Novel*
    YALE REVIEW, SPRING, 1933

Lippmann, Walter............ *The Scholar in a Troubled*
                             World
    ATLANTIC, August, 1932

Littell, Robert................ *What the Young Man Should*
                             Know
    HARPER'S, March, 1933

Lovett, Robert Morss........ *Goethe in English Literature*
    THE OPEN COURT, April, 1932

MacLeish, Archibald......... *To the Young Men of Wall*
                             Street
    SATURDAY REVIEW OF LITERATURE, January 16, 1932

Macy, John................... *George Eliot: Victorian Queen*
    BOOKMAN, April, 1932

Marquis, Don................. *New York*
    SATURDAY REVIEW OF LITERATURE, December 3, 1932

Marshall, Margaret........... *The Art of René Clair*
    NATION, June 8, 1932

Maybury, Joan............... *I Don't Like Ladies*
    HARPER'S, June, 1933

BIBLIOGRAPHY

Mencken, Henry Louis...... *A Third of a Century*
BALTIMORE EVENING SUN, January 11, 1932

Morley, Christopher.......... *Cricket on the Hearth*
SATURDAY REVIEW OF LITERATURE, December 10, 1932

Moses, Montrose J............ *A Hopeful Note on the Theatre*
NORTH AMERICAN REVIEW, December, 1932

Mumford, Lewis............. *Notes on North Sea Architecture*
YALE REVIEW, Spring, 1933

Nathan, George Jean......... *Our Premier Dramatist*
VANITY FAIR, January, 1932

Nock, Albert J............... *The Disadvantages of Being Educated*
HARPER's, September, 1932

Preston, John Hyde.......... *To the Class of 1933*
FORUM, June, 1933

Redman, Ben Ray............ *Saintsbury, the Connoisseur*
THE SATURDAY REVIEW OF LITERATURE, February 11, 1933

Roberts, Kenneth............. *An Inquiry into Diets*
SATURDAY EVENING POST, October 15, 1932

Robinson, Edward............ *Jean Sibelius*
AMERICAN MERCURY, February, 1932

Rosenfeld, Paul.............. *George Gershwin*
NEW REPUBLIC, January 4, 1933

Seldes, Gilbert............... *Have Americans Lost Their Nerve?*
SCRIBNER's, September, 1932

Spencer, Theodore........... *The Poetry of T. S. Eliot*
ATLANTIC, January, 1933

BIBLIOGRAPHY

Tate, Allen.................... *In Memoriam: Hart Crane*
              1899-1932
    HOUND AND HORN, July-September, 1932

Taylor, Deems............... *Radio—A Brief for the Defense*
    HARPER'S, April, 1933

Teall, Dorothy............... *Bourne into Myth*
    BOOKMAN, October, 1932

Teilhet, Darwin.............. *What America Listens to*
    FORUM, May, 1932

Tinker, Chauncey Brewster... *Courteous Reader*
    SATURDAY REVIEW OF LITERATURE, February 4, 1933

Tunis, John R................. *The National Game of the
                  English*
    SATURDAY EVENING POST, January 30, 1932

Widdemer, Margaret......... *Message and Middlebrow*
    THE SATURDAY REVIEW OF LITERATURE, February 18, 1933

Wilson, Edmund............. *What I Believe*
    NATION, January 27, 1932

Woollcott, Alexander......... *The Browsing Room*
    THE NEW YORKER, November 19, 1932

Young, Stark................. *Deep South Notes: Rosedown
                  Reflections*
    NEW REPUBLIC, August 10 and August 17, 1932